P9-DUZ-722

SEXUALITY
IN THE
MOVIES

It is of the cinema alone that we can say that eroticism is there on purpose and is a basic ingredient. Not the sole ingredient, of course, for there are many films and good ones that owe it nothing, but a major, a specific, and even perhaps an essential one.

André Bazin, *What Is Cinema?* Vol. 2

Sexuality
in the
Movies

EDITED BY THOMAS R. ATKINS

 Indiana University Press
BLOOMINGTON & LONDON

Published in Canada by Fitzhenry & Whiteside Limited,
Don Mills, Ontario.

MANUFACTURED IN THE UNITED STATES OF AMERICA

Library of Congress Cataloging in Publication Data
Atkins, Thomas R   1939–
    Sexuality in the movies.

    1. Sex in moving-pictures.   I. Title.
PN1995.9.S45A8   1975   791.43'0909'353   74-17564
ISBN 0-253-18071-6   75 76 77 78 79 1 2 3 4 5

For Mary Ellen

Contents

Part Three: Contemporary Landmarks

SEXUALITY IN THE MOVIES

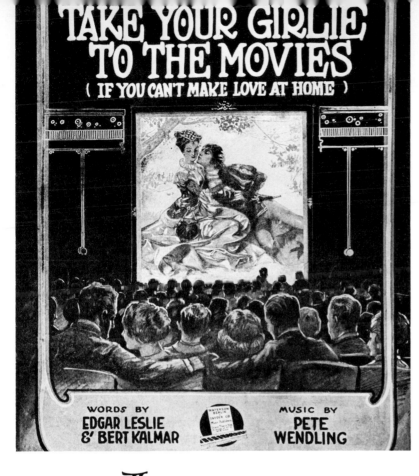

Of Prurient Interest or Shoot the Projectionist:

An Introduction

THOMAS R. ATKINS

A FEW miles south of Roanoke, Virginia, where Highway 220 winds through rocky foothills leading up to the Blue Ridge mountains, is a small drive-in theater that shows mostly X-rated movies and has a notorious reputation as a flesh pit. I discovered this seedy little theater about three years ago when, driving back home one night from North Carolina, I rounded a bend and suddenly saw a giant half-naked woman rising above the treetops. Somewhat stupefied by several hours at the wheel, I didn't question the actuality of this vision but watched as the woman, looming over the countryside like a female King Kong, unhooked her bra and flung it into the darkness. I pictured the huge bra crashing through some sleeping farmer's roof. Then, as the figure bent to remove the last stitch, it dawned on me that I was seeing a movie—an illusion flickering across an outdoor screen.

Last summer when I went to this drive-in a couple of times to see some Russ Meyer movies and *Fritz the Cat*, I found that the place lives up to its lusty reputation. The offscreen activities, in fact, were generally more interesting and often louder than those on the screen. The patrons, a truly mixed and boisterous crowd of all ages and shapes, from Roanoke and the surrounding hill country, come in convertibles, pickup trucks, vans, jalopies, hot rods, and motorbikes. Children run wild up and down the car lanes, which are littered with popcorn boxes, beer cans, and an occasional discarded condom. The evening air is sometimes laced with the faint odor of pot drifting from some of the cars. Many autos are jammed with giggling teenyboppers (the manager never asks for anybody's age), while other vehicles, with rolled-up steamed windows, show no visible signs of life. Bull bats swoop down in front of the screen, and once I spotted a fat brown rat slipping past the concession stand, a hangout for country rubes gawking at teenage girls

1

Sexuality
in the Movies

or getting into drunken brawls. Whenever a fight breaks out, the manager restores order by summoning the police on the speaker system. And there always seems to be a deputy sheriff or some representative of the law in the audience.

Like many of the early penny arcades and nickelodeons, this drive-in is a noisy, earthy place "ministering to the lowest passions" and frequently arousing the wrath of the area's moral custodians. Despite regular efforts by several local preachers and citizens to have it shut down, the theater stays open all year, closing only during the most severe snowstorms. The manager was not even discouraged when last winter, during a showing of *Women in Cages,* somebody fired a shot into the projection building. The bullet, apparently from a rifle a great distance away in the hills, made a large hole in a window and ricocheted around the concrete walls, finally coming to rest in the floor between the projectors. There are several theories about why the shot was fired, but the version I prefer is that a zealous mountaineer, enraged by the iniquitous images he saw emanating from this miniature Sodom and Gomorrah, registered his protest by trying to shoot the projectionist.

In its peculiar and often hilarious fashion, this drive-in on the fringe of the wilds of Appalachia is a good illustration of some of this book's major concerns—the inherent sensuality of movies and moviegoing, for instance, as well as the close relationship between screen content and audience mores. The audience parking under the stars to see skin flicks on an outdoor screen is not too different, in basic needs and hungers at least, from the first peepshow customers paying their pennies to watch May Irwin and John C. Rice kiss or Fatima do her "coochee-coochee dance" or slightly later movie patrons marveling at Méliès' amply-endowed chorus girls from the Folies-Bergère. And the gunslinger in the hills who attempted to end the drive-in showing of *Women in Cages* is a close cousin, in his moral indignation if not his method, to the earliest censors who accused the moving pictures and the dimly-lit places where they were exhibited of having a "prurient" influence on the public.

Long before the appearance of drive-ins, the movies already played a significant part—far more complicated than mere influence—in the sex life, real and imagined, of the American public. The drive-in was simply a practical and profitable merging of two of our most popular forms of recreation—the movie and the automobile—both imbued by our culture with an almost magical erotic power. The moviegoing habit, as it spread across the country during the first few decades of this century, became closely associated with certain widely accepted social customs and rites, particularly those determining sexual identity and behavior. For many Americans the difficult rites of passage from adolescence to maturity, from sexual ignorance to awakening, are intimately linked to moviegoing. Just as baptisms, marriages, and funerals traditionally occur in churches, the darkened interiors of our movie theaters frequently provide the setting for other ceremonies, less formalized but equally defined by repeated gestures, signs, and signals, celebrating various stages of sexual discovery and initiation.

The familiar routines and attitudes of a group of small-town teenagers in the early fifties during their regular Saturday nights at the movies are beautifully captured by Larry McMurtry in his novel, *The Last Picture Show,* which was filmed by Peter Bogdanovich. The picture show, on Main Street near the poolhall and the all-night cafe, is the repository for the adolescents' romantic dreams about life as well as the place where they ritualistically pair off in the darkness to hold hands, kiss until their lips are numb, pet above the waist, and settle into an "osculatory doze"—all of which is often a kind of foreplay to more intense passion and exploratory activity later in parked cars and pickups.

During *Storm Warning* (changed to *Father of the Bride* in Bogdanovich's film) Charlene, a stocky and homely girl who reads fan magazines and lives for movies, gets worked up into a fit of "cinematic passion" by imagining that her date, Sonny, resembles Steve Cochran. Afterwards parked by a lake Charlene lets Sonny remove her bra and feel her breasts but, because of her sense of propriety (a portrait of June Allyson sits on her dresser) and fear of pregnancy, won't allow him to go further, even though Sonny has discovered after repeated necking sessions that "there really wasn't much of permanent interest to do in that zone." In contrast, Jacy, a pretty blond who has perfected the role of a playful tease, enjoys necking with Duane in the rear of the football team bus where the other kids can watch because "being in the public eye" makes her feel "like a movie star." Sometimes encouraging Duane to do "even more abandoned things to her," Jacy uses her sex like a commodity to manipulate his feelings and have her own way.

The roles played by Jacy and Duane and the other young people of Thalia, Texas, in their sexual games and even the sensations they feel are mirrored, shaped, and to a degree sanctified by the fantasies they see each Saturday night projected on the screen at the picture show. When events in their lives distress them by not working out according to their movie-oriented expectations, they feel that somehow, as Jacy says, "Life just isn't the way it's supposed to be at all." At the end of the novel, the closing of Thalia's theater implies their coming of age, the inevitable fall from the blind innocence of adolescence into the pain, suffering, and boredom of the real adult world.

The relationship between a supposedly mature adult and the movies is explored in Walker Percy's novel *The Moviegoer,* set in New Orleans in the late fifties. A twenty-nine-year-old stock and bond broker, the hero needs movies and movie-houses to escape from "the grip of everydayness," a despairing state in which he feels like a ghost, invisible and lost to the material world. The marquee on the theater in his neighborhood reads: "Where Happiness Costs So Little." All movies, even bad ones, bring him happiness, for they possess a heightened sensuous and physical reality far overshadowing and even capable of transforming

3

William Haines and Marion Davies at the
movies in King Vidor's silent comedy
Show People.

Bruno Zanin and Magili Noel are moviegoers
in Federico Fellini's *Amarcord.*

Cybill Shepherd and Jeff Bridges emerging from a sexual initiation
in a motel room in Peter Bogdanovich's *The Last Picture Show.*

Anita Ekberg comes to life on a giant billboard ad for milk in
Federico Fellini's *The Temptation of Dr. Antonio.*

ordinary life. While seeing *Panic in the Streets,* which was filmed in New Orleans, he experiences a phenomenon he calls "certification," whereby a movie can confer upon a location its certified meaning or existence. "Nowadays when a person lives somewhere, in a neighborhood, the place is not certified for him," he explains. "More than likely he will live there sadly and the emptiness which is inside him will expand until it evacuates the entire neighborhood. But if he sees a movie which shows his very neighborhood, it becomes possible for him to live, for a time at least, as a person who is Somewhere and not Anywhere."

Binx, the hero of *The Moviegoer,* also finds that movie stars have a "resplendent reality" which can save ordinary people from the malaise of everydayness. In the French Quarter he watches a chance encounter between a plain young couple on their honeymoon and actor William Holden who is in New Orleans for the filming of a movie. Threatened by strangers surrounding him and embarrassed by the contrast between himself and the big star, the young husband manages to give Holden a light without showing his feelings. They stroll along together, talk briefly about the weather, until Holden gives them a pat on the shoulder and walks away. Suddenly the couple's honeymoon is redeemed from banality and boredom, for the young man "has won title to his own existence, as plenary an existence now as Holden's, by refusing to be stampeded like the ladies from Hattiesburg. . . . All at once the world is open to him. Nobody threatens from patio and alley." His bride responds with renewed affection, putting his arm around her neck, because she "feels the difference too. She had not known what was wrong nor how it was righted but she knows now that all is well." Holden turns a corner "shedding light as he goes."

Binx carries on imaginary discussions with one of his movie favorites, Rory Calhoun, lamenting the failure of "flesh poor flesh" in an affair with Kate, his aunt's stepdaughter, and contrasting his own behavior with what Rory would have done in the same circumstances. In the depths of the malaise when flesh fails to live up to desire and he cannot even manage "to sin like a proper human," Binx's chief solace is moviegoing. On a compulsive and disappointing trip to Chicago he and Kate "dive into the mother and Urwomb of all moviehouses—an Aztec mortuary of funeral urns and glyphs, thronged with the spirit-presences of another day, William Powell and George Brent and Patsy Kelly and Charley Chase, the best friends" of his childhood. In the romantic darkness of the old theater, Kate holds his hand tightly while they watch *The Young Philadelphians.*

In both these novels, moviegoing is characterized as a ceremonial act involving a great deal more than just looking at moving pictures. Movie theaters have their own special atmosphere and environment to put the participants in the right mood, as well as their particular rites and rules of behavior prescribed by repeated usage or custom. One of the unwritten but generally accepted rules of moviegoing at the Thalia theater, for example, is that necking must stop after the lights come on. When Jacy breaks this taboo, the other teenagers are shocked. Before entering a new movie-house in a strange neighborhood, Binx is always careful to "touch base" by chatting with the ticket seller or the manager, a rite which prevents his becoming lost inside, getting "cut loose metaphysically speaking." As a habitual moviegoer, Binx is aware that the ritual inside the theater is potent—that it deals with basic matters, such as sex and identity, and promises secret knowledge and happiness for the faithful participants, clutching their soft drinks and popcorn.

This book aims to give a general picture of the treatment of sexuality in a wide variety of different kinds of movies, from the 1890s to the present, with special emphasis on the social and cultural context in which the movies were created. Throughout the volume, the complex evolution of sex on the screen is examined in relationship to the changing, often ambiguous values of the movie-going public. The majority of the essays here are new works written specifically for this book. Several others, in different form, appeared originally in my publication *The Film Journal*; and a few come from other periodicals. As the contributors' notes demonstrate, all the writers bring unique qualifications and insight to their particular subjects. Together they provide a lively, varied, and comprehensive analysis of movie sexuality from early shorts such as *The Kiss* and *Love in a Hammock* to contemporary landmarks like *Cries and Whispers* and *Last Tango in Paris*.

The first essay in Part One, a section of essential background and theory, explores the fundamentally sensual nature of the film medium, while the next deals with the appearance and influence of various censorship codes, laws, and groups that helped shape the content of American movies. To complete the censorship study a critic, who has served as an intern on the rating board of the Motion Picture Association of America, offers an inside view of the workings and problems of the current movie classification system. The remaining essay enlarges the perspective by clarifying some of the issues involved in understanding the complicated relationship between film aesthetics and moral values.

After a discussion of sexuality in certain key Hollywood features of the past two decades, Part Two concentrates on important film genres and categories in which eroticism has been either the central focus or a crucial element. Skin flicks and hard-core pornographic movies are evaluated, as well as the frequently disguised but powerful sexual ingredients of the classic horror movies. This section also includes an investigation of movies dealing with homosexuality, including recent hard-core treatments, and a critical comparison of the different ways in which sexual subjects have been depicted by influential European directors.

Part Three culminates the entire study with appraisals of six representative movies of the late sixties and seventies. In addition to being extremely popular or widely debated, each movie discussed is a landmark in its portrayal of sexuality. *I Am Curious—Yellow* is important to film history, for instance, as a legal break-

Sexuality in the Movies

through for freedom of the screen. As the first hard-core porno movie to receive wide acceptance by legitimate theater audiences, *Deep Throat* is primarily a cultural event. Movies such as *Midnight Cowboy, Carnal Knowledge,* and *Cries and Whispers* are major artistic achievements that have not only extended the boundaries of acceptable screen content but provided creative examples for other directors.

In *The Moviegoer,* Binx points out that all movies are associated in our memory with a time and place, a certain neighborhood and season. I happened to be in Paris during the dead of winter when I first saw *Last Tango,* which was drawing crowds at a small movie-house just off the Champs Elysées. The theater staff served coffee to the spectators lined up outside in the cold. Inside the packed house responded energetically, keeping up a constant flow of chatter and laughter throughout the movie, right up to the moment when the dying Brando sticks his chewing gum under the balcony railing.

The next time I saw *Last Tango* was on an afternoon in mid-fall at the Terrace Rocking Chair Theater in Roanoke County where, except for an occasional giggle or whisper, the audience was almost totally silent. On the following day the county commonwealth attorney, with several deputies, descended on the theater, informing the manager that because of a citizen's complaint, they were going to look at the movie and decide whether they should seize the print and prosecute him on obscenity charges. Immediately the manager withdrew *Last Tango* and substituted another movie. Although *Last Tango* eventually returned to the city of Roanoke and stayed for a while, without legal interference, the initial moral uproar—not too different from furors around the country over *Carnal Knowledge* and other controversial movies—made one sometimes wish for the kind of surrealistic poetic justice that Fellini devises in his short movie *The Temptation of Doctor Antonio,* in which a gigantic, voluptuous Anita Ekberg steps out of a billboard advertisement to torment and mock a censorious, misguided reformer.

This week the drive-in on 220 is advertising a double bill of X-rated horror movies guaranteed to provoke moviegoers out of their senses. In the evening paper a letter to the editor describes the movies as "prurient garbage" and "satanic filth." The publicity will undoubtedly help to attract festive crowds of dating couples, families, tourists, teachers, and a few police officers. And perhaps tonight somewhere in the hills near the drive-in an angry mountaineer will study the screen images, raise his rifle, and take aim at the projectionist.

PART ONE

Social and Cultural Perspective

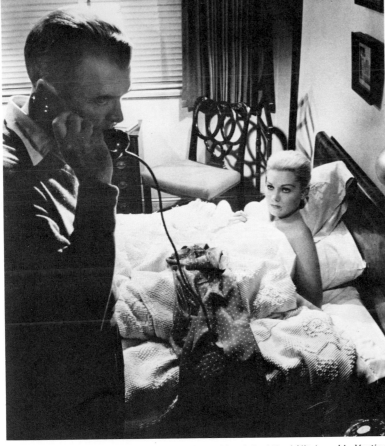

James Stewart and Kim Novak in Alfred Hitchcock's *Vertigo*.

1.
Screen Sexuality: Flesh, Feathers, and Fantasies

JOHN BAXTER

NO ART so blatantly offers sexual satisfaction to its audiences, requires its performers to fulfill so precisely the public's communal fantasies, or possesses in such abundance the tools to achieve its aims as does the cinema. With their physical advantages over the other arts for involving the audience emotionally and sensorially the movies can cater to private fantasies in a way the stage seldom approaches, while their accessibility to a mass audience creates a two-way traffic in myths and sensibilities which has allowed filmmakers to perfect their understanding of these fantasies and develop methods of catering to them. One checks one's inhibitions at the movie theater box office as completely as one discards a raincoat. Stripped of large parts of its sensorium by the controlled atmosphere, reduced light, and characterless smell of the building, the mind is doubly responsive to the physiological sedative of the flickering screen. Candy and soft drinks further lull the sense of taste, and the ubiquitous plush reduces tactile values. Sinking into the warm and limpid fluid of our subconscious, we fall easy victims to our unexpressed desires—creatures over which the filmmakers have a precise and detailed control. As we seldom are in our beds, we are in the movies able totally to exercise our sexual imagination, our senses uncluttered by the necessity to relate psychologically or physically to a partner or to our environment.

In our search for sensual fulfillment, we are aided by a community of performers unsurpassed in their drive to satisfy; the screen actor's need for our appreciation is equalled only by our own hunger. In Joseph L. Mankiewicz's *All About Eve*, the ruthless young Eve Harrington justifies her absorption in success with an almost messianic statement of an actor's aims which for most honest

11

performers must stand as a credo. At its conclusion, she sums up with the ulti-mate seduction of the stage: "If there's nothing else, there's applause—like waves of love coming over the footlights and wrapping you up. Imagine to know every night that different hundreds of people love you." *Love* is an aptly chosen word; it evokes the sexuality implicit in any public performance, an act which must, by its very reliance on submission to a communal will, place performers in a quasi-sexual relationship to their watchers. Though far from unique to actors—counter-tenors wryly describe the reaction of concert audiences to their high falsetto singing; at the first note, all eyes automatically drop to the crotch, returning to the face only after they have established that the singer is indeed male—the re-sponse reaches its peak among movie stars. Tom Stoppard perfectly isolates it in *Rosencrantz and Guildenstern Are Dead*; abasing himself before the passing pair of travellers, the leader of a peripatetic acting troupe advertises a compendium of performances ranging from the loftily artistic to the pornographic. "We can do you ghosts and battles, on the skirmish level, heroes, villains, tormented lovers . . . we can do you rapiers or rape, or both, by all means, faithless wives and ravished virgins—flagrante delicto at a price, but that comes under realism for which there are special terms. Getting warm, am I?" All the variations of sexual experience are offered as his troupe's price for the only reward it values, an audience. "We're actors" he justifies blandly. "We're the opposite of people."

Considering the opportunities offered by the conditions of movie-going and the enthusiasm of its performers, the cinema has made only fitful attempts to exploit this potential. Actors more than anxious to reveal themselves for the ap-proval of an audience have often been asked to expose their bodies but seldom their sensibilities, so that the most vivid sexual symbols of our time, their attrac-tion emphasized by advertising and publicity which underline their availability as partners in sexual fantasies, generally appear to us on the screen obscured by trivi-alities of plot and blatant falsifications of personality. Having established in the star system one of the most potent methods of guiding each member of the audi-ence to a particular ideal, a character on whom one could rely in every film for a precisely measured and identical effect, the American popular cinema hampered its own efforts by offering audiences purely physical titillation. In battling with censors for the right to expose slightly more skin or express sexual desires in marginally more explicit dialogue or plot, Hollywood missed the fact that audi-ences prefer a release offered by means of character. When films succeed eroti-cally, it is generally because purely cinematic means have achieved an effect at which dialogue can only strain. The erotic release offered by *Gone with the Wind* rests almost entirely on the skill of its directors and cinematographers; after Rhett grabs the rebellious Scarlett in his arms and storms up the red plush stairs towards bed and near rape, our expectations are perfectly answered by the next scene when, after a discreet dissolve, Scarlett wakes alone in a sunlit bed cuddled in white linen and stretches with cat-like contentment. As the two scenes emphasize, copulation is an act of color and mobility followed by calmness, relaxation, and ease—even the most explicit depiction of their moments in bed would not have offered us, the audience, any greater satisfaction. In sex, as in comedy, timing is all.

All the more disappointing, then, that so much screen time has been wasted on the merely descriptive at the expense of evocation. The introduction of censorship in the American cinema encouraged producers to expend most of their energy in devising excuses to expose a few further inches of skin or purvey marginally more graphic lines of dialogue; the arguments over whether Rhett should be allowed to say as his last line in *Gone with the Wind* "Frankly, my dear, I don't give a damn" often obscures the advances in screen sexuality achieved by the film. Before 1934, Hollywood led Europe in an adult depiction of sexuality. In 1931, Paramount could make a boldly pansexual appeal in its advertising for *Morocco* by publicizing Marlene Dietrich, already becoming famous for her affectation of male clothes and for her bluntly Lesbian nightclub sequence in Sternberg's desert melodrama, as "The Woman All Women Want to See." Sadism and a delight in the corruption of innocence could be precisely conveyed in Ulmer's *The Black Cat* with the vicious Boris Karloff sleeping like a Cocteau prince in his veiled bed accompanied by the blonde wife of his arch enemy Bela Lugosi, who returns to flay his enemy alive at the climax in a retribution regarded by filmmakers and audience alike as entirely reasonable. Without exposing more than a soft white throat, Norma Shearer in *A Free Soul* and Claudette Colbert in *Honor Among Lovers* displayed all the erotic assurance and sexual pleasure of the emancipated woman, both realistically offering themselves to men they found physically attractive, unconcerned by the inconveniences of marriage or social obloquy.

But the promise faded in the mid-thirties as the censors, in listing specifically the themes, scenes, and often the dialogue producers were not permitted to use, focused Hollywood's attention on means of defying these restrictions. Advertising now achieved its effects by misdirection, replacing a simple statement of intent with some remarkable falsifications. Since Jean Harlow could no longer display her generous sexuality on the screen—most film stories presenting her as a wisecracking New Yorker with at most a competitive interest in men—MGM sustained the sexual illusion in her advertising, distributing stills in which, clad in a black negligée, she exposed stockinged legs and appreciatively fondled her ample breasts in a masturbatory style that was to become typical of Hollywood publicity. By the forties, no star, however ill-favored, could begin work unless the press had been inundated with publicity shots of her cuddling up to propellers, ship's wheels, and other phallic objects, just as even the most pigeon-chested actor had to expose his torso to the scrutiny of the world. The gap between advertising and the thing advertised widened as the thirties wore on. Fan magazines followed the

13

Norma Shearer and Clark Gable in
Clarence Brown's *A Free Soul.*

Marlene Dietrich in Josef von Sternberg's *Blonde Venus*.

trend, shrilly publicizing articles the content of which had little relation to their headlines. "The Story Jean Harlow Never Told" in *Photoplay* turned out to be a description of how she had contracted conjunctivitis from working under hot lights and was forced to wear dark glasses for some months, and so circumspect was *Motion Picture* about the open secret of Ronald Colman's affair with Benita Hume that it was not until after their marriage in 1938 that an article remarked that they had occupied adjoining Benedict Canyon houses for some years, adding coyly, "In the shared fence there is a gate . . . its hinges are not rusty."

Locked in a competition with the censors on the issue of female nudity, Hollywood ignored almost entirely the cinema's countless erotic possibilities. In fact, the necessity to dilute sexual scenes both psychologically and photographically had the reverse effect of making the occasional achievements almost entirely unerotic. Jane Wyatt's naked dive into the pool in Capra's *Lost Horizon* and the visually rich opening of Sternberg's *Blonde Venus*, with naked female bodies surging under the surface of a lake, are so softened by the necessity to avoid censorable nipples and pubic hair that they entirely miss their effect. Just as the bleak disinterest of a stripteaser's expression can cancel out entirely the appeal of her act, so the very skill lavished on the construction of a nude scene disperses its erotic appeal, a point brought home in the less professional pornographic films, often exciting in direct proportion to the gaucherie of their performers, and occasionally in the commercial cinema; a rare example is Roger Corman's *Teenage Caveman*, where a nude bathing scene by minor—indeed, one might say non—actress Darrah Marshall is done with such obvious embarrassment that a shop-worn cliche' of popular cinema becomes momentarily believable, a sharp contrast to similar scenes in the period's jungle films, where the meticulous obscuring of the stars' bodies in their obligatory bathing scenes is as stylized as the passes of a matador, though considerably less erotic.

The new liberalism of the sixties brought home to filmmakers the long-delayed realization that, though nudity can be exciting to a film audience, it is not what the cinema does best. The filmgoer, rendered a voyeur by the very nature of the medium, prefers the unguarded and the suggestive to the explicit. Filling the screen with naked flesh, they soon realized, offered as little satisfaction as filling one's bed with women or men; and on stage, *Hair, Oh Calcutta,* and the resultant explosion of sexual extravaganzas proved conclusively that, on the contrary, mass nudity often resulted in a de-eroticizing of the material. The field was open for a return to the less specific, a re-opening of that dialogue with the audience's subconscious which had been so stimulating a feature of the early sound cinema; but, paradoxically, the filmmakers turned not to these proved methods but to a further extension of the illustrative sex characteristic of the censor-fearing thirties.

Faye Dunaway and Steve McQueen in Norman Jewison's
The Thomas Crown Affair.

Albert Finney and Joyce Redman in Tony Richardson's *Tom Jones.*

Sexuality
in the Movies

Turning its back on the visual, screen sex became almost entirely literary, exploiting the stage's new freedom of dialogue by transferring intact many of the other medium's usages, moving further from visual evocation into a schematised symbology. The most widely publicized erotic moment of early sixties cinema was a scene in Tony Richardson's *Tom Jones* where Albert Finney and Joyce Redman munch their way lasciviously through a full meal from oysters to roast before clambering into bed. Critics praised Richardson's "indirection," missing the fact that, like the stony text of volumes on "The Nude In Art," it described an erotic moment without evoking its eroticism. In *The Thomas Crown Affair* Norman Jewison had Steve McQueen and Faye Dunaway repeat the same situation—and he himself the same mistake—in a symbolic chess game, all wet lips, heavy breathing, and phallic bishops. The accepted arbiter of taste in their word-ridden field was Ingmar Bergman, whose aptly-dubbed "outspoken" attitude to sex underlined the absorption with description. His films of the fifties and sixties offer little nudity, but his characters agonize constantly about the burden of sex, the deception of the flesh. Such a form served Bergman's dour temperament, and his films do reflect an aspect of sexual need. But it was the formalized sexuality of early films like *Waiting Women* which the Europeans admired; its wryly visual depiction of a seduction, in which the man passes through a half-open door a glass of wine, a letter, a provocative figurine, and finally himself, precisely echoes the literary mode of the time. Unfortunately, the most perfect of Bergman's statements on this theme, the rich and bitter *Persona* with its interlocking erotic obsessions and the stark but stimulating scene in which Bibi Andersson describes in pornographic detail a beach orgy with a girlfriend and two young boys, had no imitators in the English-speaking film. Dialogue and literary symbolism were acceptable only as long as they obscured sexual need rather than expressed it.

The worst products of the American erotic film have a bleakness which seems to reflect self-disgust, a hostility directed not only at the sex act but at the necessity to consider any human values. While pretending to cater to an audience, many films merely exploit it like pornographers, sharing the pornographer's contempt for his "marks." To paraphrase a comparison between farce and comedy, "Pornography is heartless; eroticism sees all, knows all, understands all." (And to continue the comparison with humor, erotic film of today, which is to say erotic film at its least inspired, is more often on the level of the elaborately plotted dirty joke than the wry wit of Porter or Coward.)

This attitude had its gestation in the late forties, a cynical period which formed many modern movie preoccupations. It was characteristic of the time that the movies should have given more space and understanding to deviation than to conventional eroticism. While married couples could not, according to the dictates of the Breen office, be seen in the same bed together, sexual sadism had one of its most potent expressions in Henry Hathaway's *Kiss of Death*, with a psychopathic

Patricia Neal and Gary Cooper in Vidor's
The Fountainhead.

Jennifer Jones in King Vidor's *Ruby Gentry*.

Liv Ullmann and Bibi Andersson in Ingmar
Bergman's *Persona*.

Marilyn Monroe and Tom Ewell in Billy Wilder's *The Seven Year Itch*.

ploited the opportunities of the cinema for sexual excitement. All trade on the involvement of the audience and the suspension of disbelief, but never cynically or merely to manipulate its response. Like comedy, screen sexuality demands from filmmakers a readiness to expose themselves in return for the satisfaction of pleasing an audience. Directors are no different from actors in their willingness to turn out their souls at the request of their public, but unlike the actor, a film-maker has the higher responsibility of retaining a sense of proportion. Stoppard's actors in *Rosencrantz and Guildenstern Are Dead* wildly offer everything in return for applause; the director and screenwriter must curb this response in themselves and their performers in order to ensure fidelity to psychological realities or, on a mundane level, to the work as a whole. Above all, good erotic film demands compassion from those who make it, and an acknowledgement of shared experience common to both audience and artist.

Paradoxically, the work of the most erotic filmmakers is not always sensual; the greatest test of a director's understanding of and respect for the sex urge is whether he makes films out of it rather than about it. "Deepest feeling always shows itself in silence," says Marianne Moore; "not in silence, but restraint." Though not primarily an eroticist, David Lean has a precise and compassionate understanding of sex in all its forms, not merely its outward manifestations, though on occasion he can produce sequences which reveal sexual desire and satisfaction at their most blatant and exciting. Sarah Miles's coupling with her lover in the forest in *Ryan's Daughter* plays dazzlingly on our common experience of sex, the flickering flare of light through the trees perfectly echoing the gathering pleasure of orgasm in a way that no amount of choreographic grinding could have achieved. Lean's real genius, however, shows in his ability to introduce the sexual element into nonerotic scenes; Omar Sharif has revealed that, in directing him in the scene in *Doctor Zhivago* where he watches Cossacks sabre-charge a political demonstration, Lean told him to imagine that he was making love to a woman and trying desperately to delay his climax as long as possible. The whole scene was then taken merely on Sharif's face, creating an effect of mingled desperation and perverse excitement that lifted what could have been a mundane set-piece of violence onto another level.

Few American directors have the humanity to show sex as a force related to life rather than its sole point, and those that do generally regard it with a dispassionate, often mocking eye. Alfred Hitchcock, the most precise of Hollywood directors in his observation of sexual behavior—*Marnie, Vertigo* and *Psycho* are almost alone among American films in having stories based entirely in sexual behavior and erotic need—is bitter and self-hating in his work, betraying a revulsion for any such unseemly display of human feeling. His characters posture ridiculously like microbes on a slide while his microscopic camera, as at the opening of *Psycho*, moves inexorably towards their most private and exposed moments;

23

Sexuality
in the Movies

Janet Leigh relaxing in bed with her lover or Anthony Perkins glued to his peep-hole watching her undress are united as victims of Hitchcock's lens. Cold blondes obsess Hitchcock, and he loves to explore the erotic attraction of their ice-maid-enly appeal, as striking, he has said, "as blood on snow." Eva Marie Saint, Tippi Hedren, and particularly Kim Novak sail coldly through his films, dragging their helpless men behind them like scavengers desperate for some morsel of affection. In common with the most heartless work of Vadim, Corman, and other fifties filmmakers with an interest in the erotic, Hitchcock's characters often reveal them-selves as worshippers of the emotionally and, on such occasions as in *Vertigo*, the physically dead. His work has the heartlessness of farce—we are victims of a cruel and inhuman intellect who sees our feelings as absurd and our posturings as ludicrous.

It has been left to European directors, mainly the French, to explore sexual behavior with some respect, even without the presence of affection and without relying on titillation, though the publicity surrounding their attempts to depict sexuality with at least a vestige of realism has often distorted their work by over-emphasizing the aspects which seem to English-speaking audiences most shock-ing. Louis Malle's *Les Amants (The Lovers)* galvanized the world in 1958 with its much publicized scenes of Jeanne Moreau and Jean-Marc Bory sharing a bath, a sequence whose eroticism was underlined because the couple were casual lovers in the first heat of a relationship which lasts only until the next morning when Moreau, liberated by the experience, abandons both bourgeois husband and louche lover to set out on her own voyage of self-discovery. In the furor, few critics mentioned the remarkable range of eroticism covered by Malle; the bath is more a companionable romp than an example of sexuality, and though the film does have its explicit moments the variety achieved by Malle makes it a primer of screen sex. The camera becomes an observer, lingering with frank interest on their first coupling as the boy's head moves over her shadowed body, allowing it to disappear from the frame when its goal can be a secret to no viewer; only then does it return to the woman's enraptured face and the hand fallen with open palm on the bed, a potent symbol of complete surrender. As if to mock the conventions of bedroom sex and nudity, Malle takes his lovers into the garden for the film's most sensual moment, a gliding journey through the moonlit garden with the camera floating languorously around their glowing figures as they discover the delight of mutual attraction.

In this and later films like *Le Souffle au Coeur (Murmur of the Heart)*, Malle draws a clear distinction between eroticism and sexual behavior, a skill other French directors share. Eric Rohmer's characters in *Le Genou de Claire (Clare's Knee)*, *Ma Nuit chez Maud*, *La Collectionneuse* and *L'Amour en L'Après-midi (Chloé in the Afternoon)*, men and women alike, pursue sexual satisfaction with a single-mindedness that precludes human contact, and end up with little to show

Sarah Miles and Christopher Jones in
David Lean's *Ryan's Daughter*.

Janet Leigh and John Gavin in Hitchcock's *Psycho*.

A mating dance in Jean Renoir's *A Day in the Country*.

for it but the golden ring of the achieved end. Almost Hitchcockian in his control, Rohmer discards erotic effects in favor of more pointed observation of behavior. In *La Collectionneuse,* the young man surprises a casual girl friend in the throes of sex, but instead of lingering on the coupling pair Rohmer shares the character's embarrassment by retiring after one discreet glance. Zouzou's attempt to seduce her upright and happily married friend in *Chloé in the Afternoon* is regarded with a similar detachment, reflecting the hero's clinical disinterest in her body. These are, as Rohmer has stressed, "Moral tales," in which a cautionary point takes precedence over entertainment, but it is characteristic of his work that he offers the lesson without mocking his characters or their needs. Eroticism knows all, understands all. . . .

Of all French filmmakers, perhaps Jean Renoir has shown the most elegant and understanding appreciation of human sexual foibles, managing to combine, as few other directors have done, both the erotic and the psychologically perceptive. The moment in his American film *The Southerner* when sharecropper Zachary Scott shares a cigarette with his wife Betty Field as they relax in bed at the end of a hard day has the instinctive respect for a moment of common affection and physical ease which the work of native American filmmakers never achieves, while in his delightful fragment *Partie de Campagne (A Day in the Country)* the seduction by two slick city men of a buxom woman and her nervous virgin daughter is observed with all the psychological insight of Rohmer, combined with a sensuality at which most directors merely strain. The girl's brief struggle and dazed surrender under the willows remains touching no matter how aware one becomes on sustained viewing of Renoir's technique, and the moral point of the film's conclusion when the two lovers, both now married, meet embarrassedly some years later on the same spot, is no less effective for the sympathy that Renoir shows for them all, even the girl's loutish husband, an unimaginative city boy dominated since childhood by environment and his elders.

Most modern French directors, in contrast, have adopted a Hitchcockian detachment rather than a Renoiresque respect; François Truffaut in particular regards sexual foibles with contempt, notably in *La Nuit Américaine (Day for Night)* where his film crew characters screw with all the emotionalism of rabbits. The coldest and most Hitchcockian moment in Truffaut's work is that of *Le Peau Douce (The Soft Skin),* where Françoise Dorleac, enjoying a "dirty weekend" with her middle-aged lover at a country resort, plays precisely on his sexual tastes as a means of revealing her superiority over him. "Do you see that one over there," she says, pointing to a slightly overdressed woman chatting to a friend; "Women who wear leopard skin like to do it," and smiles thinly to see the revelation fan his jaded lust. It is a moment of truth made all the more unpleasant for its lack of feeling.

Erotic film need not rely entirely on the balance of psychological insight and

27

shared experience shown by Renoir; the commercial film remains tied to the patterns of mythology which it must exploit or fail at the box office. But there are areas in which imaginative directors can expand their technique to achieve new erotic effects. The most tawdry films can often be the most sexually exciting, and the least likely relationships can produce remarkable erotic tensions. The movies have few more sensual moments than those in Jack Arnold's *Creature From the Black Lagoon* where the heroine's white-clad body attracts the attention of the gill-man lurking on the floor of the mysterious lagoon. As she swims unconcernedly on the surface, the monster becomes a demon lover twisting beneath her on a parallel path, imitating her explicitly seductive motions in a stylized representation of sexual intercourse until excitement drives him to rise and clutch at her fluttering legs.

Occasionally, the electricity of a particular film or series of films can depend entirely on a unique relationship between an often indifferent director and star. Without the participation of his then-wife Brigitte Bardot—and sometimes when she withheld something of herself from the films they did together, as in *Les Bijoutiers de Clair de Lune (Heaven Fell That Night)*—Roger Vadim produced mediocre films, as did Bardot when she worked with other directors, but in collaboration their exploitation of the erotic possibilities of film was masterly. Vadim is at best a decorator with a feel for surfaces. His worst films have the unreal slickness of TV commercials, their lush flock wallpapers and greasily slick walls dissipating all atmosphere, all eroticism. In *La Curée (The Game Is Over)*, the couplings between Peter McEnery and Jane Fonda, reflected in a flexing plastic wall to the accompaniment of biliously twanging Indian music, seem a funhouse parody of sex, while even with its Gothic imagery and inspired Jean Prodromides score, his vampire film *Et Mourir de Plaisir (Blood and Roses)*, starring yet another of his wives, Annette Stroyberg, is at its most hilarious in an inserted dream sequence of naked bodies and red rubber gloves where Vadim is trying to be his sexiest. With Bardot, however, some shared lust communicated itself to the audience, and throughout *Et Dieu Créa La Femme (And God Created Woman)*, and *Le Repos de Guerrier (Warrior's Rest)* one has the sense of eavesdropping on a personal obsession.

The Vadim/Bardot films illustrate the second, and perhaps most readily acceptable aspect of successful screen eroticism, the use of a wider sensorium. Sex does not lie entirely, nor even partially, in simple description, but in an evocation of mood. Vadim sensed the erotic potential of certain simple effects and used them in all his films. Perhaps the most powerful was the juxtaposition of white cloth with a tanned body. From Bardot's first famous appearance, in *Et Dieu Créa La Femme* sunbathing naked on a Riviera patio amid drying sheets, Vadim knew he was on to a good thing and used it both in this film and later. Bardot wanders down to interrupt the wedding party dressed only in a sheet, and in *Le Repos de*

Jean Desailly and Françoise Dorleac in François Truffaut's *The Soft Skin*.

The Gill Man watches Julie Adams in Jack
Arnold's *The Creature from the Black Lagoon*.

Brigitte Bardot masturbating in Henri-Georges
Clouzot's *The Truth*.

Guerrier she captivates her lover by displaying herself provocatively against the same white linen. The trick was a minor one and was used to equal effect by Louis Verneuil in *Une Parisienne* with Bardot, but its disproportionate success illustrates the impact which can be achieved by a director and star with even the slightest intuition concerning their own natures and those of the audience.

Fabric in its aural and tactile as well as its visual nature can be powerfully erotic. One thinks of the electric crackle with which Bette Davis undoes a taffeta bow while seducing Richard Barthelmess in *Cabin in the Cotton* (an effect richly, almost comically sustained by her husky singing of "Minnie the Moaner" and calm cornpone comment "I'd kiss yah but ah jes' washed mah hair") and of Lola Albright's stripteaser in *Cold Wind in August* slipping into a whispering silk blouse before setting out to seduce young Scott Marlowe. In *Dr. Jekyll and Mr. Hyde*, Rouben Mamoulian plays on the same contrasts in the bedroom confrontation between Fredric March and Miriam Hopkins, where her plump leg swings negligently from under the bedclothes and her frilly underwear contrasts with Dr. Jekyll's elegant full-dress suit. All these movies show a heightened response to the possibilities of materials and a polished sense of shared erotic experience.

During the late fifties, tactile values assumed increased importance, particularly in the Asian cinema, whose photographers pioneered a new interest in textures. Sand on the naked body seemed in particular to interest them, and *Woman of the Dunes* achieved its greatest moments in the closeups of a woman washing from her lover's skin the grains of sand which speckled it. Alain Resnais's *Hiroshima Mon Amour* exploited the same effect in its opening love scene, in which the bodies of Emmanuelle Riva and Eiji Okada—later to star in *Woman of the Dunes* —were covered with sliding sand to accentuate, as Buñuel had done with ants in *L'Age D'Or*, the skittering of nerves beneath the surface, and to provide in Resnais's case a chilling transition to the blistered skin of atom bomb victims. This explicitly erotic use of texture contrasts hilariously with the "beach party" films then enjoying a vogue in America; their teenage stars, notably Annette Funicello, Sandra Dee, and Jimmy Darren, leaped athletically about the sands of California with never a grain clinging to their pneumatic bodies and taut costumes. This dry, sexless environment, with its preoccupation with relationships, offered no purchase for the few flecks of sand which might have given these rubbery bodies an erotic life or their characters a believable sexuality.

Psychological fidelity and the exploitation of the full panoply of our senses are two vital tools in the full exploration of sex on the screen. But the most important of the techniques available to erotic filmmakers is also the most complex and generally requires a total understanding of both its predecessors for full effect. Sexual symbolism has been misused so often in the film with its excessively literary obsession with metaphor that its deepest and most significant form has fallen into disrepute. It is easy for us to smile at a broad simile like Hitchcock's recurrent use of a train plunging into a tunnel to indicate sexual intercourse, but it is less simple to appreciate, as Freud and particularly Jung revealed, that certain subconscious archetypes carry the seeds of man's deepest erotic emotions and that the language of dreams rather than that of the body is the best means of exploring these preoccupations. Elliptical, often confusing, this symbology is our surest insight into the subconscious, a fact that a few filmmakers have discovered and exploited. Used in isolation, it can be as cloying or barbaric as a piece of music written entirely for brass: the films of Ken Russell, a director with a deep and instinctive appreciation of such symbology, are cases in point. Few films of recent years have explored sexuality more effectively than *Women in Love,* and its best images—the corpses of two lovers curled naked in the mud of a drained lake; the clash of flesh in the nude wrestling match between Gerald and Birkin, echoed by a delirious free fall of the latter towards his mistress in a wheat field; notably Gudrun's lascivious dance to the cattle and final swooning collapse at Gerald's feet—are dazzling exercises in erotic symbolism. But frequently the dream language is not wedded to compassion for or understanding of the characters, and their excesses became for some viewers exhausting and intolerable.

Erotic film reaches its peak when an intimate understanding of sexual symbology is combined with the use of a wider sensorium and a compassionate appreciation of character; the result is best expressed in the words of Fellini's Duke de Villalonga in *Juliet of the Spirits* as he offers Juliet a glass of sangria: "They say it takes away all thirsts from those who drink it—even that thirst which is never acknowledged." Only a few filmmakers have reached this peak. Fellini himself, even at his best, seldom achieves this sense of the unexpressed, though the ambiance of *Juliet* and notably Sandra Milo's nude glide into her bath boudoir come close. By far the most important master of screen sexuality is Josef von Sternberg, whose films outdistance in every respect the efforts of other Hollywood directors. Partly through chance, a little through good judgment, Sternberg brought together under his control the richest assortment of ingredients ever offered to a director of erotic film. Through his relationship to and absorption with Marlene Dietrich, he had a subject on which he could lavish all his directorial and photographic skill, while Paramount, during the thirties a company preoccupied with the perfection of visual technique through effects of photography and decor, provided a perfect experimental laboratory. His best work also precedes the days of Breen office influence, and though he did encounter trouble with *Blonde Venus* in 1932 —in a huffy memo rejecting his first script, the censor commented that Paramount more than any other studio seemed preoccupied with sexual exploitation—he was able in *Morocco* and *Shanghai Express* to achieve erotic effects never attempted elsewhere. But the ace in Sternberg's pack was his instinctive knowledge and understanding of sexual symbolism and of the archetypes psychologists had isolated as expressing man's dreams of sex. In common with Buñuel, whose relation-

31

Fredric March and Miriam Hopkins in Rouben Mamoulian's
Dr. Jekyll and Mr. Hyde.

Richard Barthelmess and Bette Davis in
Michael Curtiz's *Cabin in the Cotton.*

Sandra Milo slides into her bath in Fellini's
Juliet of the Spirits.

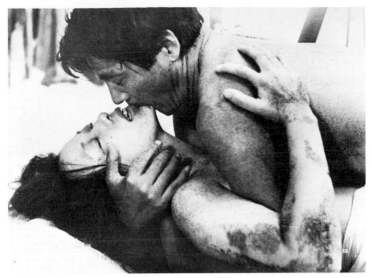

Kyoko Kishida and Eiji Okada in Hiroshi
Teshigahara's *Woman of the Dunes*.

Gary Cooper in von Sternberg's *Morocco*.

Anna May Wong and Marlene Dietrich in
von Sternberg's *Shanghai Express*.

ship with the surrealists provides a direct link to the work of Jung, Sternberg grasped that connection between certain animals, objects, and personae and the evoking of our deepest erotic emotions.

For Sternberg, the bird, one of Jung's most potent sexual archetypes, a creature in whose connotations of flight and physiological comparison to male and female genitalia much of the unacknowledged language of reproduction is encapsulated, became a lifetime preoccupation. He called Dietrich "my bird of paradise" and dressed her always in feathers, plumes, and boas. His films abound in all manner of birds, used both for decoration and with precise symbolic effect; imperial eagles spread their wings and dip their phallic necks over the Russian court of *The Scarlet Empress* and dominate both the Roman senate in *I Claudius* and the courtroom in *Blond Venus*. Doves coo in her home in the latter film, and in *The Devil Is a Woman* caged birds aptly symbolize her capture of the besotted Lionel Atwill. No film more effectively displays the remarkable synthesis of all these elements than *Shanghai Express,* Sternberg's greatest work and one which explores every avenue of screen sexuality. Shanghai Lily's black plumes decorate her costume and serve Sternberg's need to evoke the bird comparison, but they are also used to dazzling effect in suggesting the constant motion of the train on which the film is set; brushed by a draught, shaken by the carriage's slight undulation, they are in constant stirring movement.

Shanghai Express has no subject but sex, and all its confrontations between Shanghai Lily and her old lover Doc Harvey, played with willowy disdain by Clive Brook, revolve around their mutual desire less for love, which both have left far behind as a preoccupation of the trivial-minded, but for immolation, a total mutual devouring of one another. Their best scenes are barbed adagios of painful memory; chatting on the observation deck of the speeding train, Lily and Doc review their parting and the desolation which followed. Opening his watch, Doc displays the photograph he has always carried of her, a face half-drowned with sex, blind with desire, and though she responds passionately to his advances, allowing herself to be kissed as, in a brilliantly placed insert, Sternberg shows the train capturing a message from a hook placed by the track, her flip disregard for his appeals keeps her totally in control. "Wouldn't you have changed anything, Madeleine?" he begs as they discuss the empty years since their parting, and she remarks tartly, "I wouldn't have bobbed my hair."

Shanghai Lily is the ultimate sexual heroine, the woman of such self-contained feelings and personal insight that, for all her understanding of and love for Harvey, she can always remain in control of her own emotions. Her attraction to both men and women is eternal and immutable; no director can hope to achieve again so archetypal a character, and no film so sexually potent a scene as that in which Lily and Doc make their peace. Strolling along the corridor of the speeding train in her black negligée, Lily slips into Doc's compartment and begs a light for her cigarette. Her relaxation has a fatigue that is hauntingly like the aftermath of sex, and though nothing is said, desire is as palpable as the tendrils of smoke in the still air. Reluctantly, agonizingly, Doc yields a half-statement of belief in her explanation of the events that divide them, a symbolic surrender to her stronger will, and she returns to her room. Leaning against the door, she drags on the cigarette, and the camera moves in to show a shocking tremor of her body and hands, a sign perhaps of the train's motion but equally of her own excitement, or distress. The exhaled smoke flares before her face, she looks up into the light—triumphant, fulfilled, alone. In this sequence, Sternberg and the cinema come to the heart of our sexual needs, revealing our natures to ourselves in a way which carries the movies to the peaks of art. At such moments it is possible to feel that the price of contempt and derision demanded by the screen in return for a fleeting insight is not too high to pay.

Joan Crawford in Henry Beaumont's *Dance, Fools, Dance*, an early thirties pre-Code movie.

2.

A History of Censorship of the American Film

ARTHUR LENNIG

THE SILENT FILM

ᗷACK in 1893, the midway of the Chicago World's Fair featured a belly dancer named Fatima who proved a sensation with her exotic skills of undulation. Although science and industry had erected monuments to technological progress, they could not quite equal the peculiar effect Fatima had on her gaping spectators. She vibrated her hips sideways, she pumped them back and forth, she twirled them around. The lady—"Hardly a lady!" the blue-noses sniffed—showed most graphically what a thousand-year-old tradition of eroticism could do for a tired and depleted Sultan with a hundred competing wives.

Fatima from the East created in America's midsection more than just a glow. She was "something to behold!" and therefore it seemed good business to capture her provocative and aphrodisiacal ambiance on film. The unquestionably moving image that resulted provoked one of the earliest instances of motion picture censorship. Her gyrations appeared in two versions. The uncensored one showed her heavily clothed body writhing about; the other showed the same action as through a fence darkly, with two white grids obscuring her movements both top and bottom. The effect was a bit like finding lint in the keyhole.

Although Fatima was not as natural a wonder as Niagara, which had recently been recorded on film, audiences preferred her slides and slips to Niagara's falls. In short, the public expressed considerable interest in the many manifestations of that old three-letter word: Sex. At the same time, officialdom expressed considerable interest in denying them that golden opportunity. Censorship was already extending its tentacles into the film industry.

Feminine pulchritude did not necessarily have to emanate from the East. The servants' quarters would also do. In the mid-nineties, a twenty-two-foot Biograph film for a peep show had the title: *How Bridget Served the Salad Undressed*. A maid misinterprets an order and, according to the catalog, "Brings in the salad in a state of dishabille hardly allowable in polite society."[1] What was "hardly allowable" in the 1890s probably had the girl swathed in enough material to form the main sail of the Santa Maria. Still, the film hinted of naughtiness, as did such early peep show and movie titles as *The Kiss, Love in a Hammock, Trapeze Disrobing Act*, and *Peeping Tom in the Dressing Room*. If Bridget had really come in "nekkid," the police—after taking a good look themselves—would have raided the penny arcade immediately. All the natural wonders of the world could be shown with the new magical invention except for the one that apparently many people wanted to see: the nude human body. The public instinctively knew what some learned critics refuse to recognize: that movies at least partially appeal to the audience's latent voyeurism. For this reason, it is the medium that has been plagued—and, ironically, aided—the most by censorship.

The basic issues of censorship were cogently argued in the seventeenth century by John Milton. His *Areopagitica* stated that a cloistered virtue is no virtue at all, and that it is, by no means, a personal triumph over vice but merely the prevention of its realization. His persuasive reasoning notwithstanding, most societies have seen fit to limit freedom of expression. In the history of the United States, this limitation has applied more to sexual mores than to political and religious beliefs. Divergent attitudes, though hardly appreciated, have been tolerated. Revolutionaries, white supremicists, anarchists, fascists, communists, and monarchists, as well as Papists, Zionists, Mormons, Quakers, and all kinds of religious sects have all been allowed their say, along with various degrees of harassment. But sex was not to be discussed publicly or written about in any detail. It was not so long ago that Margaret Sanger was arrested for dispensing birth control information.

How did such official repression come about? Laws always somehow reflect the mores of a people. And the general attitude toward sex in the nineteenth and early twentieth centuries was simply that it should not be mentioned. In America such evasiveness and prudery was a direct carry-over from Victorian England and has been referred to, at least by the literary fraternity, as the "genteel tradition." This attitude was a far cry from the directness of the Elizabethan age and such lines as "the bawdy hand of time is on the prick of noon" from *Romeo and Juliet*; Hamlet's laying his head in Ophelia's lap and announcing, "That's a fair thought to lie between maids' legs"; and even such puns as "firk you" in some Shakespearean comedies. Such license was stopped in 1642 after Cromwell and his Puritans closed the theaters in an attempt to legislate morality. When Cromwell went the way of most rabid reformers—out—King Charles returned from France and assumed the crown. He brought with him continental sophistication and supported the amusing and occasionally salacious Restoration plays.

In 1697, Jeremy Collier, a British clergyman who occasionally went to the theater, convinced himself—and later others—that "nothing has gone further in Debauching the Age" than the plays of his time and wrote *A Short View of the Profaneness and Immorality of the English Stage*. The already existing censorship of political matters and of outright obscenity was not sufficient. Collier advocated a "moral" censorship. He examined in depth the content of plays and wished to remove anything that disagreed with his own sense of propriety. The purpose of theater was not to entertain or to reflect life: "The Business of *Plays* is to recommend Vertue, and discontenance Vice. . . . " He was convinced that the theater of his day was in "the Enemies' Hand, and under a very dangerous Management."[2] The reverend moralist had a fine nose for evil and could sense its presence in almost every stage production. He was not only opposed to jokes or insults levelled against his holy profession, he was also allergic to any risqué dialogue. "Such licentious Discourse tends to no point but to stain the Imagination, to awaken Folly, and to weaken the Defences of Vertue."[3] He concluded that "the *Stage* is faulty to a scandalous Degree of Nauseousness and Aggravation."[4] Despite many rebuttals, Collier won the day and the English theater cleansed itself, and as a result became considerably duller.

Although the eighteenth century attempted to be an age of reason and modeled itself artistically after the classical period, personal behavior still remained relatively unrefined. Alexander Pope, annoyed at a fellow critic, slipped him an emetic and described his discomforture with great glee. By the beginning of the nineteenth century, however, a sense of propriety began to intrude. Bodily functions, and in particular sex, were no longer mentionable. Most poets, except for Byron, were perfectly "safe" for any youngster. Novelists too became far more discreet. The lustiness of Fielding's *Tom Jones* could not be found in nineteenth century English and American novels. Pressures of society plus the self-imposed limitations by publishers kept most writers in line.

One of America's leading critics and novelists, William Dean Howells, although a progressive for his time, could not escape the Victorian *Zeitgeist* and seriously contended that books should take into consideration the pure mind of an innocent young girl and should not, under any circumstances, bring a blush to her virginal cheeks. What was going on under that long dress and those heavy bloomers and what shocking fantasies were flickering through her mind would not be revealed until Freud pulled away the fourth wall of the sacrosanct bedroom and peeled back those rumpled sheets.

The laws and customs of American society in the late 1800s and early 1900s reflected Victorian attitudes to such an extent that not only new outspoken works but often older ones were trimmed to preserve morality. Even Shakespeare was

Alla Nazimova in the 1923 version of *Salome*.

Early examples of screen sex: May Irwin and John C. Rice in Edison's *The Kiss*, a scene from *Kissing*, and Sally Rand's famous fan dance in *Streets of Paris*.

not spared, at least in popular editions. He remained whole in other versions, but the obscurity of his language was considered a sufficient shield and no one seemed to explain his off-color meanings. Scholarly tomes that otherwise examined every line and word of the bard were curiously silent with passages touching upon sexual matters, such as Ophelia's lines: "Young men will do't, if they come to't; By Cock, they are to blame."

Although censorship affected the written word—the definition of obscenity was a broad one—books and articles were far more free than the medium of the movies. This increased concern was due to a number of factors: (1) cinema affected a lot of impressionable people; (2) it catered to the lower classes who in particular needed strict guidance; (3) it was a medium that was yet to be considered "art"; and (4) it was too graphic and immediate about life itself. The unwritten rule is that the closer to life an art form comes, the more it must suffer from checks.

Since cinema was explicitly realistic, considered by almost everybody to be only entertainment and not by any means worthy of the protection of freedom of speech, the movies incurred the suspicion and ultimately the wrath of the censors. Nor was their concern wrong. An erotic drawing will never have quite the same lustful power as an equally erotic photograph, for the latter has the real flesh of a specific person. In contrast, the artist's pencil or brush can somehow raise the most sordid details into an artificial and therefore aesthetic realm. Thus the tourist had a right to be disappointed when he bought a Parisian vendor's packet of "feelthy pictures" only to find out they were reproductions of nude paintings. He saw just as much flesh as he had hoped for, but he felt cheated (and had a right to feel cheated) for the poses and the aesthetic control of the artist ruined the more basic appeal of the body as lust object. As a result of this difference, the artist could paint and exhibit a nude far more easily than a photographer could exhibit an equally explicit photograph. And even the still photograph, because it was not as "alive" and therefore further removed from reality, was still more abstract (and therefore less dangerous and corruptive) than a motion picture of the same subject matter.

Although from its very beginning the motion picture was involved with stag films, these productions were only for a specialized clientele and were not shown to the general public any more than photos of a like nature were readily available. What caused the growth of film censorship in the U.S. and interested the first censors was, of course, the product being shown in local theaters—the official product stamped with the approval of society as a whole—and the effect of that subject matter on what was correctly presumed to be a more impressionable and less mentally gifted public: the motion picture audience.

As nickelodeons spread across the country during the first decade of the century, legislators, educators, and various civic groups in New York, Chicago, and other cities felt that the movies—that peripatetic and ubiquitous sideshow—were taking people out of the churches, libraries, art galleries, and concert halls. Dimwitted dime-novel readers and budding Horatio Algers were hampering their reading skills and possibly foregoing gainful enterprise to wile away their formative years watching movies about philandering husbands, mischievous maids, female acrobats, wild Indians, and train robbers. Pulpits, auditoriums, and city halls around the nation thundered and echoed with moral indignation against the new disease which threatened to ruin the eyesight, blight the mind, and corrupt the morals of millions of the young.

By 1907 newspapers like the *Chicago Tribune* were condemning the nickelodeons as ministering to "the lowest passions of children. . . . Proper to suppress them at once. . . . influence wholly vicious. . . . They cannot be defended. They are hopelessly bad."[5]

That same year in Chicago the police were given the authority to preview movies to determine whether they were fit for public showing. In 1909, under pressure from organizations such as the Children's Society, the mayor of New York temporarily shut down all the nickelodeons and movie houses in the city. To prevent similar actions an organization of influential New Yorkers, the People's Institute, working in cooperation with certain producers and segments of the budding movie industry, formed a self-appointed review committee, the National Board of Censorship of Motion Pictures, which later became the National Board of Review. Within a few years some variety of local censorship existed in a number of states.

Despite these pressures, producers continued to offer movies focusing on crime or risqué subjects—but they were careful to see that the movies had "moral" endings. After a life of crime the villain was always apprehended, and after a life of pleasure the rake or woman of loose virtue must die some horrible death. Although technically the "bad" characters received retribution, in the audience's eyes, identification, and sheer affection, these characters were usually the real heroes. And this approach, of course, has remained the same for decades.

In 1913 a movie called *Traffic in Souls* played to packed houses because of its exposé of white slavery. People went to see it not because of its indictment of sin, but to get at least a vicarious thrill. Although this film encountered a large amount of litigation, it was allowed to play in many places. At that time laws were not consistent, and whether or not a film was shown depended on the whims of local officials around the country. The protection the movies should have had under the First Amendment was denied in 1915, in an Ohio law case involving a local distributor versus a town censorship board. When it was appealed, the United States Supreme Court decided that the movies were "a business, pure and simple,

41

originated and conducted for profit," and that they were therefore unworthy of constitutional protection. This decision, which encouraged the passage of censorship laws in additional states, was not overturned until 1952.

But the noose that was being tied around the movies would take a long time to tighten. In 1916 D. W. Griffith's *Intolerance* was able to present some temple maidens relatively unclothed—the breasts of one girl were exposed. (When the film was later revived in 1942, the New York Censor Board decided that scene had to be cut. In fact, *Intolerance* could not possibly have been made after 1934, when the stringent Hollywood Code took effect.) In the film Griffith castigated the "Uplifters," a group of reformers opposed to drinking, dancing, and the joys of the flesh. One remarkable scene shows the do-gooders closing a brothel. The "girls" trounce out to a paddy wagon as the masculine, middle-aged, and unattractive women uplifters watch. Also observing the exodus are two men in the uplifters' employ who effeminately smirk. Only women who can't get a man and male homosexuals would favor the closing of brothels, implies Griffith. This kind of outspokenness would become impossible during Hollywood's later years of tight censorship.

In addition to Griffith's temple maidens, movie audiences during the silent period were also treated to such sights as Annette Kellerman in the buff in *Daughter of the Gods* (1916), Theda Bara in *Cleopatra* (1917), Gloria Swanson bathing in *Male and Female* (1919), and Betty Blythe in *Queen of She*ba (1921). Valentino in *Blood and Sand* (1922) and Erich von Stroheim in *Foolish Wives* (1922) conveyed a strong sensuality. Although the screen was relatively free from major interference at this time, the state censors around the country often encroached on more subtle matters and exerted a strong sense of provincialism, by generally discouraging controversial topics and more mature treatments of sex and by insisting that the films reflect a simplified morality. These first censors sat humorlessly through all of the Hollywood products and snipped indiscriminately, without any consideration as to whether the films were artistic, sincere, or merely junk.

In the first decade the nickelodeons had been replaced by larger, more elaborate movie theaters and palaces, which were drawing in a new audience from the middle class. The postwar years saw the attitudes of middle class America swiftly change, aided by such factors as a widespread cynicism (the war had demonstrated that man obviously was no longer on an inevitable path to progress), increased material prosperity, the mobility of the automobile, and the influence of Freud who had suggested that the Id was the prime mover behind human behavior. Science had agreed that evolution was a fact—except perhaps in Tennessee after the Scopes trial—and began to analyze modes of behavior, concluding that morality was relative rather than absolute. Paradoxically as the tension between the old Victorian standards and new modes of life began to be felt in the twenties, the local censors and various reform groups became more insistent that the movies reflect proper standards of morality.

Pressures, however, were not levelled just at the movies. The stage too had its Savonarola, a remarkably clear echo of Jeremy Collier of over two hundred years before. His name was John S. Sumner, the Secretary of the New York Society for the Suppression of Vice. During the postwar years, he was an outspoken opponent of anything that seemed conducive to sin and had a strong nose for sniffing out the salacious. He was appalled by the change in American life, but directed most of his ire against the New York stage, Broadway to him being the Devil's own highway. Long incensed at the steady progression of evil on the boards, Sumner issued this purple pronunciamento in 1923, entitled "The Sewer on the Stage": "Our muddle-headed producers are substituting mental sewers for those physical, and they find customers who desire to inhale the aroma of noxious mental products." He goes on to blame the newspapers. "If they would stop pussy-footing and would come out openly and tell their readers that the Messrs. Panderer are producing an unclean and demoralizing show at the Cesspool Theatre, there would soon be an end of such nefarious activities."

Sumner goes on to lament that at a matinee performance of "one of these degenerate brain children" at least 50 percent of the audience were girls between sixteen and twenty years of age. He shivers to think of the effect. Representing the Puritan ethic *in extremis*, Sumner felt, "that with the increase of leisure among women, as among men, immorality will increase, because idle hands and Satan's work are as closely related today as ever. Attendant conditions of our present day civilization have left millions of people with insufficient honest work to occupy their time. The hardest problem for some of these people to solve is what to do next. Girls and young married women are largely in this unfortunate class. They must be educated in methods of properly utilizing this new freedom from what they disdainfully call drudgery."[6] He concluded simply that theatre managers "should be clubbed into a sense of decency." Fulminate as he did, Sumner could not stop Broadway from proceeding on its merrily indecent way. But he and his kind eventually had better success with the films.

The conflict between movies and the growing censorship forces came to a head in 1921. A general outcry was raised throughout the country against the transformation of young women from God-fearing maidens who valued their virginity into hedonists who exposed their legs, bobbed their hair, went unchaperoned, and indulged in gross familiarities in parked cars. Hollywood seemed to be the leading exemplifier of this kind of evil. In the world depicted on the screen almost everyone appeared to be rich, spoiled, young, and brash; every man had a bevy of girls; every woman a host of lovers. As a matter of fact, the films in the twenties were by no means so "modern" and dangerous. For the most part the girls were still good, and the heroes, except in Erich von Stroheim's pictures, were generally unsullied by desire or corruption. Most American films of this period were remarkably proper, and only seemed to be sinks of iniquity in the perspective of the Puritan-Victorian tradition. To many of the screen's more vocal critics, however, Hollywood continually and irresponsibly offended the Protestant ethic of hard work, just rewards, and deserved but muted pleasure. Such hedonism had to be stopped.

Unfortunately, Hollywood in 1921 proved quite vulnerable. There were some juicy scandals, in particular, the still unsolved shooting of director William Desmond Taylor and comedian Fatty Arbuckle's alleged rape of a girl named Virginia Rappe, who died of some scandalous internal ailment. Her death roused every woman's club from its tea cups, YMCA leaders out of their crowded showers, and ministers from their thundering imprecations, to cry out against the Sodom and Gomorrah of Hollywood. A chorus of righteousness rose up from all the lecterns, single beds, and local reading rooms: "Stop these fiends of decadence."

The movies suffered in silence—in more than one way—as the opposition readied its forces. The General Federation of Women's Clubs, the International Reform Federation, The Lord's Day Alliance, New York Christian Endeavor members, The Central Conference of American Rabbis, as well as specific church groups such as Baptists, Episcopalians, Methodists, Presbyterians, and, of course, Roman Catholics, all fulminated against the evils. In 1919, The General Federation of Women's Clubs found over 20 percent of the movies objectionable.[7] And by 1921 this situation had not changed. Most crusaders demanded federal control of the movies. Although The National Board of Review, which had been founded earlier, was used as a standard for censorship and many states followed its recommendations, many people felt that the Board was far too lenient toward sin. Various states including New York, Pennsylvania, Ohio, and Kansas, and cities like Chicago had created their own censorship boards. Some repressive laws were challenged as a violation of the First Amendment, but the Supreme Court upheld them.

The Hollywood scandals of 1921 had created a ground swell of revulsion against the motion picture industry. To forestall further proliferation of censorship boards and the threat of a federal board, the industry offered to reform itself. It drew upon the traditional American opposition to governmental interference and the general fear that the Federal board would soon grow beyond its bounds. Many newspapers, though decrying the sins of the movies, while, of course, writing up those sins in sensational articles, were leary of federal censorship, fearing for their own freedoms.

To short-circuit the growing indignation, Hollywood formed the Motion Picture Producers and Distributors of America (MPPDA) in 1922 and hired Will Hays to be its Czar of Morality. At the time, Hays was in President Harding's cabinet and had a lot of personal prestige. This elder of the church was able to placate the moral vigilantes while at the same time fending off their more repressive attempts. Hays in the ensuing years oscillated between satisfying the producers and the public. He was probably a necessary evil, although the first Code that he administered in the twenties partially constrained the freedom of the screen. The list of "Don'ts" and "Be Carefuls" that his office eventually sent to the studios disapproved of people drinking liquor, forbade the ridicule of any religion, and banned the use of ministers as villains or as comic characters. The Code also established that crime could not be shown sympathetically, nor should specific details be explicitly described. But its main concern was sex. Besides stating that "the sanctity of the institution of marriage and the home should be upheld," it advised that "low forms of sex relationship" be avoided. Adultery, the age-old preoccupation of a number of people, "must not be explicitly treated or justified, or presented attractively." Scenes of passion should not be presented in a way to "stimulate the lower and baser element" nor should seduction or rape be "the proper subject for comedy."

Hays, thanks to his aura of respectability, was immediately effective. In November 1922, a referendum in Massachusetts for censorship was defeated two to one, a far better result than the victory of the censors in New York of the previous year.

Hays suggested and then ordered that the studios not make films from certain risqué plays and novels which were being produced and printed, but which might offend the sensibilities of the American public. Although his control was strong in the beginning, Hays bowed to the bolder producers who tried to go as far as they could. Typically, ninety minutes of sin on the screen was followed by five minutes of redemption, which, at least technically, satisfied the Code. But reformers were still annoyed at the movies, and pressures started again for more and more control.

Meantime, the transformation of America was still taking place, and the movies also changed with their audience. The films of the twenties picked up a certain continental sophistication, and the naive farm boys and innocent young girls of Griffith quickly became passé. Many of the more daring films, such as those of Lubitsch or von Stroheim, were almost censorproof; innuendo and unexplicit references made clear to alert audiences what was going on without being too obvious about it. More than once the censors themselves missed the implications of some of the charming little tidbits offered on the screen. Perhaps the slyest director (and actor) of them all was Erich von Stroheim. Whether seducing a woman at the foot of a cross as in *Blind Husbands,* sniffing his middle finger and later raping a retarded girl in *Foolish Wives,* or raising and lowering his sword in some kind of phallic obedience in *The Wedding March,* he created a world that only a knowing audience could really appreciate.

But this new continental approach was not unreservedly liked, even by the

45

An artist and his model in film shot by Edwin S. Porter at
Edison Studios in 1902.

The Babylonian harem in D. W. Griffith's
Intolerance.

The Uplifters raiding a brothel in D. W.
Griffith's *Intolerance*.

Annette Kellerman in *A Daughter of the Gods* and in a 1917 ad promoting chewing gum.

Betty Blythe in full regalia in
The Queen of Sheba.

Mack Sennett's Keystone Bathing Beauties in 1917.

sophisticated press, though it was a step forward in many ways. As one newspaper article said:

> These new plays [the films of Lubitsch, von Stroheim, and others] of sugges-tion, innuendo, and sidelong glances are unearthly clever. Everyone loves them for a change. They give us all a pleased feeling of being highly intelligent. But they don't touch the heart.
>
> They reflect the feelings of an old civilization which has learned, with bitter-ness, that nothing matters very much, that life is only a cruel jest; that if the villain ravishes the poor "gell"—well, the chances are a thousand to one she wouldn't have stayed pure, anyhow—so what's the difference![8]

In contrast, the article praises the films of D. W. Griffith, which did touch the heart, but such praise did not compensate for their declining appeal at the box office.

Even Griffith did not escape censorship. Admittedly, he did not indulge in what he once referred to as "lingerie ads," but censors took exception to his honest and therefore often controversial subject matter. Most film historians think that Griffith suffered from censorship only because of his and Thomas Dixon's view of Reconstruction in *The Birth of a Nation* (1915). But his next film, *Intolerance,* incurred the wrath of a number of people, who blamed him for criticizing chari-ties, prohibitionists accused him of being a "tool of the liquor interests," and do-gooders were angry at his dubious Freudian conclusion, "When women cease to attract men they often turn to reform as a second choice."

The rest of his films were innocuous enough, but the early censors kept after his choice of subject matter and his occasionally too realistic treatment of vio-lence. In *Hearts of The World* (1918), a shot of blood spurting out of the chest of a bayoneted French soldier was eliminated. In *Way Down East* (1920), Lillian Gish's labor pains were too realistically depicted and were cut. *The White Rose* (1923) was banned in a few states because of its story about a hypocritical clergy-man who seduces an orphan girl (Mae Marsh) and unknowingly leaves her preg-nant. There was too much violence in *America* (1924), according to the New York censor. Griffith's sympathy for the Germans in *Isn't Life Wonderful* (1924) was not politic and after the film's first showing the too-German-sounding "Hans" became "Paul," and the Germans became Polish refugees. Even his last film *The Struggle* (1931), suffered a number of cuts.

Perhaps C. B. DeMille best caught the flavor of the postwar period, and in fact helped create it, by his sophisticated showmanship. Although DeMille is often thought of as the stager of great spectacles, his works in the teens and twen-ties were not, except for *Joan the Woman* (1917), *The Ten Commandments* (1923), and *King of Kings* (1927), of such large canvas. His films were modish, almost as up-to-date as the daily newspapers. In *Old Wives For New* (1918) a marriage falters because a wife loses interest in making herself attractive to her

Nita Naldi and Rudolph Valentino as a matador in Fred Niblo's hit of the early twenties *Blood and Sand*.

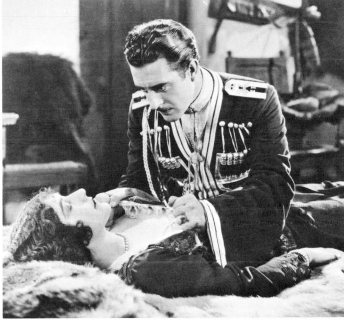

John Gilbert and Aileen Pringle in the twenties film *His Hour*.

Erich von Stroheim as a lecherous count spying on a halfwitted girl in *Foolish Wives*.

Sexuality in the Movies

husband. In *Don't Change Your Husband* (1919), the male was the slovenly one. In *Why Change Your Wife?* (1920), DeMille continued to examine the domestic scene. These box office successes were not films which examined the poor or the rural folk à la Griffith. DeMille was interested in the rich or almost rich. He didn't care about idealized emotion or about the faithfulness of his actors to real life. He was interested in showmanship. The ladies of the audience and some of the more appreciative men wanted to see what was almost a fashion show. The audience witnessed all kinds of high falutin' conduct and fancy dresses—scenes and costumes that would satisfy the fantasies of his popcorn audience. The men looked at the pretty stars in the beautiful dresses and said, "Wow." The girls looked at the same dresses and went home to try to copy them.

When Gloria Swanson went for her morning bath in *Male and Female*, the movies left realism and entered instead a fantasy world that few people then or now could take quite seriously, but a world that somehow they still wanted to see. Certainly it paid off at the box office. Compare the simple, primitive one-room apartment of the modern story of *Intolerance* to the sumptuous bathroom in *Male and Female*. The audience was teased and titillated by Gloria approaching her sunken bathtub with two handmaidens to remove her dressing robe as she immerses herself in the water, just cheating us of the opportunity to observe her forbidden flesh. The task of washing off grime and sweat was elevated into a kind of pagan ritual. This was no longer "takin' a bath" but an obeisance to Eros. The audience with its collective jaw hanging open watches a beautiful woman in an unbelievably luxurious bathroom caressed by sparkling water, then rinsed in rose water and dried with towels held by her attendants. From a point of dramaturgy this scene ostensibly tried to show how spoiled she was, but its effect on the audience was different. It made an exotic rite out of a necessity and brought light into the darkened world of people who had only prosaic bathtubs at home. (In 1923 von Stroheim filmed a sardonic analogue to this scene. The rakish hero of *The Merry-Go-Round* is about to take a bath in an elaborate tub. The valet measures the temperature and makes sure that everything is entirely satisfactory for his master. Meantime, the hero's dog jumps in the tub. The valet shoos him out and the master unknowingly steps into the same water, a grotesque parody of high living.) DeMille created teases and presented the perfect essence of what has ever since been called "Hollywood."

Gloria Swanson, Pola Negri, and others may have been big stars dressed to kill from the bottom of their manicured toes to the top of their plumes, but they were not the only leading ladies. Mary Pickford remained popular with her portrayal of poor waifs and Lillian Gish continued to suffer in *The Scarlet Letter* and *The Wind*. The "woikin goil" still appeared, but she never made the literal and figurative splash that her high living sisters did. *Seventh Heaven* (1927) is more sentimentalized, cloying, and confectionized than anything Griffith ever presented, yet it was an outstanding success. Much of the same audience paid to see these almost diametrically opposed types of heroines. The dressed-to-kill upper-class type became one kind of wish fulfillment; the poor-but-eventually-growing-financially-comfortable-and-sometimes-even-rich-type became the other.

Although censorship had grown in strength during the twenties, it by no means had the thorough control that it would achieve after 1934. There were still a few ways of evading a strict interpretation of the rules administered by the Hays Office. Only after 1934 was the machinery of complete control perfected. By that time censorship problems were less obvious, because the censorship was enforced before the film was made or released and thus overt cases were not as frequent. Studios quickly found that there was no purpose in shooting a scene that could not be used or in producing a film that could not be shown. In the twenties films could still be blessed by Hays and the Motion Picture Producers and Distributors Association and yet be damned by local boards. Of 579 features released in 1928, for example, only 42 escaped some kind of cutting throughout the country.[9]

While the modifications were often minor, mere kibitzing, in some cases they were major and thus detrimental to the film. In the German picture *Variety* (imported in 1926), a serious and well made work, the censor's efforts were catastrophic. In the first reel the motivation of the tragedy was clearly established. A carnival worker (Emil Jannings) longs to return to the circus as a trapeze performer. Both he and his wife had once been star acrobats but a severe fall ruined their career. After a while the trouper succumbs to a younger girl and allows her to tear him away from his wife and child. Director E. A. Dupont took care to show that the big fellow's attachment for the other woman represented more than illicit love; she is a means by which he can again resume his career as an acrobat. In *Censored: The Private Life of The Movies*, the fate of this film at the hands of the American censors was described:

> Thus, when he has left his wife and child and been at once a servant, trainer, and lover to the girl, you can understand his killing the man who takes her from him. . . . No healthy normal man or woman could have detected the slightest note of vulgarity in its portrayal. It was human, earthy tragedy. Yet the censors in every state, with the exception of New York and a few cities, cut it almost to pieces. They cut out the first reel entirely, thus destroying the motivation of the tragedy, implying that the acrobat was married to his Eurasian temptress. From the treatment given *Variety* you can easily understand why it is almost impossible to produce a great movie in this country. There is no such word in the censors' vocabulary as "taste".[10]

Sadly, *Variety* is known in America only in this cut version, even though the missing footage exists in the Library of Congress and could easily be restored to current prints.

Censors not only worried about men living with their mistresses, they also

worried about the tightness of their trousers. In *Drums of Love*, a film made by D. W. Griffith in 1927–28, the censor ordered:

> Cut scenes showing hero in tight trousers bowing and standing at top of stairway. Cut view of him walking (still in tight trousers).[11]

The heights (or depths) of absurdity were reached when the Maryland censors ordered two scenes cut from Murnau's masterpiece, *Sunrise:* one, a "scene of a woman and man reclining" and two, a "scene of a woman wriggling and dancing and a man embracing her." Both were intended to show the sensual interest a farmer had in a woman of the city and how in his passion he is tempted to drown his wife, but apparently these two episodes were seen as corruptive.[12]

In *The Unholy Three* (1925) for example, Lon Chaney, portraying a ventriloquist at a circus, has a girl friend (Mae Busch) who picks the pockets of visitors to the carnival and gives all her proceeds to Chaney. That the two are living together in sin is hinted at financially, but not sexually, except for one rather mild kiss. Later when Chaney and a strong man and a midget start a life of crime, the girl falls in love with a clerk in the pet store they are using as a front. The clerk is completely asexual; this seemingly impotent creature wears glasses, has a mild manner, and is stupidly credulous—a most unsatisfactory replacement for the more virile and imaginative Chaney. That she could leave him for such a milquetoast seems unbelievable, but the reasons are obvious: Chaney, though interesting, is "bad"; the clerk, though dull, is "good." If she were to leave Chaney for another man with sexual potential, she would appear cheap, but leaving him for such a nothing makes her decision a moral one with no hint of the flesh in it to sully her decision. As can readily be seen, censorship caused the major issues of life to be sidestepped. Instead of providing serious conflicts with the tormenting panoply of choices that the world baits us with, films offered simple stories without moral ambiguities.

And so the twenties proceeded, refracted comfortably in a medium that was not allowed to depart substantially from the moral limitations imposed upon it. Some films questioned the old values, but none was allowed to go straightforwardly against them. As a result, the roaring twenties were mostly a mindless roar, but the sound of the Depression, at least for a few years, would make a different noise. And so would the talkies. The collapse of the economy brought about a new cynicism, and allowed innuendo and even more explicit language to be presented to the public.

THE SOUND FILM

Despite the growing freedom in the first few years of sound, the screen was still somewhat hampered by censorship. Unable to depict stories of moral ambiguity and unable to touch upon some of the realities of sex, the American screen specialized in various kinds of teases. In one of the first musicals, *The Broadway Melody* (released in February 1929), the maturity of the screen at that time can be readily observed. Two sisters come to New York to do a song and dance routine. One sister has a boyfriend, a rather ineffectual fellow who sings and even composes. In the course of the film the other sister finds herself attracted to him and, even worse, he returns the interest. Although they both attempt to repress their inclinations, they finally get together and marry, and even invite the single sister to live with them! Sex in this film seems to be little more than a brief hug and kiss. Any real indications of the frustrations of the principals and the realities of the Broadway world are skirted over.

And what else is skirted over is skirts. Whenever the director can, he shows the girls in their underwear. They are constantly drawing baths, changing clothes, and marching around in abbreviated costumes. Even the hero, in a completely bland scene, stands around in his undershorts arguing with the girl. The tone of the film reminds one of some five-year-old children trying to be naughty. Unaware of sex, the best they can do is show people briefly clad. This is Hollywood's puerile sexuality at its most absurd.

The films in the following four years from 1930 to 1934 dealt more honestly with certain facts of life. These facts were not explicit in a visual sense—there was no nudity, for example—but at least they accepted the fact that people lived together without benefit of matrimony and had desires. In Ernst Lubitsch's *Trouble in Paradise* (1932), one of the most brilliant and witty films ever made, there is no question that the male lead (Herbert Marshall) and the female crook (Miriam Hopkins) are living together.

The thirties were the morning after the binge of the twenties. The glow of the candlelit night that had transfused a mundane world into beauty vanished in the harsh glare of dawn. The collapse of the prosperity and fun of the twenties into the seriousness of the Depression destroyed the confidence of the people in moral as well as in economic values. The films reflected this disillusionment. A plethora of malevolent gangsters, monsters both supernatural and natural, trim-legged chorus girls, and smart, clever, and disrespectful Broadway-like dialogue filled the screens. The soft-focus romanticism of the silent screen came into sharp and uncompromising clarity. In *Footlight Parade* (1933), there are an alimony-hungry wife, crooked partners, a designing female, a disloyal colleague, and a general air of dog-eat-dog ambition. Even the heroine, Joan Blondell, is not a clinging vine but a no-nonsense secretary who is shrewd and clever in her own right. Other films of the time are equally realistic not only in their content but in their titles: *Smart Money* (1931, a sympathetic story of a Greek gambler), *Gold Diggers of Broadway* (1933, a musical), *She Done Him Wrong* (1933, Mae West exuding sexuality), and even *Dr. Jekyll and Mr. Hyde* (1932, showing that sex

55

should not be repressed). The innocent maiden did not entirely disappear, but she was far less in evidence. The new girl knew about sex, knew its price, and sometimes she accepted the payment.

As the Depression tightened its grip upon the country, the movies came in for more and more condemnation. Despite the complaints, profits were not adversely affected at first. In fact, the movies seemed to be the one industry untouched by the collapsed economy. The reasons for the good earnings reports were two-fold. One, people wanted to be diverted from their own grim prospects and thus flocked to the movies to escape themselves. Two, they also found the talking pictures a fascinating phenomenon. It was almost a new medium, a medium that was changing and in certain ways definitely improving every day. If the art of the film grew quickly, so did the indignation about the content. The moralists became more and more discontent. Some of the nation's problems, they felt, came from the disregard of the people for the good, solid, moral values. The Depression was the result of the decadence and erosion of ideals that were so rampant during the twenties. If the nation were to survive, the emphasis would have to be shifted from sex and crime and criticism of established institutions to more healthy and uplifting subject matter. In short, the mouth of this new and obstreperous medium would have to be washed out with soap.

How was this cleansing act to be performed? It would be aided by the pubcation in May, 1933, of a book called *Our Movie Made Children*, which surprisingly turned out to be a best seller. It authoritatively declared what a malign influence the cinema had on the youth of the nation of which one third was illhoused, ill-clad, and ill-fed, and unfortunately also ill-advised by a Hollywood lacking morality and taste. The book pointed out that of a sample 115 pictures, 59 contained murders that were either attempted or committed. Furthermore, 71 violent deaths occurred in 54 of the pictures.[13] Such an influence did not bode well for the youth of a nation. The book graphically and logically pointed out just how effective films were in shaping the attitudes of audiences. The medium's influence was proved to be immense, a fact that the moralists made good use of when they asked for further restraints.

The book did not blame just the talking pictures. It cited the effect that the 1925 *The Phantom of the Opera* had had on audiences:

> Children would scream all over the theatre; many of them would dash out and mothers would leave the theatre with frightened and hysterical children clinging to them. . . . And at times the children would vomit as a result of their emotional condition.
> According to one trained nurse, *The Phantom of the Opera* caused "eleven faintings and one miscarriage" in a single day. Four of the eleven who fainted were men. The average was three or four faintings a day during the run of the picture.[14]

Filming chorus girls in *Painted Angel*.

The hall of human harps in *Follies of 1934*.

Maidens in *Roman Scandals*.

The Honeymoon Hotel number from *Footlight Parade*.

The silent classic *The Phantom of the Opera* with Lon Chaney was cited in the 1933 book *Our Movie Made Children* as having an overpowering effect on audiences.

After the 1934 *Tarzan and His Mate* the studio was forced by the Breen Office to provide Johnny Weissmuller and Maureen O'Sullivan with less revealing costumes.

Joan Crawford as chorus girl in *Dancing Lady*.

MOTHERED BY AN APE—HE KNEW ONLY THE LAW OF THE JUNGLE — *to seize what he wanted!*

TARZAN THE APE MAN

with
Johnny **WEISSMULLER**
Neil **HAMILTON**
C. Aubrey **SMITH**
Maureen **O'SULLIVAN**

Based upon the characters created by
EDGAR RICE BURROUGHS

Adaptation by
CYRIL HUME
Dialogue by
IVOR NOVELLO

ANOTHER MIRACLE PICTURE
directed by
W. S. VAN DYKE
Creator of "TRADER HORN"

METRO-GOLDWYN-MAYER

Edwina Booth in W. S. van Dyke's jungle
film *Trader Horn.*

Osgood Perkins watches as Paul Muni inspects
Karen Morley in Howard Hawks' pre-Code
gangster film *Scarface.*

Mae West in *I'm No Angel* before the 1934 Code diluted
her image and bawdy humor.

Sultry forties heroines
Veronica Lake and Ann Sheridan.

Fred Astaire and Ginger Rogers

But the horror films were not what the moralists were worried about. They did not put up a fuss about *Dracula* or *Frankenstein* or the later sequels. They said they were concerned with the values of the whole society and how those values were being eroded for box office success. But their main interest was sex. The authors of *Our Movie Made Children* complained about the disappearance of the once innocent heroines: "Virtue may have been at a premium once—but apparently it slumped along with the other leading stocks."[15]

During the teens and early twenties women tended to be of two kinds: the good maiden and the evil vamp. But this polarization faded and in its stead came the new woman, essentially still an innocent, but acting like a vamp. Like Joan Crawford in *Our Dancing Daughters* (1928), she flirted and radiated sex, but she held herself back. The new breed of woman may have been more realistic, but she also helped influence the behavior of millions of girls who, in turn, affected the reality which Hollywood was supposedly reflecting. In short, there was feedback. As a result, the decade of the twenties wrought a behavioral change in women which was absolutely unprecedented in world history. New modes of conduct snowballed into a revolutionary avalanche and the New Girl emerged.

In *Our Movie Made Children* there were also complaints about Hollywood's preoccupation with love and courtship. Although marriage was the end goal, the connubial state was seldom depicted. In real life over 60 percent of the males were married, but in the movies only about 15 percent had succumbed to the noble institution.[16] Love became the be-all and end-all and marriages concluded most films. Such a criticism did not take into account that many novels and plays also concerned themselves with the same situation. Of course the movies depicted love. Their fantasy world was the perfect place to deposit its delightful but often temporary presence.

Films, the book complained, not only placed a false emphasis on the transient joys of love, they also instructed young people in the art of love-making (at least in its beginning stages). As one boy who copied John Gilbert's ardent style put it:

> I place the blame not on my inability to imitate what I have seen on the screen, but on someone else's inability to imitate Greta Garbo's receptive qualities.[17]

But if our embryonic John Gilbert lacked an adequate partner, so did many a young Garbo long for a Gilbert. Each was faced with a formidable problem: to find a mate as attractive, romantic, and polished as the great profiles on the screen, an impossible quest in a prosaic universe plagued by alarm clocks, pimples, and financial worries.

Our Movie Made Children's examination of the sociological and psychological effects of the movies demonstrated with statistical and seemingly scientific information how powerful an effect movie-going had on audiences. Its evidence

61

might have been weathered had not the Depression finally affected the industry. Profits were good in 1930 and 1931, but by 1932 and 1933 disaster struck. Warner Brothers, which had shown a fourteen million dollar profit in 1929, lost that same amount in 1932. Fox in 1932 was sixteen million in the hole, Universal one and a half million, RKO over ten million in 1932 and over four million in 1933. Paramount did the worst of all. After an eighteen million dollar profit in 1930, it plunged to a fifteen million deficit in 1932, and then went into bankruptcy. The only two studios which showed a profit were MGM and poverty-row Columbia.

In the meantime, certain groups in the United States were growing more adamant about the kinds of morals that films were promulgating. The most powerful and vocal body was the Roman Catholic Church. "An admission to an Indecent Movie is a ticket to Hell," said placards wielded by some parochial children.[18] In October 1933, a high church official spoke to an annual convention of Catholic Charities in New York:

> Catholics are called by God, the Pope, the Bishops and the priests to a united
> and vigorous campaign for the purification of the cinema, which has become a
> deadly menace to morals.[19]

Martin Quigley, who edited two powerful movie trade magazines, and Joseph Breen, a layman in the church, decided to create a Legion of Decency in an attempt to force the eight major studios to conform to their standards. Thus in 1933 the church set up its own censorship organization to pass upon the virtues and vices of individual films. Ironically, Americans who were just escaping from the punitive pressures of prohibition were now to be faced with another encroachment on their freedoms. The Legion of Decency threatened to order their ten million members to boycott Hollywood's films. The sunny colony of ulcerated moguls looked up fearfully from their red-inked financial reports, considered the problem, and capitulated. Rather than suffer the box office losses threatened by the church, Hollywood finally decided to cooperate with the Legion and to allow its scripts to be tailored to meet the church's new demands.

A new Motion Picture Code had been adopted at Hays' suggestion in 1930, but it had not been taken seriously by the studios. To guarantee its enforcement a Production Code Administration, headed by Joseph Breen who had helped write the Code, was established four years later in Hollywood and the Code itself was amplified. Financed by the studios, the Production Code Administration was authorized to grant a "Seal of Approval" only to movies that adhered to its guidelines. Any movie without the Seal, according to studio agreement, would not be distributed or exhibited in any theatres.

This Code was established by the industry in 1934 as a self-regulating device not only to prevent the loss of Catholic audiences but to forestall the possibility of more state censorship boards and perhaps even Federal regulation. The guidelines adopted by the MPPA were very similar to the Legion of Decency's standards. The Code was not concerned with art but morals. It stated that pictures would not be produced which would "lower the moral standards of those who see it." Only "correct standards" of life could be shown. Words like *lustful, lecherous, brutal, indecent* ran through the document as if they were definite entities rather than subjective terms. "The treatment of bedrooms must be governed by good taste and delicacy." Nobody could swear by saying God, Lord, Jesus Christ, Hell, S.O.B., damn, Gawd or any other earthly or heavenly expressions. Adultery could not be "explicitly treated or justified or presented attractively." The Code proceeded to spell out many other matters to be avoided, such as methods of crime, drug traffic, drinking of liquor unless basic to the plot, excessive kissing, sexual perversion, white slavery, miscegenation, and subjects reflecting on the integrity of the government and its officials. Two of these forbidden matters were not really the concern of the Catholics, but were added to satisfy other pressure groups. The limitation against excessive drinking was included to make the Drys happy, although it was seldom enforced. The other was miscegenation which was included to pacify the South's deep neurosis on the subject.

This new code sounded straitlaced, and indeed it was. Some people in the industry felt that it would easily be violated, but that proved not to be the case. Scripts had to be submitted before production to Breen's Production Code Administration office which approved or rejected them. Then the film, made from the approved script, was submitted for further checking to be sure that no impurities crept in during shooting. This method of precensorship was a quiet and painless way of laundering the product before the public would ever have been in a position to take sides in a borderline case. When the Code was ratified by the MPPA, Hollywood gave up its own freedom, although ostensibly to itself, since the Code was supposedly administered by its own people. Industry spokesmen neglected to say outright that the church's demands and the Code were almost synonymous.

The Legion had three categories of film classification: A, B, and C. The A rating explained that a film was entirely pure, the B that there were certain dangers, and C that it was condemned and must not be seen. Although the C rating had temporarily been applied to a few films made by the major studios, no film was actually issued with a C rating for many years and thus there were at first no *causes célèbres*. The producers were too afraid to sustain a Roman Catholic boycott and so each condemned film was reedited or reshot to escape its supposed economic damnation. As a result, the Legion was 100 percent effective with films issued by major studios and 97 percent effective with overall American produc-

63

Sexuality in the Movies

tion. The church's official attitude towards the new art can be seen in Pope Pius XI's statement in 1936:

> The cinema speaks not to individuals but to multitudes and does so in circumstances, time, place and surroundings which are the most apt to arouse unusual enthusiasm for good as well as for bad and to conduct that collective exaltation which, as experience teaches us, may assume the most morbid form.
> A motion picture is viewed by people who are seated in a dark theatre and whose faculties, mental, physical and often spiritual, are relaxed. . . .[20]

The Legion of Decency's code and the MPPA Code were repressive and narrow-minded in the worst way, reflecting the most parochial and puerile attitudes of the audiences they were trying to shield. Films had been relatively lusty, hard-hitting, and biting during the early thirties, as exemplified by the humor and cynicism of *The Dark Horse* in which a nincompoop gets nominated for governor; the bawdy implications and satire of the Marx Brothers; criticism of the popular press and the depiction of a sleazy, unfrocked cleric (Boris Karloff) in *Five Star Final*; the indictment of injustice in *I Am a Fugitive From a Chain Gang*; the affirmation of the sex drive in *Dr. Jekyll and Mr. Hyde*; the incisive humor of *Footlight Parade*; the open implications of sex by Mae West in *She Done Him Wrong*; the sophisticated milieu of Sternberg's *Morocco* in which Dietrich appears in a man's tuxedo and kisses a girl on the lips; and the high style of comedy in Lubitsch's *Trouble in Paradise.* All of these films would have had to be modified if made after the Code. These pictures were intelligent and honest and by no means "immoral" by the standards of Western civilization of the last few centuries, but in the early thirties they seemed to the censorious to glow with unrelieved sin, salaciousness, and cynicism, and to be foul exudations upon the pure landscape of America.

With the bite, thrust, and wit of films hampered by the 1934 Code, moviemakers tried to imply as much as they could. How much could they slip across before the censorship board would rap their fingers? A man and a woman sleeping together outside of the bonds of matrimony had to be broached so subtly that the very fact was unclear. Audiences always had to infer. In short, every reference or innuendo had to be scrubbed and cold-showered. The man-about-town who comes back to his bachelor apartment every night at three or four o'clock in the morning hardly gets a chance to kiss his female guest before something interferes to keep her not only unsullied but, as the film implies, in a permanently virginal state. Such plots eventually had the hero sleeping in the bathtub or, more comfortably, on the couch while the girl lay ensconced in a boudoir barricaded as if Vandals and Goths stood at the door. Admittedly such plots could be found

64

in pre-Code films, but the possibility of more blissful joys in the wee hours of the morning had been at least hinted at. The Code could best be summed up, at least sexually, by "Bedrooms are for sleeping."

But sex was not the only concern of the Code. It also worried about the treatment of the clergy, avoided references to drugs, and omitted homosexuals (the Franklin Pangborn type of sissy often appeared but did not ooh or ah if he portrayed a tailor measuring an inner seam). The Code placed some restrictions upon treatments of crime and violence, stating, for example, "Brutal killings are not to be presented in detail." Nevertheless, the Code was more lenient on violence than sex.

Some American intellectuals berated the low state of cinematic realism and honesty and from the mid-thirties on through the sixties blamed censorship for the failure of the American cinema to grow up. They felt that the Code was far too strict and that the Legion of Decency was even less reasonable. The Legion with its concern for morals frequently recommended mediocre films and disapproved the more intelligent ones that broached subjects offensive to its sense of propriety. The Legion also wielded what was in effect a veto power on any American film. The prospect of its condemned rating so frightened the producer that he invariably recut or reshot the picture.

Garbo's last film, *Two-Faced Woman,* had the famous actress play a ski instructor whom Melvyn Douglas, a big-time publisher, marries because of her unsophisticated nature. Once back in New York, however, he starts to backslide. Garbo goes to New York and pretends she is her own twin sister, a sophisticated vamp. Douglas falls for her, not knowing that she and his wife are the same person, and tries to make love to her. This was too shocking for the Legion, for the film implied that men are capable of sleeping with women other than their wives. Whatever comedy value the film had was lost when the studio was compelled to insert in the middle of the film a scene showing the husband telephone his wife and thus discover that she and the twin were one and the same. The plot thereafter made little sense, and whatever wit and fun that were in it fizzled badly.

The Legion's narrow interpretation of screen morality was even more obvious in its judgments on foreign films (which were made, of course, without the benefit of the Code). The Legion condemned a number of foreign films, such as *The Blue Angel, La Ronde,* and *Miss Julie,* that were and still are considered masterpieces. Although *The Outlaw* with Jane Russell had caused considerable censorship trouble and its director Howard Hughes had raised questions about the Code's legality, it was a controversial Italian film titled *The Miracle* that was largely responsible for permanently weakening the power both of the Legion and of the Hollywood Code.

65

THE CONTEMPORARY FILM

The bridle of censorship was kept upon the cinematic steed for close to two decades with hardly a protest until *The Miracle* started what eventually turned out to be a stampede. Roberto Rossellini made this short film in 1948 about a Catholic peasant, played by Anna Magnani, who believes that her child was fathered by St. Joseph. When *The Miracle* came to New York in 1950, it was approved by the state censor and shown in a New York art theater in December. There was at first little reaction, but soon the Catholic leaders heard of it and exerted pressure on the theater. When that didn't work, the City Commissioner of Licenses was prevailed upon to stop its presentation. A brief court action rescinded the Commissioner's ruling. Pressure then shifted upstate to the Censorship Board. Telegrams, letters, and personal contacts by the Catholic hierarchy caused the board to revoke its former approval. The case was then brought to the United States Supreme Court which decided that the law invoked against the film violated the Fourteenth Amendment as prior restraint, interfered with the separation between church and state, and employed the term *sacrilegious* too vaguely. In May 1952, the Supreme Court decided against prior restraint and affirmed, at long last, that film was entitled to the same guarantees of freedom as the press.

As a result of the Supreme Court decision the first breaches in the imposing fortress of censorship were made in the fifties. Although the movies had won their constitutional freedom at long last, they exercised that freedom rather gingerly at first because of the strong economic and civil pressures of the church. In 1951 Elia Kazan's film of Tennessee Williams' *A Streetcar Named Desire* suffered a number of cuts because of the Legion. When Kazan did another Tennessee Williams script, *Baby Doll*, in 1956, he had control of the final cut. When he wouldn't knuckle under to the Legion, Cardinal Spellman, Archbishop of New York, ordered all Catholics within his archdiocese to avoid the film under "pain of sin." In Albany, Bishop Scully, long connected with the Legion, tried to coerce the Strand, a local theater, not to show the film. When the theater refused, the Bishop not only forbade Catholics to see the film but punished the Strand by ordering Catholics not to patronize that theater for six months. Earlier, in 1953, the Bishop and veterans groups quietly forced another Albany theater (the Delaware) to discontinue showing *Limelight* because it was made by Chaplin, whose sex life and politics were objectionable to the church. In the fifties and even up to the early sixties the Legion still had its strength in heavily Catholic areas, but it could no longer exert the same kind of pressures it once had on the studios.

The Code, too, weakened as a repressive force after such films as *The Pawnbroker* (1965) and *Who's Afraid of Virginia Woolf* (1967) were given seals. At long last great screen artists were allowed the same freedoms that the novelists had earlier won. They would be able to refer to all the actualities of motivation

Marlon Brando and Kim Stanley in final
scene of Elia Kazan's *A Streetcar Named
Desire*, among the first Hollywood films
made primarily for adult audiences.

Anna Magnani in *The Miracle* which provoked
a landmark censorship case in New York.

Despite controversial use of nudity, Sidney
Lumet's mid-sixties film *The Pawnbroker*
received Code seal.

Birger Malmsten and Gunnel Lindblom in
Ingmar Bergman's X-rated *The Silence*.

and to depict the whole range of human conduct. But most of the great artists—such as Lubitsch, Sternberg, Mamoulian, and James Whale—had either retired or died by the sixties, and the kind of audiences that once would have appreciated wit and style and sophistication had also either died or no longer went to the movies. If the old masters had vanished, new ones, it was hoped, would soon develop, although the ratio of artists to hacks and opportunists has never been impressive.

The freedom from silence which ushered in the thirties was equalled by the freedom from censorship in the sixties. The results were not, however, equally impressive cinematically. The movies were no longer a basic part of American culture. Television had usurped that role. Entertainment had shifted from the theaters to the home, and society as a whole had shed many of its old values and moved into a different atmosphere. Socially, morally, and economically, the sixties turned out to be twentieth century America's most revolutionary decade, far more so even than the twenties. Within ten years whole areas of thought and behavior had changed.

The movie world also experienced serious changes. The star system virtually disappeared. New faces cropped up, enjoyed great popularity for one or two films, but passed from view when they did not guarantee high returns at the box office. Hollywood, so long dominant, further declined as the movie-making capital of the world. Union demands raised costs to astronomical heights and property taxes made studio lots too expensive to maintain. With more portable equipment, smaller crews, and cheaper foreign labor, Hollywood films were made almost every place but Hollywood. The glamorous panache disappeared and film output declined. Large budgeted productions vanished in the sea of the red ink they left behind. Major firms like MGM teetered and tottered and other important studios were bought up or merged. Suddenly, the aging studio executives realized that what they once thought was sure-fire entertainment no longer appealed. Somehow there was a new crowd out there, one that apparently did not care about stories with a beginning, a middle, and an end, didn't mind average-looking leading men (Dustin Hoffman), and rather homely women (Barbra Streisand). Furthermore, that new crowd saw films not in large downtown theaters (many of which had been turned into parking lots) but in small theaters seating a couple of hundred, or in drive-ins where various rites of initiation were sanctified by wafts of rancid popcorn. The movie audience shrank, production budgets shrank, and even some industry egos shrank. Of the films made, only a handful were real money-makers; most of the others failed. People definitely went out to see a particular film, not just to "go to the movies."

Hollywood had to try to offer something more enticing than the free TV at home. In the fifties it had tried large screens (later dropped because films in CinemaScope could not play easily on the television tube), color films (but TV got

color too), and stereophonic sound, but audiences continued to decrease. One way
of gaining larger attendance was to offer new and shocking subject matter, something that could not possibly be shown in the living room. Hollywood's defiance
of its own Code and the Legion was caused partly by the realization that the
screen needed freedom to entice customers and that the risk of offending some
groups was equalled and surpassed by the advantage of pleasing others.

The new freedom, however, had its own particular limitations. Ethnic humor
(and slurs) were unofficially banned. The lazy, good-for-nothing Negro, the Irish
cop with his brogue, the Jewish peddler, the Italian gangster, and many other
stereotypes disappeared. But if this kind of freedom was hindered, other kinds
opened. The hero (he was not really a hero any more, just a male lead) could sleep
with a woman without being married to her, and she could sleep with him and
conceivably have slept with some other men before and not be compelled to die
under the wheels of a train or to waste away from some dread disease. Boys and
girls and men and women could do on the screen what they often did in real life.
As most of the old taboos disappeared, film finally became capable of touching
upon any subject it chose.

Unfortunately, problems beyond mere youthful romance, that is, subject
matter that might appeal to older people, were not often treated on the screen
for the simple reason that there were not many mature people in theaters to support the films. Thus the subject of a woman over forty trying to find meaning to
her life (such as in the 1926 picture, *Dancing Mothers*) could now be made with
no censorship problems, but no young audience would have empathy with the
woman's problem. Thus the new freedom for filmmakers had to contend with a
new limitation: the narrowness of its audience's interests. Many good scripts were
now rejected, and those that were accepted often had to have sensationalism
added (either of sex or violence or often both) in order to have "contemporary"
appeal at the box office.

The films that best reflected the problems and desires of young people became the box office winners, such titles as *The Graduate* (1967) and *Easy Rider*
(1969). *The Graduate* echoed young people's resentment of the establishment,
and *Easy Rider* showed their urge for wandering and their paranoid fears of being
destroyed by a hostile society. While many films took an "anti" approach, few
were willing to handle the lives of people past twenty-five. Contrary to what the
screen illustrated, reality for most people after college did not consist of seeking
a new sex partner, engaging in violence, racing motorcycles, surfing, or wandering around the world. Instead life was often composed of a rusting car, fraying
furniture, bulging waistlines, "why Johnny can't read," crabgrass, and a sullen
horizon of fractured dreams. Such matters were frequently the *real* reality, but
the screen avoided this kind of subject matter even more than did the films of
previous decades. Yet many people took the screen's four-letter words, explicit

69

action, and the frequent presence of ugliness and unpleasantness, as reality, not realizing that such unlovely details could be almost as spurious as the glamorized world of the movies' past.

The changes in movie entertainment did not occur overnight. The transition was slow but seemingly inevitable between the rigors of the Code and today's complete permissiveness. The Supreme Court and economic pressures had caused the transformation. *The Miracle* had been supposedly sacrilegious, but obscenity became the next legal hurdle. This was not a problem confined solely to film. Literature first fought the battle. In 1957 in *Roth* vs. *the United States*, the Supreme Court decided that while obscenity was "utterly without redeeming social value" and not protected by the First Amendment, explicit sex—if encased in a work of value—was not necessarily obscene. The test, the Court said, was "whether to the average person, applying contemporary community standards, the dominant theme of the material taken as a whole appeals to prurient interest."

In the next few years, however, the Court began reversing obscenity convictions, finding that even the most doubtful works had some "redeeming" value and thus that fewer and fewer works were "obscene." Then in 1967 the Court confessed its own confusion and more or less retired from the field except when the material was being "pandered," when it was going to juveniles, and when it was "thrust" upon the public. It was during the middle sixties that nudist films began to be shown with the obligatory volleyball game in which genitalia could be glimpsed by the quick-of-eye.

As a result of these legal decisions, more sensational sex films like *I, a Woman* began to appear in neighborhood theaters. This Swedish movie about a nymphomaniac contained somewhat explicit language and was soft-core; the film showed the heroine's breasts and implied the sex act but avoided glimpses of the "privates" in action. The immense amount of money this film took in prompted further imports and encouraged producers in Europe and importers in America to top the previous film by further explicitness.

In October 1969, another Swedish film, *The Language of Love*, was seized by American customs as "obscene." The distributors, Chevron Pictures, piously claimed that their film "is a lecture and it has educational value." Although Chevron had never previously expressed interest in "educational" pictures, it now took its self-appointed and profitable mission seriously and innocently wondered why anyone should be offended at their pedagogical aims.

In *The Language of Love* a panel of experts discussed sex and a number of couples demonstrated various positions.[21] This film contained hard-core elements that were supposedly sanctified by the learned panel. For a thorough evening of arousal audiences had to tune out but view in. Once these graphic sexual elements were presented, it was only a matter of time before more sex and less talk began to get by. Finally film viewers would have to live without the benefit of the learned

90 minutes
of violence,
excitement
and
SEX

...he's X rated and animated!

Screen sex after the demise of the Hollywood Code:
*Alex in Wonderland, Myra Breckinridge,
The Lickerish Quartet, Fritz the Cat.*

Everything you've heard about Myra Breckinridge is true!

At last,
the book that couldn't
be written is now
the motion picture
that couldn't be made!

voices and derive the educational message from the bouncing images alone. Viewers managed quite well.

Another Swedish film, *I Am Curious—Yellow*, made history in 1969, attracting lines around the block in New York City and other cities because of several explicit and widely-publicized sexual sequences. *I Am Curious—Yellow* came in for a large share of litigation, which, of course, only swelled its fame. The various communities which declared it obscene lost in the higher courts. In November 1969, a Superior Court justice in Massachusetts declared the film obscene but a month later Boston permanently lost its previous fame as a city of blue noses. The Federal Court there ruled that state authorities "cannot prosecute theater operators for showing the film."[22]

American independent filmmakers immediately tried to equal and then to surpass the imported productions. The major Hollywood studios—those that still remained—decided that they too would cash in on the public's seemingly insatiable interest in sex. Hollywood was certainly adept at the subject, but it had been confined to exploiting breasts in tight-fitting sweaters and showing off bodies in bathing suits. In the days of the Code the girl might slip into the bathroom, dodge coyly behind the shower curtain, and parade around in her bra and panties. Hollywood decided that the audience would like to see her take the shower.

When the courts ruled in favor of total permissiveness on the screen, the motion picture industry began to worry that local laws would be invoked and that distributors and exhibitors would be mired down in expensive and time-consuming litigation in various cities and towns throughout the United States. "Contributing to the delinquency of minors" was a valid and seemingly incontestable law. To forestall the institution of new kinds of censorship, either state or federal, Hollywood invented a rating system which took effect on November 1, 1968. It would forewarn people as to whether a film was general entertainment or whether it contained explicit sexual material. A year later, in 1969, a leader of the exhibitors agreed that the new system was "the only vehicle which has stemmed an all-consuming tidal wave of anti-pornography, anti-violence restrictive legislation and concomitant censorship."[23]

The MPAA rating system had been created by the types of films being offered. Explicit sexual behavior obviously was not considered wise fare for children, and rather than lose the whole market the industry decided to lose just a part of it and hoped that limiting a film to adults with an X rating would bring in those customers who had become displeased with Hollywood's tame depiction of the world.

The 1968 rating system had a G (for general audience), M (for mature ones), R (for people over 18), and X (for those over 21). In 1970 the M was changed to GP (general patronage), since the M scared away too many people. In the following years other modifications were made. The GP was changed to PG (parental guidance), the R was opened to people under 17 if accompanied by parent or guardian, and the X opened to those over 17 and closed to everyone under that. Thus within five years the producers and exhibitors managed to erode the classifications so that the lucrative 17-21 year bracket could go to the theaters. Ironically even some films with a PG rating, and thus acceptable for all audiences, could not even have been made during the years of the old Code. In fact, some now rated PG might have landed the theater owner in jail a decade before.

By 1970 Hollywood took full advantage of its freedom: anal rape in *Myra Breckenridge*; frontal nudity both male and female in many regular studio feature films; fornication with a pig in *Futz* and with a chicken in *End of the Road*; explicit language, first referring to female genitalia as "the big C" in *The Arrangement* and then all four letters in *Quiet Days in Clichy* and *Carnal Knowledge*; and nudging ads, "It puts you in the cockpit" for *The Stewardesses*.

Unfortunately, the principles of the rating system were not always so strictly observed by the rating board members or the studios. The categories were soon haggled into relative meaninglessness. Each company tried to inject sex into its film and then, when the MPAA gave it an "adult" rating, the company complained that such a rating would hurt at the boxoffice. For example, in 1971 MGM was upset about the R rating for *Ryan's Daughter,* appealed, and won a GP without cutting anything. A GP film had not earlier been interpreted so freely, for the film contained some nudity that, at least in previous years, would not have been considered necessary to the emotional and narrative needs of the film. In other cases the rating board, while officially disavowing censorship, has functioned like a censor by encouraging studios and directors to make cuts in their films to avoid an X rating and possible loss of box office revenue.

Deep Throat, a hard-core pornographic film, was one of the most notorious and thus profitable films of 1972. Known more discreetly in some advertisements as just plain *Throat*, the film depicts the adventures and travails of a maiden whose organ of sexual pleasure has developed near her larynx. To satisfy herself, and incidentally to give pleasure to her male acquaintances, she performs what years ago used to be called "an unnatural act."

The film not only saw magnificent box office returns but also considerable litigation as well. When it came to trial in late 1972 various defense witnesses spoke of its "very amusing premise," its satirical intent, and its ability "to expand viewers' sexual horizons." But the New York judge who had listened to all the explanations, studied the testimony, and witnessed the film was not convinced. In a thirty-five-page opinion he decided that *Deep Throat* was "indisputably and irredeemably" obscene. He referred to it as a "feast of carrion and squalor," a "nadir of decadence," and "brazenly explicit." The judge concluded that "This is one throat that deserves to be cut." The World Theater in New York, where the film had been playing since June 1972, stopped exhibiting the film in March and put on its marquee: "Judge Cuts Throat, World Mourns."[24]

Life became even more complicated for the movie industry when the Supreme Court in June 1973 decided that pornography could no longer be judged nationally, but that the question whether a work was obscene or not depended on the standards of the community where it was offered. The Court stated that the standards of Maine or Mississippi might be different from those acceptable in Las Vegas or New York. As a result, some films are protected by the First Amendment in some states, but not in others. Unfortunately, the first major film to be prosecuted for obscenity after this decision was not an out-and-out porno movie but *Carnal Knowledge,* a film that had explicit language, some explicit action, and also a mature theme. In 1974 the U.S. Supreme Court overturned the Georgia conviction of *Carnal Knowledge,* implying that the film was not obscene enough to lose its First Amendment protection, even though it might have shocked the community standards of Georgia.

The problem of censorship and obscenity in films has by no means been solved. *Variety,* as befits a trade paper, has invariably favored freedom from censorship, but even it acknowledges that "reasonable people of all political persuasions find hardcore pornography appalling."[25] Some reasonable people, however, do not find it appalling and argue that nothing should be prevented on the screen.

But sex is not the only thing being explicitly portrayed in contemporary movies; another is violence. Audiences had been kept from seeing too many gory details in the thirties and forties by the Code. The horror, gangster, and western films had violent action, but gross examples of sadism were avoided. In *Dracula* (1931), the vampire leans over to bite the throat; he does not lap up the blood nor does the heroine heave her bosom with orgasmic delight. The murders and carnage in earlier films were either referred to suggestively or kept in discreet long shot. Eyes did not bulge out and tongues protrude in strangulations, as in Hitchcock's *Frenzy* or *The Godfather.* The classic aesthetic distance of the ancient Greeks, who omitted violence from their stages, has now been eliminated. Oedipus blinded himself off stage, whereas today we would see the pins go into his eyes and the bloody aftermath of his empty sockets.

Censors, when faced with the problem of violence versus sex, have usually adhered to the unwritten motto: better slay than lay. They preferred that people make war rather than love, for the one, though sometimes fatal, was considered less dangerous—and in some cases advantageous—to the preservation of society. It was considered morally better that a nation lose its men in fighting than lose its women in debauchery. That violence could also be a kind of debauchery was not admitted, despite the views of many people that too much brutality brutalizes, just as too much hard-core porn may demean.

As audiences once enjoyed the mindless but often beautiful films of the thirties, so we tend to endure the mindless but often ugly films of today. The new permissiveness of the screen did not quite reveal the green pastures the intelligent public had so patiently awaited. Andrew Sarris, critic for *The Village Voice*, confessed his own mixed feelings about the new era:

> I mean long live the sexual revolution and freedom of expression and all that. But why don't I feel happier now that all the tabus, topless and bottomless, are being shattered on the screen? Heaven knows I have always followed the crowd in gazing at the slightest intimation of forbidden fleshiness. More often than not I've drifted down into the quasi-criminal depths of depravity in search of mysteries society hypocritically deplored. I have always been against all censorship, but, as I have always suspected, all the freedom in the world need not necessarily inspire aesthetic excellence, and aesthetic excellence is the name of my game. . . .[26]

Many people defend explicit sexual content in films as if it were performing some great aesthetic service. In some cases it has. *The Silence*, for instance, and more recently *Carnal Knowledge,* conveyed points that would have been thoroughly impossible under the old Code. But for every effective use of the new freedom, there are dozen of abuses.

Despite the arguments of experts that no one can prove that films with graphic sex or violence have a harmful effect on viewers, there seems little doubt that films do have some effect on society and that all of us live with such effects. Either censorship is brought back (with all its old problems) or the consequences of complete freedom (with all its new problems) will confront us in the future. The question of how society will function when all the checks that a few thousand years of civilization have imposed (however repressive, unjust, and hypocritical) are weakened has yet to be answered. Perhaps there is an ecology of the human spirit. If so, can there not only be destruction of physical resources but the destruction of psychic ones as well? Can society, like the earth itself, become so polluted that it can no longer cleanse itself? Such an apocalyptic vision may seem too hysterical, for mankind usually manages to find a way through its troubles. At least it has up to now. But in the present situation the way isn't going to be easy.

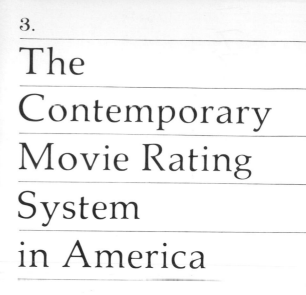

EVELYN RENOLD

Susan George, Ken Hutchison, and Del Henney following the rape sequence which was shortened to avoid an X rating in Sam Peckinpah's *Straw Dogs*.

3.
The Contemporary Movie Rating System in America

ONE of the most important and controversial American films released in recent years was Sam Peckinpah's *Straw Dogs*. In this bold, disturbing film, the director works out his familiar themes—man's innate propensity for violence, the link between sex and aggression, the power of the male bonding instinct—in new and provocative ways.

However, the version of the film seen by most critics and by the general public was not quite what the director had intended it to be. Just before release, *Straw Dogs* was cut—not at the behest of the studio that had finished the film, but rather according to the instructions of the Motion Picture Association of America's Ratings Board. The climax of the film, in which the erstwhile shy, inhibited mathematics professor goes on a bloody rampage, brutally murdering a group of ruffians who have raped his wife and tormented him, was shortened; more importantly, the daring rape sequence was severely cut, thereby obscuring the meaning of the scene, and, to some extent, the meaning of the film itself. (The wife is assaulted twice; she responds with pleasure and excitement to the first attack, but is horrified by the second, a more violent, anal rape. In the release version of the film, the second rape is almost eliminated.)

Unfortunately, the last-minute alteration of *Straw Dogs* does not represent an isolated instance of Ratings Board interference. Far from it. Close to half the commercial films made in the United States are in some way reshaped by the movie industry's censors, an isolated group of seven people who work in Beverly Hills, California.

The ratings system, largely the brainchild of MPAA President Jack Valenti, was inaugurated in fall 1968, with the blessings of the nine major studios (the

76

member companies of the MPAA) and of the organizations representing industry exhibitors (NATO—National Association of Theater Owners) and distributors (IFIDA—International Film Importers and Distributors of America). In announcing the newly devised ratings scheme, Valenti officially sounded the death knell for the industry's highly restrictive Production Code, which had governed the content of American films since 1934 had lost much of its potency by the mid-sixties. As the social climate in the country changed, and the movie-going public indicated its readiness to accept more sophisticated, adult material on the screen, studios began releasing films without the sanction of the Production Code seal. In 1966, the Code was watered down considerably to accommodate the subject matter of the more daring films that were surfacing; at the same time, the Code office was empowered to designate such films "suggested for mature audiences." Finally, the decision was made to scrap the Code and formulate a new structure.

The original rating categories announced by Valenti were (as also noted by Arthur Lennig in the previous chapter): G—general audiences, all ages permitted; M—suggested for mature audiences (later changed to GP and then to PG—some material may not be suitable for pre-teenagers); R—restricted, under seventeen requires accompanying adult; and X—no one under seventeen admitted. The ratings system was billed as a self-regulatory classification device, pure and simple—one designed, in other words, to provide information about films, and not to censor them as the Code had.

From the outset, however, the ratings operation bore more than a casual resemblance to the Production Code program it had ostensibly replaced. The ratings system, despite pious proclamations to the contrary, was basically conceived as a holding action, a protection against the threat of censorship beyond the confines of the motion picture industry. That same threat had breathed life into the Production Code, some thirty-four years earlier. (As former Code office official Jack Vizzard notes in his book, *See No Evil:* "The Code was signed into existence because of the growing threat of censor boards—both on the state and municipal level.") This is not to suggest that the industry's concern about censorship is unjustified or exaggerated; the recent Supreme Court rulings on obscenity, which I will discuss later, are ample evidence that the concern is appropriate indeed. Nevertheless, ratings spokesmen have confused the issue, by insisting the system is a public service, whose sole purpose is to aid parents in deciding what films to allow their children to see.

Considering the MPAA's eagerness to create a new, independent identity for the ratings system, it seems curious that several Code office veterans were allowed to make the transition to the Ratings Board. These included Eugene Dougherty, who became the Board's first chairman, after serving for many years as secretary to Code office czar Joe Breen; Al Van Schmus, a twenty-year member of the Code office staff, who acted as interim ratings chairman following the resignation of Dr. Aaron Stern, the Board's second chairman, in December 1973; Janice Montgomery, who had worked as a Code office clerk; and Richard Mathison, a journalist who had come to the Code office in 1965. (Mathison and Montgomery still sit on the Ratings Board; Dougherty resigned shortly after Stern's appointment.)

Although it would be fatuous to argue that the Ratings Board is as repressive as the Code office was in its heyday, the basic tactics of the "raters" are similar to those of the censors in several respects.

The Code office played an active role in the entire filmmaking process, offering advice and suggestions even during the preproduction stages. The Ratings Board functions similarly in at least one important respect. It is now a matter of policy for the major studios to submit screenplays to the Board, before production, in order to secure tentative ratings. The Board members examine these scripts carefully and then propose alterations and deletions. Ironically, every script letter which leaves the Ratings Board office bears the same admonition included on all script correspondence issued by the Code office: "You understand, of course, that our final judgement will be based on the finished film."

Movie critic Pauline Kael, in an introductory note to the shooting script of *Citizen Kane* (included in *The Citizen Kane Book*), touches on another connection between the Code office and the Ratings Board: "It was customary for scripts [in those days] to include bargaining material—that is, scenes or bits of business and lines of dialogue that the moviemakers didn't expect to get Production Code approval for, but that they included for trading purposes—so they could get by with a few items they really wanted. Thus the final, 156-page shooting script . . . has a bordello scene that was eliminated. . . .

"Today these games are still played with the Rating Board, and now as then, the joke is that often the most flagrant material put in for swapping purposes sometimes gets by, while relatively innocuous material is considered objectionable."

This kind of swapping or horse-trading is, in fact, standard operating procedure today (although it usually occurs after a finished film has been submitted). In a typical bartering session, the Board will try to eliminate as much as possible from a film before granting the desired rating, while the studio or filmmaker will attempt to retain as much as possible without sacrificing that rating.

The Ratings Board classifies films largely on the basis of a set of guidelines, most of them formulated by former Board chairman, Dr. Aaron Stern. (The substance of the guidelines will be discussed later.) While these guidelines are certainly not as numerous or prohibitive as the provisions of the Production Code— which banned everything from the depiction of "illegal drug traffic" to miscegenation to "excessive and lustful kissing, lustful embraces, and suggestive postures and gestures"—they are enforced just as rigorously. In the light of con-

Dustin Hoffman confronting his attackers during the climactic siege which was trimmed to satisfy the Ratings Board in Peckinpah's *Straw Dogs.*

Bogdanovich's *The Last Picture Show* was released with R rating without cuts due to last minute negotiations between the studio and Ratings Board.

Bibi Andersson and Elliot Gould are lovers in Bergman's R-rated *The Touch.*

temporary social and sexual mores, some of the guidelines almost seem as arbitrary, and finally as ludicrous, as the old Code regulations.

Under the old censorship system, when a film failed to meet the standards of the Code, it was denied a Production Code seal; today, when a film is rated X that same seal is withheld.

The Code office censors considered it one of their main duties to "advise" filmmakers on how to steer clear of trouble with the Catholic Legion of Decency— a powerful church-controlled group that kept a vigilant eye on the film industry and whose "condemned" classification could destroy a movie's box office potential. Legion of Decency approval was so important, and so difficult to attain, that filmmakers were sometimes forced to cut their films for the Legion even after a Production Code seal had been granted. Nevertheless, the Code office and the Legion of Decency worked hand in hand, and almost all films which got a Code seal ultimately escaped the onus of the condemned classification. Although the Legion is still operative, its influence has diminished greatly and its classifications are no longer taken very seriously.

Today, the Ratings Board uses the threat of obscenity prosecution against filmmakers in much the same way that the Code office officials used the threat of Legion of Decency condemnation. In a similarly "helpful" spirit, the Board will indicate to filmmakers what they should excise from their films in order to avoid court action (and, by extension, financial loss and almost certain box office ruin). The Board's motivation in providing this kind of advice is the same as was that of the censors: to extract as many concessions as possible from filmmakers.

From August through October of 1971, I served as a student intern on the Ratings Board. The internship program, instituted by Mr. Valenti in 1969, was ostensibly set up to provide some representation on the Board for the young people who constitute the largest segment of the nation's movie-going audience. Although presumably the program existed to *encourage* the presentation of dissenting opinions (and, at the same time, to bring the Board into closer contact with the young film audience), it was my experience as a member of the Board that dissent was not tolerated. The internship was to have lasted for one year, but I resigned after three months.

Shortly before I joined the Board, Dr. Stern, a New York psychiatrist, had assumed the chairmanship. (Stern was succeeded in July 1974 by a communications consultant, Richard Heffner.) His appointment, which climaxed a particularly tumultuous period in the Board's brief history, apparently was intended to appease critics of all persuasions: his avowed concern with the levels of violence permitted in the GP category and his academic credentials seemed certain to impress liberals, while his early pledge to restore credibility to the ratings system by making it less susceptible to studio pressures seemed sure to hearten conservatives. Instead, Dr. Stern ushered in a period of heightened controversy.

As an intern, I quickly became aware that the Board was actually engaged in censorship. I also learned that despite the Board's democratic veneer, the members consistently acceded to the chairman's wishes, carrying out his orders as would the most conventional of employees. Finally, I came to understand that the strength of the ratings system—or, more accurately, its durability—largely rested in the Board's determination to conduct its business in almost total secrecy and to avoid public scrutiny altogether. Moviegoers have yet to be granted access to the most fundamental information concerning the composition of the Board and the premises and tenets by which it operates.

During the three months that I served on the Board, some 107 films were rated; of these, 48 were in some way cut according to the specifications of Dr. Stern and the Board, so that lighter, more commercially viable ratings could be achieved.

The official Ratings Board position is that a filmmaker can play whatever he likes in his film, provided he is willing to accept an appropriate rating, or, to quote Dr. Stern, as long as he "pays the price" for what he has put on the screen. While this approach may sound reasonable in theory, it fails to take into account several practical realities: (1) Economic factors in the film industry make it impossible for studios to accept the more restrictive ratings in many instances; (2) The Board actually encourages the editing of films; and (3) Unless a director has a "final cut" clause written into his contract—a privileged arrangement which only a handful of luminaries enjoy—it is likely that the final negotiations will be conducted without his participation and he will be forced to abide by whatever decision his studio or distributor makes.

The studios, in fact, will sometimes use the Board to coerce reluctant filmmakers into making cuts that the studios deem desirable. Although aware that this kind of manipulation occurs, the Board is extremely sensitive about the editing issue, to the point of refusing to acknowledge that they have anything whatever to do with the cutting of films.

While I served on the Board, six major studio films were rated X; of these, only one, *The Decameron*, sustained its original rating. Columbia Pictures ultimately secured an R rating on *The Last Picture Show* without making any cuts in the original version of the film. (This change came about following eleventh-hour, behind-the-scenes negotiations between the studio and Dr. Stern; the Board members, after being pressured into unanimity on the X rating, were not even consulted about the switch.) The remaining films—*The Last Movie, Macbeth, Dirty Harry*, and *Straw Dogs*—were all cut, according to the dictates of the Board, before R ratings were granted.

Sexuality
in the Movies

While it is true that the studios involved had the option of accepting the X rating, all were reluctant to take the financial risk carried by that classification. (United Artists' willingness to accept the X on *The Decameron* is easily explained because the film was independently financed and picked up for distribution purposes only: with relatively little money riding on the film, the studio could better afford to take a chance on the rating.) Studio executives and filmmakers alike argue that it is difficult for the public to make the proper distinction between "quality" X films—e.g., *Midnight Cowboy, A Clockwork Orange, The Devils*— and pure exploitation films, most of which are self-rated Xs. (The X is the only rating which can be self-applied.) Several newspapers around the country aggravate the problem by refusing to accept advertising for any X-rated film, or, as in the case of the *Los Angeles Times,* grouping together ads for X-rated films, legitimate and otherwise. In the *Times,* ads for such critically acclaimed, mainstream X films as *Heavy Traffic* and *Le Sex Shop* were made to coexist with lurid ads for the raunchiest of exploitation films. In promoting its highly praised, X-rated *Last Tango in Paris,* United Artists took out segregated, full-page ads, partly to avoid the problem of guilt by association. Too, certain drive-in chains, and some theaters—notably in the Midwest and in the South—will not play X-rated films at all. It is not surprising, then, that a film stands to lose as much as 50 percent of its potential revenue if it is rated X instead of R. Studio anxiety about finances is such that increasingly films are *contracted* to be released with certain ratings—which means, of course, that filmmakers trapped in such arrangements will be obliged to do whatever the Board tells them in order to gain the promised classifications.

As previously noted, the Board's role in the editing of films begins at the script level. Unless the script is particularly important or controversial, it will be read and evaluated by one Board member only. Rather than merely assign a speculative rating, the Board member will almost invariably list in minute detail the "troublesome" aspects of the script (complete with page numbers and line references) and will indicate what would have to be removed in order for the finished film to earn a lighter rating than the one assigned to the script. Sometimes, a script will be doctored and resubmitted several times until the studio secures the Board member's assurance that the final draft has been sufficiently altered to qualify for a lighter rating. This happened with the script for the Woody Allen film, *Play It Again, Sam,* which originally drew an R rating, primarily on the basis of some ribald dialogue. At least one whole scene was rewritten—and purified—before the script was deemed suitable for the GP category.

Ironically, although the Board is instructed to write tough script letters, the members are still free to disregard those letters, when arriving at a final decision on the rating of the finished film. However, the Board still uses the letters as ammunition against the studios. In the case of *Sometimes a Great Notion,* Universal was warned at the script level that in order for the film to be considered for the

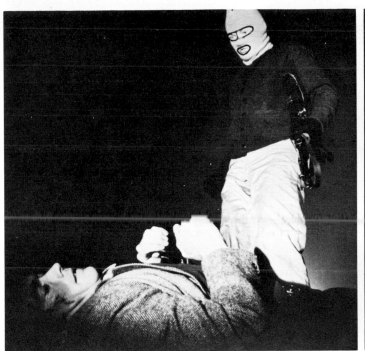

Andy Robinson in his Scorpio disguise kicks
Clint Eastwood in Don Siegel's *Dirty Harry*
which was trimmed slightly for R rating.

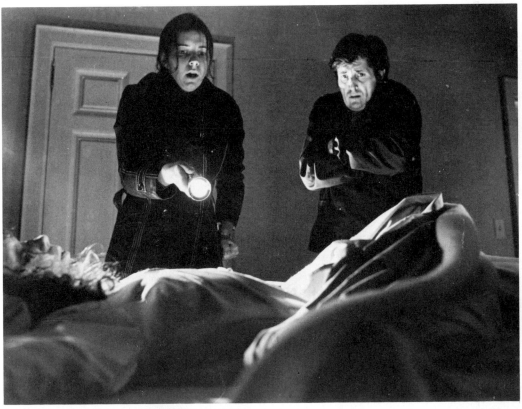

Jason Miller watches Linda Blair during possession
sequence from William Friedkin's *The Exorcist* which
received a controversial R rating.

GP category, the climactic scene, in which the "fuck you" finger gesture figures prominently, would have to be removed or somehow modified. When the film arrived with this scene intact, the Board member who had written the script letter became indignant; the rest of the Board was divided on the question of whether the scene could play in a GP film, but it was decided that since the studio had been warned, and had chosen to ignore the warning, that the Board ought to press for the alteration. (The scene was finally shortened by a few seconds, and the film got the lighter rating.)

During the screenings, each member of the Board is required to take copious notes on any and all items which might place the films beyond the G category. Individual lists, sometimes running to several pages, may include anything from an isolated use of the word *hell* to a description of a nude lovemaking scene or some brutal act of violence. A master list is compiled from the separate lists and, if the studio is unhappy with the rating assigned, this new list becomes the focal point of negotiations.

Usually, the studio or filmmaker is told that specific words, shots, or even scenes must be excised before the desired rating can be achieved. On occasion, a film is judged to have a "quantitative" (or cumulative) problem—usually too much nudity or too much profanity—for a given category. In this case, the filmmaker is allowed to use his own discretion in deciding exactly what to eliminate. However, the Board will admonish him that he is taking a "calculated risk" which means that they reserve the right to retain the original rating even after cuts have been made. Almost invariably, the desired rating is attained, although the Board may continue to demand additional cuts before it is finally satisfied. Low-budget, independently-made films seem to be hit harder when it comes to this kind of editing, mainly because the independent filmmaker has less clout than the filmmaker working in conjunction with a powerful studio. In addition, the Board tends to be very respectful of the big-budget film whose box-office fate will bear significantly on the financial health of a given studio. (Witness *The Exorcist*'s R rating, widely criticized as being too lenient.)

Once the cuts have been made, the Board may elect to rescreen the entire film to determine if the general impact has been changed appreciably; it is more common, however, for the Board to reevaluate only those parts of the film which were earmarked for editing. Small segments of film will be shown, completely out of context, sometimes as many as a half a dozen times, before final approval is given.

For the first month or so of my internship, the editing was conducted in a fairly arbitrary fashion—that is to say, there were no set standards or criteria governing the Board's decisions. During this period, it was difficult to predict just what elements in a film the Board might choose to fasten on and rate against. In the case of *Medicine Ball Caravan*, for example, Dr. Stern demanded that a shot of

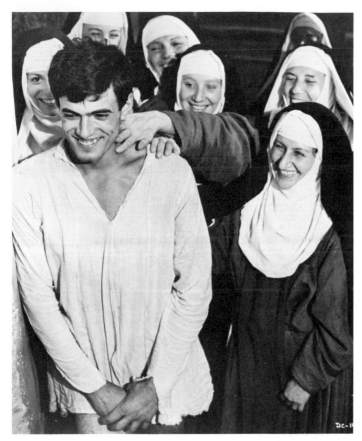

Pier Paolo Pasolini's X-rated *The Decameron.*

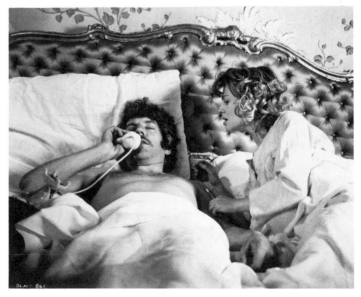

The violent conclusion of Roman Polanski's *Macbeth* which was slightly cut to make it acceptable for the R category.

Portions of the love-making sequence between Donald Sutherland and Julie Christie were deleted in Nicholas Roeg's *Don't Look Now* to escape an X rating.

a young mother nursing her infant and smoking a joint at the same time be deleted to earn the film an R. Dr. Stern also decreed that the scene in *The Last Picture Show* depicting the sexual initiation of the mentally retarded boy by the town whore was strictly X material and would have to be edited before an R rating could be conferred. (He had originally insisted that the film had a cumulative problem and that no one scene was of X quality by itself.) Referring to the same film, another Board member insisted that the sound of the bed creaking in the love scene between the young protagonist, Sonny, and the coach's wife was beyond the limits of the R category and ought to be somehow modified. As previously noted, the studio somehow prevailed and the film was released in its original form with an R rating.

Nevertheless, as haphazard as this process was, and as foolish as many of the individual judgments were, at least some real attempt was made to assess the general suitability of films for young audiences. However, after a short time, a new modus operandi began to evolve. Responding to what he claimed was a mandate from Jack Valenti and the company presidents who comprise the MPAA, Dr. Stern started to formulate a number of very precise guidelines for the individual categories. When I left the Board in November 1971, the following rules were being strictly enforced: (1) The portrayal of sexual intercourse was prohibited in any form outside the X category; (2) Nudity—including minimal breast and buttocks exposure—was forbidden outside the R and X categories; and (3) The use of the word *fuck*—or any of its derivatives—was barred from the G and GP categories. Also, although some modes of profanity (e.g., *bastard* or *shit*) were permitted in the GP, if such words surfaced repeatedly in a GP film, the filmmaker or studio would be asked to reduce their frequency. If these standards had been in effect six months earlier, films such as *The Go Between, The Touch,* and *Ryan's Daughter* would have immediately drawn X ratings. In accordance with the guidelines, a tame, youth-oriented film about the plight of the American Indian called *Journey Through Rosebud* was rated X because of a brief (ten seconds or so) scene of nude lovemaking, shot through a gauze-like filter; *Buck and the Preacher*, a comedy-adventure film, was initially rated R on the basis of a single bare buttocks shot in a non-sex-related context; Elia Kazan's *The Visitors,* a sober study of the common human impulse to commit acts of violence, was originally rated X because of a brief rape-seduction scene, done in long shot, with no nudity involved; and *A Safe Place,* an obscure, fantasy-like film, was rated R because of a scene involving tongue-kissing (a more informal prohibition for the GP category) and one off-screen, barely audible use of the word *fuck*. Interestingly, once the offending love scene was removed from *Journey Through Rosebud*, the film dropped two whole categories.

The prohibitions on the various categories still appear to be in effect as of this writing, although the intercourse taboo has apparently been relaxed somewhat as evidenced by the ratings of such films as *Don't Look Now* (R) and *Our Time* (GP).

The guidelines were enforced singlemindedly while I was on the Board, with absolutely no regard for such elements as context or treatment. But the imposition of the guidelines did not signal an end to the earlier, more capricious editing practices, as the Board members continued to seize on arbitrary items not covered by the regulations. Thus, the guidelines emerged as an additional frame of reference as opposed to a substitute. Filmmakers who initially welcomed the guidelines, thinking that they finally had an objective, unimpeachable set of standards to refer to, quickly discovered that they now had to maneuver through an even more intricate maze of rules and regulations.

Inevitably, the inflexibility of the guidelines occasionally permitted a very mature film—a film which by all rights *should* have been restricted—to earn an unrestricted rating, because it failed to violate any specific guidelines or because it was edited in such a way as to circumvent the guidelines. The film *Going Home*, for example, was rated GP despite a scene in which a young child watches his drunken father savagely murder his helpless mother, and a later sequence in which a youth (the child grown up) rapes his stepmother-to-be. A grisly British horror film called *Fright*, replete with graphic physical violence and terror-inducing devices, was initially rated R and then rerated GP after modest cuts had been made.

About the same time that the guidelines came about, a new twilight-zone category, the "GP Tag" was put into effect. Designed to accommodate films which the Board considered appropriate for teenage audiences and over (the legend read "contains material which may be unsuitable for pre-teenagers"), the category was to give younger audiences access to films with more mature themes. Actually, the GP had originally been conceived as a teenage category, but the legend (general audiences—parental guidance suggested) was thought to have misled many parents into believing that the category was not substantially different from the straight G. However, while open to sophisticated themes and ideas, the new "GP Tag" remained closed to visual and verbal "explicits." The impossibility of intelligently distinguishing between theme and treatment for rating purposes is perhaps best illustrated by Dr. Stern's evaluation of *The Hospital*. The film contains several conversations on and references to impotence, orgasm, and masturbation, all of which he was willing to allow in the "GP Tag"; however, a flash shot of a woman's partially bared buttocks, and a brief shot showing a faint grimace on the woman's face during a love scene—interpreted as a response to penetration—were ruled unacceptable (and were subsequently cut). What this decision said, in effect, was that it was perfectly acceptable for a teenager to hear a mature conversation on sexual matters, but somehow unacceptable for him or her to see a woman's naked buttocks for a couple of seconds.

87

(The handling of *The Hospital* by the Board also serves to point up the inherent absurdity of the guidelines themselves: the phrases "getting screwed," "getting laid," and "getting zapped," were all allowed to play, but the word *fuck* had to be deleted before the film could get its "GP Tag".)

In January 1972, the GP and the "GP Tag" were incorporated into one category, the PG, which carries the same legend that the "GP Tag" did.

The irony of the Ratings Board censorship program is that it ultimately accomplishes so little. On a major studio film, the final cuts frequently involve only a minute or two (or even less) of film time; in many cases, scenes will merely be shortened rather than deleted. While this kind of trimming can easily throw off the rhythm or emphasis of a scene and so distort its meaning, the overall impact of the film cannot really be changed. It is hard to imagine how the elimination of a few blows and a shot of some spurting blood in *Dirty Harry* could make this film a more acceptable R—or how the removal of a few shots of bare breasts in *Diamonds Are Forever* could miraculously turn that film into a PG. The potential harm from this kind of intervention by the Board is great, but there is really no way that the movie-going public can possibly benefit from it.

The Board influences film content in more subtle ways as well. For example, Dr. Stern would often *advise* a studio executive—in a very informal manner—as to what rating he (Stern) thought would be most viable commercially for a certain film. Midway through the Board's first screening of Roman Polanski's *Macbeth*, Dr. Stern conferred with the studio representative in charge of the film, and told him that he would be "crazy" if he didn't cut the film for a "GP Tag" rating. After seeing the second half of the film, however, Dr. Stern changed his mind. On occasion, he would offer the opposite advice—he would suggest to a studio representative that the film in question had enough commercial potential to survive with a tougher rating, and that it would be doing the film a disservice to cut it. However, even this seemingly well-intentioned kind of advice is inappropriate at best. The chairman of the Ratings Board—or any member of the Board—has no business engaging in such a dialogue with studio personnel.

The Board's enthusiasm for editing is partly a reflection of a basic insensitivity to film as a legitimate art form. The members are very much tied to the old concept of film as mass entertainment. Film is basically regarded as a marketable commodity which can justify its existence only by making money for the industry which spawned it. I don't mean to suggest here that the members of the Ratings Board should be film historians or scholars; nonetheless, some familiarity with the medium—extending beyond an understanding of the economics of the film industry—would certainly be useful.

Dr. Stern would sometimes try to justify the Board's role in editing films by suggesting that film is a collaborative medium, and that the finished work, unlike a painting or a sculpture, bears the imprint of diverse hands. He would also argue frequently that the filmmaker could not and should not expect absolute creative control, because of the tremendous expense involved in making a film. While it is certainly true that a number of professionally trained, creative people are involved in the making of a film, and that, because of financial necessity, a filmmaker frequently must be responsible to the studio which finances him, this in no way justifies the intrusion of an outside group with neither a creative nor a financial stake in the project. The Hollywood lore about films damaged or destroyed by insensitive moguls is voluminous; that filmmakers must do battle not only with the company executives but with the Ratings Board as well is sad indeed.

Still, Hollywood filmmakers as a group have not resisted the encroachments on their freedoms forcefully enough. The reasons for their reluctance to tackle the Ratings Board are fairly obvious. With the possible exception of some of the young filmmakers who are new to the game, most directors and screenwriters are well schooled in the art of compromise. To these veteran filmmakers, the demands of the Ratings Board may seem only the last in a series of obstacles, the final arena for compromise. Too, by the time their films reach the Board, the filmmakers may be weary of fighting—at this point, they are very much interested in getting matters expedited so their films can be released. Finally, most filmmakers are aware that they will eventually have to return to the Board and face the same group of people with their next film. The Board doesn't exactly give blatantly preferential treatment to "friendly" filmmakers or vice versa, but the members do have long memories. Some misguided filmmakers, apparently hoping to ingratiate themselves with the Board, have actually written the chairman, thanking him for improving their films by forcing cuts on them. While I was on the Board, Dr. Stern would use these letters to try to bring recalcitrant filmmakers in line, to convince them that the Board had their best interests at heart.

Once a studio has decided to acquiesce to the Board, there is not a great deal that a filmmaker can do. Individual ratings decisions can be protested before a special Appeals Board—but winning an appeal is no easy task. (The filmmaker cannot even mount an appeal without the go-ahead from the studio or distributor.) Originally, a rating could be overturned by a simple majority of the Appeals Board members; that provision was changed, however, and now a two-thirds vote is required. Made up of representatives from the MPAA, NATO, and IFIDA, the Appeals Board is even more prone than the Ratings Board to protect big-budget films at the expense of smaller, independent productions. The Appeals Board has retained the R rating on such tame fare as *Harry and Tonto*, *The White Dawn*, and *Thieves Like Us* (all relatively inexpensive films) while overturning the R on the graphically violent *Papillon* (budgeted at a cool $13 million).

Clearly, then, the most effective avenue of protest is public statement. Unfortunately, if a filmmaker feels that his own film has not been seriously damaged by the Board's reediting, he is unlikely to take a public stand against censorship; and if his film *has* been hurt by the cuts, he may fear that admitting as much publicly will jeopardize the film's chances at the box office. Nevertheless, some prominent members of the film community have spoken out against the Board's policies. Since Dr. Stern's departure, in fact, the number of public complaints lodged by disaffected directors seems to have increased. In the April 1974 issue of *Action*, the magazine of the Directors Guild of America, director LaMont Johnson voices his complaints: "Four frames of film in which a barely perceptible view of a 12-year-old boy's penis appeared in an underwater sequence gave my . . . movie *Visit to a Chief's Son* an R rating until the objectionable subliminal flash was blown up to eliminate it. That my film, from its conception to its final cut an unabashed family, kids-and-animals in Africa picture, should have the same rating as *The Exorcist* is an obscenity symptomatic of our national disease of censorship. . . ." Robert Radnitz, producer of family-oriented films such as *The Little Ark, Sounder*, and *Where the Lilies Bloom*, has also been outspoken about the Board: "I always said the rating system would come back to haunt us," he is quoted in an article in the *Los Angeles Herald Examiner*. "It was designed as a ploy to ward off federal legislation, but we have in fact since got closer to it. It comes down heavily on sex but lets a lot of violence go by. . . ." Radnitz goes on to say that he almost got an R on *The Little Ark* because the girl in the film undresses and her male co-star says the word *Jesus*. Even Clint Eastwood, a political conservative and a sometime supporter of the Board, has publicly protested the R rating on his film *Breezy*. Also quoted in the *Herald Examiner*, Eastwood says, "They [the raters] say they don't want to become censors, yet in effect they are."

The actual business of rating movies is conducted in a singularly undemocratic manner, with the chairman wielding tremendous power over a largely subservient Board. The members are basically functionaries, who execute the policies and the specific decisions handed down by the chairman. Former Ratings Board intern Stephen Farber, in his book *The Movie Ratings Game*, comments on the relationship which existed between the Board members and the chairman during the Dougherty administration:

> The Administrator has a great deal of sway, and usually the group will go along with whatever rating he wants to assign a film—and whatever cuts he feels should be demanded. In some cases the board would decide on a rating and then discover that Eugene Dougherty was negotiating for cuts and promising a less restrictive rating without consulting the group. The other board members did not take offense when the democratic process was bypassed, for they believed the Administrator *should* have authority to act on his own.

The Board members remained similarly impotent during the Stern administration. During a trip to New York and Europe, for example, Dr. Stern personally rated two films—*Fiddler on the Roof* and *Mary Queen of Scots*—which the Board was never allowed to see. (Curiously, advertisements for *Fiddler*, which were placed before even Dr. Stern had a chance to see the film, carried the G rating.) In Europe, he also saw *Diamonds Are Forever* and provided the studio with a specific run-down of what would have to be eliminated for the film to receive the desired "GP Tag" rating. (The Board was later given the opportunity to see and rate the *titles* of the film.) In addition, Dr. Stern attended a special screening of Sergio Leone's *Duck You Sucker* in Italy, and explained to the director what would have to be deleted for that film to qualify for a "GP Tag" rating. Finally, he saw *The Hospital* on his own, and informed the studio that the film could be rated "GP Tag" if substantial cuts were made. Although the Board was allowed to see this film intact after Dr. Stern returned to Los Angeles, it was understood that the rating had already been determined and that the members were to consider the necessary deletions only, although a couple of the Board members strongly felt that the film deserved an R rating and that too much would have to be cut in order to bring it in line for the "GP Tag."

Frequently, Dr. Stern would not be present during the initial screening of a film; if the Board members felt that the film presented special problems or was particularly controversial, Dr. Stern would then see the film on his own time and report back to the Board. The film *Black Jesus*, an allegorical account of an African nationalist leader who is martyred by his white colonial adversaries, was rated R by all the Board members save one, who voted X. However, the members were slightly uneasy about the intensity of the violence in a couple of scenes, and as a result, Dr. Stern was asked to see the film. His "report" to the Board came in the way of a simple declarative sentence: "*Black Jesus* is an 'X'." The film had been made in Italy and sold to an American distributor who proved to be quite willing to cut anything to secure an unrestricted rating. The film was finally released as a "GP Tag", a rating which seemed as inappropriate as the X had been.

In the film *One on Top of the Other*, an Italian-made suspense yarn, there are two shots of a decomposed skull, which appear at different points in the film. Dr. Stern insisted that the second shot be deleted before the film's original X rating could be reversed, arguing that this shot, unlike the first, was gratuitous in that it didn't serve to further the development of the film's plot. (This line of reasoning—i.e., that which is extraneous to the barebones plot of a film is "gratuitous" and therefore expendable—was frequently used by Dr. Stern and a couple of the Board members to justify cuts. They were unresponsive to the argument that elements of a film which don't bear directly on the plot may be essential to the larger purposes of the film and are not by definition gratuitous.)

A scene in *Winter in Mallorca* shows a child peeking through a keyhole and seeing her mother and her mother's lover lying in bed. Dr. Stern insisted that children who have seen their parents engaged in the primal act can incur severe psychological damage. The fact that the child in the film did not witness any such act did not impress Dr. Stern; the child's curiosity, or desire to witness the act, was sufficiently disturbing, as far as he was concerned, to require the removal of the shot to make the film acceptable for the "GP Tag" category.

Another time, Dr. Stern was asked to pass judgment on the bloody, climactic scene in a low budget horror film called *Sweetkill*; in explaining to the filmmakers why the scene would have to be trimmed for the film to get an R rating, he referred to the "subliminal, psycho-erotic force" of what was portrayed on screen. To underscore his point, he described the following experiment: the message "you are thirsty" was flashed on a movie theater screen at a speed too fast for the audience to perceive it consciously; the theater management then tabulated the number of soft drinks sold during intermission, and reported that the figure was significantly higher than under ordinary circumstances. Dr. Stern went on to suggest that Swedish filmmaker Ingmar Bergman was the one responsible for developing a cinematic technique designed to reach audiences on a subconscious level.

Dr. Stern has repeatedly insisted, however, that he never considered the "unconscious psychological effects" of a film; in fact, he would even go so far as to say that his psychiatric background was incidental, and in no way related to the work he was doing as a rater. In an interview with *The Hollywood Reporter*, he said, "Would you like some half-assed psychologist sitting back and telling you what's good or bad? That's thought control! . . . The rating system in no way ever tries to make judgments on what's good or bad for children. That's censorship, and, by definition, that's the beginning of a loss of freedom."

The ballots which Board members are required to fill out following each screening are largely a formality. On those occasions when he would sit in on a screening with the Board, Dr. Stern would frequently ask for a voice vote at the conclusion of the film. This practice prevented the members from reflecting on their decisions, and, more importantly, encouraged conformity. While he maintained that the members were free to change their votes on the formal ballots, he was adamant about securing a preliminary "commitment" as he called it. Immediately following the screening of *The Decameron*, Dr. Stern asked, "Is there anyone who *doesn't* vote X?" There were no dissenters.

While at times the Board members seemed to resent the chairman's methods, they appeared basically to sympathize with his aims, and to agree that the Board had to present a united front to the industry and the public. Contrary to my initial expectations, the members turned out to be an educated, fairly urbane group who, for the most part, were not personally offended by the more explicit and provocative films to which they were exposed. Yet often they felt obligated to disregard their own instincts and responses, and to guide themselves instead by the imagined responses of more conservative persons. (If the Board is really supposed to rate for the "average citizen," why then are there no "average citizens" on the Board?)

Although Dr. Stern certainly put his own very personal stamp on the ratings, his role and influence ought not to be regarded as entirely singular or distinctive. Eugene Dougherty, his predecessor, maintained a lower profile, but was as much an autocrat as Stern, and ran the Board in a similar fashion. Dougherty had obviously learned the rules of the game during his long service in the Production Code office; Stern, although he was never associated with the Code office, played his part like an old trouper. Unless the basic premises which govern the ratings system are rethought, there is no reason to believe that the current chairman, or any future chairman, will conduct himself in a vastly different manner, or have a vastly different impact on the ratings process.

In June 1973, the United States Supreme Court handed down a landmark obscenity decision, which seemed certain to have a profound effect on the motion picture industry, and, by extension, on the ratings system. The Court toughened federal obscenity guidelines and, in the same breath, gave individual communities broad powers to legislate against and prosecute obscenity offenders.

Three guidelines were provided by the Court for the preparation of anti-obscenity legislation: (1) The average person, applying contemporary community standards, must find that the challenged work appeals to prurient interest; (2) The work must depict or describe in a patently offensive way sexual conduct explicitly defined by the law; and (3) Taken as a whole, the work must lack serious literary, artistic, political, or scientific value. (Previously, the Court had held that a work must be proven *utterly* without redeeming social value in order to be judged obscene.)

One month later, the new obscenity definition was put to the test. A jury in Albany, Georgia, found *Carnal Knowledge*—a highly respected R-rated film—to be obscene, and held that the manager of the Albany theater which had been showing the film was guilty of distributing obscene materials. In a decision that sent shock waves through the movie industry, the Georgia supreme court upheld the lower court action, ruling that a local jury has the right to decide what is obscene in a particular community in Georgia.

Hollywood lost little time reacting to the Supreme Court decision and to the *Carnal Knowledge* ban. Controversial films scheduled for production before the court decision were abandoned altogether; many other films dealing with relatively innocuous subject matter were modified considerably to head off possible censorship action. As several observers noted, the new obscenity guidelines, while ostensibly aimed at hard-core pornography, seemed more likely to injure "mainstream" Hollywood films in the long run—mainly because porno films,

93

made on tight budgets, can usually earn back their production costs with a few bookings in a few major cities, while Hollywood films, most of them budgeted at several million dollars, must play all over the country to stand a chance of making a profit.

In a television interview in Los Angeles, Robert Wise, president of the Director's Guild of America (which took a public stand against the Supreme Court action), spelled out some of the problems created by the obscenity flap:

> Filmmakers are concerned because several of them have had projects that were to go and were "R" pictures—not "X" pictures even—that were put on the shelf the minute that decision came out because the producers were afraid to go out and put money into something that might not get shown widely enough. . . .
>
> A friend of mine made a picture at MGM. It's a story dealing with rape. When he made the film . . . he was instructed to have an "R" film. They wanted an "R" film. He made the "R" film. Now they are taking the picture over and doing anything that they can to it to cut it to a "PG".

Director John Frankenheimer was quoted as saying that he personally knew of eight films which were not made as a result of the Court action. Stephen Farber and Estelle Changas, in an article in the *New York Times*, cited two specific examples: *Last Exit to Brooklyn*, a novel about an unlikely love affair between a middle-aged trucker and a young transvestite by Hubert Selby Jr. which was to be filmed by Arthur Hiller, with major studio financing, and *Cruising*, a novel about a homosexual killer by Gerald Walker, which had been purchased by *French Connection* producer Philip D'Antoni.

The Court decision had other less dramatic, but nevertheless dismaying, effects. Studio executives, for example, accelerated their demands on directors to provide so-called "cover" footage for scenes involving profanity, nudity, or other provocative material. In the past, such alternate footage had been shot only so that the films could ultimately be sold to television; suddenly, the studios seemed prepared to use the substitute clips when the films were released theatrically—if circumstances so dictated.

On June 24, 1974, the U.S. Supreme Court, in a unanimous decision, ruled that *Carnal Knowledge* was not obscene after all. Although the decision was immediately hailed by Jack Valenti and others in the film industry, it was far from a clear-cut victory for Hollywood. While declaring that the film did not depict sexual conduct in a "patently offensive way," the justices upheld the right of local juries to base their obscenity determinations on the moral standards of their respective communities. And the Court's specific defense of *Carnal Knowledge* did not appear to bode well for such films as *Last Tango in Paris* or *Don't Look Now*. The justices declared that *Carnal Knowledge* was not obscene partly because "the camera does not focus on the bodies of the actors" during the scenes in which "sexual conduct, including 'ultimate sexual acts' are understood to be taking place."

Rather than clarifying their original decision, the justices succeeded only in confusing matters further. As was noted in an opinion filed by the Court minority (which supported the *Carnal Knowledge* decree but took issue with the confirmation of the powers of local communities to judge obscene material), the Court may now be pulled into the "mire of case-by-case determinations." But the Court will not have time to hear every such case which arises; thus, important obscenity cases could well be decided by appellate courts across the country. The prospect of facing such courts on a semiregular basis cannot be attractive to the studio chiefs. The only way for them to avoid it, of course, is to continue their self-censorship program in earnest. Which they probably can be expected to do.

Although as I have pointed out, the ratings system was conceived as a protection against the kind of extra-industry censorship that the Court decisions have encouraged, the position of the Ratings Board has, ironically, been strengthened by the rulings. Studios which were once merely reluctant to accept X ratings are adamantly refusing to consider that classification under any circumstances. And, as indicated by Robert Wise, the studios are becoming increasingly wary of the R rating as well. What this means is that the Board can exercise even greater control over film content, now that the studios are desperate to get lighter ratings.

One bright spot in his otherwise bleak picture is that state legislatures, at least as of this writing, have not jumped on the censorship bandwagon. In May 1974, *The Hollywood Reporter* announced that only thirteen states had come up with new or revised obscenity laws as a result of the original Court ruling. And in California, the already existing obscenity law was declared unconstitutional in June 1974, a decision which immediately terminated all obscenity prosecutions in the state, including a scheduled retrial involving the film *Deep Throat*. (Prohibition of the exhibition of obscene materials to minors was not affected by the ruling.)

Meanwhile, the MPAA, under Valenti's direction, has been promoting its own, so-called "model legislation," designed to draw a clear distinction, for law enforcement purposes, between hard-core films and quality adult films. The concept has not been widely embraced by filmmakers, who argue that the distinction is largely a matter of personal taste and cannot be precisely articulated. Says Robert Wise: "In our view [i.e., the Director's Guild] the decision is a wrong decision. It's unconstitutional . . . and it's an infringement on our civil rights. There should be no qualification between a pornographic film and a nonpornographic film."

In light of the regressive Supreme Court rulings and the resultant panic in studio executive suites, it may be difficult to effect liberalizations in the ratings system in the near future. On the other hand, the censorship crisis has clearly given the creative community in Hollywood a sense of shared purpose, of common cause. Filmmakers may be starting to realize that if they join together and if they are determined enough, their voices will be heard. The Court decisions have served to focus attention anew on the Ratings Board; now that it is abundantly clear that the ratings system has failed to shield Hollywood from "real" censorship, perhaps filmmakers will press harder for changes.

What form should such changes take? First and foremost, the coercive elements embedded in the ratings structure must be abandoned to make way for a completely advisory structure, one in which the ultimate decision on what should and should not be seen by young people would be left in the hands of parents. This revision would be in line with Mr. Valenti's original concept of the ratings system as a device to help parents make their own decisions on what to allow their children to see. A lessening of the onus on the adult categories would almost definitely accompany such a change; presumably, the studios would be less reluctant to accept tougher ratings as long as those ratings didn't automatically keep large numbers of movie-goers out of the theaters. The industry should also consider the total elimination of the X category, which has surely proven to be the weakest, most troublesome link in the ratings structure.

Revamping the ratings system along the lines I have suggested need not entail an abdication of responsibility on the part of the Board. On the contrary, an advisory program could provide more information on film content to concerned parents. The Board could issue a regular bulletin with plot summaries, and brief descriptions of the more "adult" aspects of new films. Such bulletins might be published in daily newspapers, or posted at theater box offices, or both.

Finally, the internal workings of the Board should be changed. Even though the Board is a part of the MPAA, it must achieve some measure of autonomy. Individual ballots and votes must be respected; and the censorship of screenplays and finished films must be stopped completely.

Defenders of the ratings system have consistently argued that film censorship in other countries is far worse than it is in the United States. They go on to insist that the ratings system, as presently constituted, is a necessary evil, and that we should be thankful that it does as comparatively little damage as it does.

While it is true that films are censored with greater abandon in many foreign countries, certain factors should be kept in mind: (1) Censorship bodies in most other countries are clearly identified as such and are not permitted to hypocritically masquerade as classification systems designed to help the filmmaker; (2) The sensitivity to explicit sexual material on the screen is far greater here than it is in most European countries; and (3) Since Hollywood is regarded as the film capital of the world (run-away production notwithstanding), it stands to reason that our approach to film censorship *should* be more enlightened in this country.

It is also important to remember that the damage done by the Ratings Board

cannot be measured in excised film clip
helped to create an atmosphere of tensi
by the Court rulings) and has functior
studios and filmmakers into taking fewe
film fare. In this sense, the damage must

While every artist, regardless of th
some concessions to those who can affo
public's attention, it is safe to say that fil
share of dues to the business communit
cinematic works of art have been produ
sures and meddling, filmmakers have
the demands of the men who hold the p

The ratings system, like the Production Code program before it, has imposed yet another set of debilitating restraints on artistic freedom in the film
industry. Unless the power of the Board is checked, the ratings system—fueled
by the fears of the studio moguls and the whims of the citizen censors—will continue to take a heavy toll on creative expression on the American screen.

4

Sex, Morality, and the Movies

LAWRENCE BECKER

*A*NY serious analysis of sexuality in film has to shake off two naïve dogmas: (1) the false dichotomy which insists that there are films which exploit sex, as opposed to ones in which sex is merely an ingredient; that there are mixtures of the two; but that the exploitation of sex diminishes a film's worth; and (2) the false conflation which insists that moral and aesthetic values are somehow inter-connected.

The first of these dogmas leads to a sterile line of criticism: sex should not be exploited. It should, rather, appear as a "natural" ingredient, integral to the whole. Nudity should not be forced or implausible—rather, it should be *necessary*—organic to the film. Any attempt to contrive a place for sex is exploitation. To build a *whole* film around explicit sexuality is exploitative in the extreme, for here the entire filmmaking process, from beginning to end, is a contrivance to get sex on the screen. Sex is legitimate in a film to the degree to which it is organic to the narrative. It is natural and necessary in *Women in Love*. But Angie Dickinson's seduction-for-a-friend in *Point Blank* is exploitation.

The bankruptcy of this line of criticism is obvious: it leaves no room for the use of sex as a dispensible but powerful metaphor. And it leads to downright confusion over a whole wave of films—beginning, perhaps, with *I Am Curious—Yellow*, including *Blow Up, Clockwork Orange, WR: Mysteries of the Organism* and, most recently, *Last Tango in Paris*. Sexually explicit scenes are *used* in these films, and not merely included to be honest about something that is natural and necessary to a narrative. The conceptual trap laid by the dogma insists that these films must be exploitative, and hence somehow damaged. But that will not do.

They are deeper, more important than that. What works as a way of assessing the qualitative difference between the usual run of 42nd Street skin flicks and *Women in Love* breaks down when applied to *Last Tango*. A more precise set of analytical tools is required.

Try, for example, the following definitions: films *about* sex are those whose dominant themes are *merely* about (as opposed to *of*) sex, and whose sexual material may serve a variety of purposes. A relatively pure example might be a Planned Parenthood documentary on contraception. Films *of* sex (henceforth: sex films, as in political, horror, war films) are those whose dominant themes are of (as opposed to merely about) sexual activity, and whose sexual material is not used as a device to achieve some other purpose within the film. A relatively pure example is Stan Brakhage's *Lovemaking.* Films which use sex (i.e., exploit it in the nonpejorative sense of the term) are those whose dominant themes are *not* sexual ones, and whose sexual material *is* used as a device to achieve some other purpose within the film. A relatively pure but rather silly example is the use of bedroom scenes in *Strategic Air Command*. Most films which involve sex are, of course, mixtures of two or three of these types.

The exploitation of sex *in* a film should not be confused with the exploitation *of the film* by the inclusion of, or reference to, sexual material (as, for example, in *The Outlaw*). Any film can be so exploited, and sex is not the only tool for doing it. Consider violence, the presence of stars, fashionable issues. Whether a film gets this sort of exploitation or not—indeed, whether it lends itself to it or not—has no direct bearing on its aesthetic worth. One may want to criticize Marlon Brando for the exploitation of *Last Tango* made possible, even inevitable, by his stature in the industry. But his conduct must not be confused with the exploitation of sex *within* the film, and criticism of his conduct must not be taken for criticism of the film.

The use (exploitation) of sex within films is as legitimate as the use of any other form of human behavior. It *should* be used as a metaphor, as a dramatic device. Like any metaphor, any device, it can be well-used and ill-used. But also like other metaphors and devices, whether it is well or ill-used will be determined by its potency, originality, clarity and illuminatingness in doing what the film-maker wants it to do. And those things have no necessary connection with natural-ness or literal honesty in a narrative.

In short, sex films are as distinct and important a genre as political, horror, western, or war films. The exploitation of sex is as legitimate and important a device (aesthetically) as the exploitation of any other fundamental human interest. The best sex films, like the best films generally, are too complex to be adequately described *only* as sex films. Dusan Makavejev's *WR*, for example, is a sex film, a political film, and a comedy, and each element is exploited as a metaphor for the others. The result is a richness of affective and intellectual response which would

99

not have been possible had Makavejev followed the canons implicit in "sex-as-a-necessary-narrative-element."

So much for the first naive dogma. Any remaining reluctance to see its misleadingness comes, I think, from tacit acceptance of the second: that moral and aesthetic values are somehow interconnected. It will be worthwhile spending a little space demolishing that assumption, for it represents a deep confusion and unfortunately pervades a great deal of the discussion of films like *Last Tango*.

People who are morally outraged at sexual explicitness feel compelled to speak of it as artistically degenerate as well. People who merely have moral qualms about it, also try hard to have aesthetic qualms—and talk about how dull it all is, or how "gratuitous." (Just as an aside, it should be remarked that qualms have not received enough attention as an important moral category. I once had a student who claimed she had no moral principles—just a lot of qualms.) In any case, defenders, as well as critics, of sexual freedom in film argue for this sort of value-correspondence. Catharsis (almost always involved with sex in one way or another anyway) is said to be good for the soul. Sensuality is beautiful and beauty is ennobling—reinforcing our sense of the dignity and sanctity of the individual. Depravity (e.g., sadism) is not illuminating . . . And so on.

All such talk is muddled. The truth is that while there may be, in special cases like documentary film, a parallelism between certain moral values and analogous aesthetic ones, in general, nothing could be clearer than that moral and aesthetic values in film are radically independent of each other. Everyone will agree that just because a film is bad aesthetically (sloppily made, unintentionally dull or whatever) nothing necessarily follows about its being bad morally, whatever one may mean by that. Sex education films, often pathetically unaesthetic, are a case in point. But there is a curious reticence to see the converse—to see that just because a film is bad morally (subtly racist, perhaps) nothing necessarily follows about its being bad aesthetically.

We resist this latter conclusion because we don't like to be caught admiring, in any way, something we seriously disapprove of. (I say "seriously disapprove of" to eliminate the case of "fashionable evils" like witchcraft.) Yet doesn't this completely obfuscate the fact that some fascists, as well as some sex educators, are a lot better at making films than others? And that the way we know they are better is by how hard it is, when viewing their films, to experience them *only* through our moral sensibilities? We are dismayed to find subtle racism in a film, and we infer from the fact that the film was spoiled as an aesthetic experience for us, that it was flawed aesthetically (i.e., as a work of art).

This is nonsense. *Of course* art cannot properly be isolated from morality. *Of course* our experience of art can never be isolated from our moral point of view. Nor should it be. But it is no use pretending that moral and aesthetic values are

100

interlocked. Reflect, again, on aesthetically trite and cinematically clichéd educational films.

Ah, but you say, think how much better they would be "for the cause" if they were well made. Surely this indicates an interrelation of moral and aesthetic values.

Not at all. It indicates a relation, perhaps, between a film's aesthetic value and its effectiveness as a piece of propaganda, but that is a different matter. A film is not moral merely because it is convincing. If its content is of moral worth (good or bad), then its aesthetic excellence may increase that goodness or badness by making it effective in moral education. But it is important to notice that even this is not necessarily so. A slick documentary on the need for abortion reform may be unconvincing just because of its aesthetic value. I, for one, get suspicious of message films made with adequate money and a lot of talent; I wonder if I'm being manipulated too thoroughly. I wonder if I'm being lied to. A sloppily cut, badly printed film whose point of view sticks out tastelessly is infinitely more reassuring.

Now of course there are some moral values (e.g., honesty, directness, integrity) which have their analogs in the aesthetic or particular sorts of film. Documentaries are better, both morally and aesthetically, by virtue of being honest and direct. But I think this is a very special case, and at any rate it is hard to find such parallels for cinematic sex of the frankly erotic sort.

Take honesty. We all know what that does to the intense (though ultimately claustrophobic) aesthetic values of a hard-core skin flick. Pornography *depends* on dishonesty; women must be perpetually willing, always available, aroused, and insatiable; men must be perpetually interested and indefatigable. Above all, the action must not have any nonsexual consequences: there may be pain, but there must not be an incapacitating injury. All of which is thoroughly dishonest. Yet the eroticism of pornography—around which all its aesthetic values are built—fails totally without it.

Surely though, you say, it is possible for a film to be erotic without being dishonest. And precisely what relegates pornography to the status of a low—if not non—art form is its failure to reflect anything approaching the real complexity of human erotic experience. Here, then, is how a single value (honesty) can be determinative of both moral and aesthetic worth (assuming we can brush aside those who don't want art to be honest about sex).

On examination, however, this rather attractive argument fails. For eroticism in films ultimately fails or succeeds in just the way all art does: not by its possession of moral virtues, but by the novelty and clarity of its vision, its inventiveness, and the excellence of its execution. A film doesn't fall short of being the highest sort of aesthetic experience merely by being a sexual fantasy as opposed

103

to an "honest" account of how things really are. There is beauty in honesty, but not all beauty is there.

Moral values can interfere with or alter aesthetic experience, of course. And indeed they should. It would be odd and more than a little disquieting if men now could watch the obligatory male dominance bits of business from the good old days without flinching a little (was that really me?). And how do you feel these days watching the Candice Bergen orgasm—her lover being unbelievably in control and nicely self-possessed? (This is neatly mocked in Alan Pakula's *Klute*.)

But moral and aesthetic values are interconnected simply because (for most of us, at least) moral values are overriding. They control, to some extent, what we can experience as beautiful or otherwise aesthetically valuable—or if not precisely what we can so experience, then the way in which we experience it. Ken Russell's *The Devils* draws this line nicely. Some people get nothing but nausea followed by dumb shock. Not very high on the index of aesthetic experience, whatever rationalizations viewers may add about what they learned about themselves and human nature. For others, the experience provided by the film is more complex.

Such conflict in aesthetic experience provides a fertile field for confused arguments: my lack of ability to appreciate something you find compelling may be seen (by me) as a consequence of my superior moral sensibilities. You may see it as a pathetic limitation imposed by stupid moral attitudes, and proceed to argue that it is important to be open to the sort of aesthetic experience I reject—important for moral reasons.

Now this is a straightforward moral argument and is one link in the necessarily long and convoluted chain of arguments about censorship. But it is just the point at which people are most tempted to ring in the film's aesthetic values to help decide the moral/political/legal question. And, of course, aesthetic values are largely irrelevant to such questions. You cannot decide the "redeeming social value" issue by proving that the film was well made—indeed, that it is a work of art. Those pure souls who reckon that anything which has high aesthetic value can do naught but good (in the long run?), or is, merely by virtue of being aesthetically good, morally good as well, have not, I fear, thought far enough. Or else they have covertly imported their ideological convictions and moral standards into their definition of aesthetic worth—a hopelessly confusing thing to do.

Better to keep the question of moral worth where it belongs—quite distinct from notions of aesthetic value. Human value experience is very complex, and it does no good to disguise its complexity by papering over important distinctions. I can, after all, find myself horribly fascinated in a medieval torture chamber (Fantastic workmanship on that iron maiden, eh Maud?). But that doesn't mean that I would recommend to anyone that he open himself to the experience it offers.

PART TWO

Categories and Genres

James Dean and sidekick Sal Mineo rest in Natalie Wood's lap in the fifties' most famous movie *Rebel Without a Cause.*

5.

Troubled Sexuality in the Popular Hollywood Feature

THOMAS R. ATKINS

MARLON BRANDO in a leather jacket astride a motorcycle in *The Wild One.* Marilyn Monroe's skirt lifted by a sudden breeze from a subway grating in *The Seven Year Itch.* Burt Lancaster and Deborah Kerr embracing in the surf in *From Here to Eternity.* Jayne Mansfield clutching two bottles of milk against her breasts in *The Girl Can't Help It.* Rosalind Russell ripping off William Holden's shirt in *Picnic.* Jack Lemmon and Tony Curtis in drag in *Some Like It Hot.* Elvis Presley singing and gyrating in *Jailhouse Rock.* Carroll Baker in a crib sucking her thumb in *Baby Doll.* Natalie Wood going berserk in the bath in *Splendor in the Grass.*

The popular erotic icons that Hollywood offered its public in the fifties and early sixties are often strikingly different from those of any other period. Some of the screen images are satiric, some serious, others downright silly; but most are characterized, like the decade itself, by a curious ambiguity, a sometimes schizoid duality. All are transitional images—products of what André Bazin called American film's "long, rich, byzantine tradition of censorship" and precursors of the more permissive cinema of the next decade. In their deviousness and cleverness these images belong to the past, to the years of the Production Code administered by the Breen office which forced directors to deal indirectly with sex through suggestion and innuendo; but they point to the future in being unmistakenly and often blatantly obsessed with sex, particularly the frustrated and compulsive variety.

Contrary to the popular notion of the Truman-Eisenhower years as bland and passive, the era was actually seething with contradictions and conflicts: a time of the McCarthy hearings, the Rosenberg executions, the Korean police action, fallout shelters, flying saucers, and Sputnik. The cool, seemingly disengaged exterior style of the fifties—its world of crew cuts, duck tails, pegged pants, sock hops, hot rods, and drive-ins—masks a turbulent interior, which erupts with violent impact in the late sixties and seventies. The cultural and sexual revolutions of the next decade, the protest movements that split and altered American society, resulted from forces that were smoldering and festering beneath the square, apathetic facade of the fifties.

The Graduate, Easy Rider, Carnal Knowledge, The Last Picture Show, Walking Tall, and many other contemporary box office hits are based on formulas and themes that evolved in the previous troubled decade. In *Badlands* the renegade hero seems modeled after James Dean; and *American Graffiti,* a nostalgic and extremely funny tribute to teenagers' lifestyles in the early sixties, relies upon many of the same stock characters and situations that can be found in *Rebel Without a Cause.* Although these later movies are more graphic verbally and physically— superficially more liberated—they still reflect basically the same stereotypes of human identity and divided attitudes toward sexuality as their earlier counterparts, but usually without the pervasive sense of repressed anxiety and ambiguity that makes many fifties movies so compelling.

Stanley Kubrick's use of the Gene Kelly title song as a counterpoint to Alex's violent antics in *A Clockwork Orange* is especially appropriate, for *Singing' in the Rain,* which appeared in 1952, is one of the last pure examples of old-style Hollywood escapism at its best—a lavish musical satire about show biz in the Roaring Twenties, featuring Kelly as a popular movie star, Debbie Reynolds as a nice young actress, and Jean Hagen as a blonde sexpot who tries to become a sound star using Reynolds' dubbed-in voice. The mood is light, spontaneous, confident, with no trace of the ambiguous undercurrent of troubled sexuality that flows through many fifties films.

By the time *Singin' in the Rain* was made, the monopolistic studio system it satirized was already dying, its demise hastened by U.S. antitrust decisions which ended studio control of theater chains around the country, by television which began to drain away its mass audience, and by the investigations of J. Parnell Thomas and the House Un-American Activities Committee, which wrecked the careers of countless actors, writers, and directors and eroded what was left of Hollywood's sense of community. Moreover, changing postwar social and moral attitudes had begun to undermine the power of the Breen office, whose censorship Code had once spoken not only for the film industry but for the popular values of the general American public as well.

As the general public or "home audience" switched to TV for their escapism and entertainment, the television networks developed their own censorship— a set of guidelines regulating program content and ethics that, as formulated in

1951, were even more puritanical and conservative than the movie censorship of the mid-thirties and forties. Ostensibly designed to protect the sensibilities of the family audience, the television code was actually a reflection of the commercial values of sponsors and advertisers who, while professing moral decorum, utilized sexual association and innuendo to market their products in much the same manner as Hollywood exploited sex to sell movies. The popular early TV shows, featuring such stars as Milton Berle, Gertrude Berg, Jackie Gleason, and Kukla, Fran and Ollie, were usually completely devoid of sex; but the commercials were experimenting with lines like "Why don't you pick me up and smoke me sometime?" for cigars and "Does she or doesn't she?" for a hair dye.

Meanwhile, Hollywood tried desperately to compete with the magic box with a series of technical gimmicks, such as 3-D and Cinerama, and by turning out expensive blockbusters, historical epics like *The Robe, The Ten Commandments, Ben Hur,* and the forty-million-dollar flop *Cleopatra* or adaptations of bestsellers like *Marjorie Morningstar, Not as a Stranger, Magnificent Obsession,* and *Giant.* In spite of these spectacular efforts, television continued to win the battle for audiences; by 1955 sixty-five million viewers watched Mary Martin soar through the air in a TV version of *Peter Pan.*

The influx of foreign movies that were attracting audiences in smaller theaters in New York and other major cities suggested another lucrative possibility to Hollywood: movies on adult themes that were too hot for TV. Such films as Max Ophüls' *La Ronde,* Ingmar Bergman's *Monika,* Alf Sjöberg's *Miss Julie,* and Henri-Georges Clouzot's *The Wages of Fear* dealt with sexuality in a more mature fashion than ever attempted in Hollywood. Ulla Jacobsson went skinny-dipping with her boyfriend in *One Summer of Happiness,* and later in the decade Brigitte Bardot in *And God Created Woman* and Jeanne Moreau in *The Lovers* displayed more skin than had been available previously on U.S. movie screens.

Bolder European directors and performers encouraged Hollywood filmmakers to take the first tentative, insecure steps in the direction of movies made chiefly for adult audiences. In 1951 when television presented its viewers shows like *I Love Lucy, Amos 'n' Andy, The Cisco Kid,* and *Mr. District Attorney* (all based on early movie or radio formulas), the film industry offered *A Streetcar Named Desire,* adapted by Tennessee Williams from his own play, and starring Marlon Brando, Vivien Leigh, and Kim Hunter.

Director Elia Kazan fought with the Breen office to preserve certain essential elements of the script, particularly the crucial scene where Stanley Kowalski rapes his sister-in-law Blanche DuBois and Blanche's story of the suicide of her young homosexual husband. The Code Board permitted a modified version of the rape, but Kazan and Williams had to cut references to homosexuality and soften the movie's ending by implying that Stella Kowalski rejected Stanley for his brutal

111

Timothy Bottoms and Cybill Shepherd in
The Last Picture Show, set in early fifties.

Sissy Spacek and Martin Sheen in Terrence
Malick's *Badlands*, based loosely on
Charles Starkweather killings of late fifties.

Gene Kelly and Cyd Charisse in number
from fifties musical *Singin' in the Rain*.

Dean as Jett Rink in George Stevens' *Giant*.

treatment of her sister. Later without Kazan's knowledge, the Catholic Legion of Decency pressured Warner Brothers into making further changes, such as dropping "on the mouth" from Blanche's line to the young man from the *Evening Star*, "I would like to kiss you softly and sweetly on the mouth."

By 1956 when Kazan filmed the black comedy *Baby Doll*, he was able to refuse to make any changes that would weaken the heady sensuality of Williams' script—partially because the Code had gradually become more tolerant and also because he had shot it on location in Mississippi away from Hollywood studio politics. In open defiance of the Legion of Decency, Kazan placed a huge ad on Broadway showing Carroll Baker as child-bride Baby Doll Meighan in a crib with a thumb in her mouth.

Two years after *Streetcar* independent director Otto Preminger demonstrated the weakening power of the Code board by releasing *The Moon Is Blue* without a seal of approval. A banal bedroom comedy with William Holden and Maggie McNamara uttering such taboo words as *virgin, mistress,* and *pregnant, The Moon Is Blue* was successful at the box office and showed other directors that the Code was not all powerful. Controversy also surrounded Fred Zinnemann's film version of James Jones' *From Here to Eternity,* about Army life in Hawaii shortly before Pearl Harbor. The Code board was disturbed by an affair between a sergeant played by Burt Lancaster and an officer's wife, Deborah Kerr, and particularly by their love-making scene on the beach which was later exploited in the ads for the movie (and satirized by Billy Wilder in his 1955 sex farce *The Seven Year Itch*). The beach scene remained, but even the mildest four-letter words were deleted and an important Honolulu whorehouse setting was changed to a social club. A considerably cleaned-up but still powerful interpretation of the barbarity of the military life, *From Here to Eternity* won eight Academy Awards, including Best Picture.

But a movie that did not win any Academy Awards in 1953 was probably the most significant, sociologically if not aesthetically. Laslo Benedek's *The Wild One* concerns the terrorizing of a small town by two packs of motorcyclists, one gang led by Marlon Brando and the other by Lee Marvin. Actually a blend of the Dead-End Kid formula and the Western genre, using motorcycles instead of horses, the movie is a sentimentalized and safe comment on the problem of juvenile delinquency.

Despite a few menacing episodes such as the sequence where the gang frightens the telephone operator and temporarily cuts off the town's communication with the outside world, most of the rebels are characterized as misguided but fundamentally good boys who speak jive talk and just want to scramble with girls. To further glamorize the subject, Brando's character has a romance with a policeman's daughter who longs to escape the town. But the real importance and power of *The Wild One* lies in the effective portrait of the claustrophobic small-town

113

environment and its petty-minded, fearful citizens—a dominant motif of the fifties—and in Brando's inarticulate, tough/tender, sexually ambiguous rebel leader.

In the role of Johnny in *The Wild One*, as well as with his performances as Stanley in *Streetcar* and the longshoreman in *On the Waterfront*, Marlon Brando established the basic outline for the major cult figure of the decade and the dominant acting style that still prevails in American movies today. James Dean, Sal Mineo, and Elvis Presley are variations on this basic rebel image; and actors like Dustin Hoffman, Jon Voight, and Jack Nicholson use essentially the same Method acting techniques.

Derived from Konstantin Stanislavsky's rehearsal methods at the Moscow Art Theatre and interpreted by the Group Theatre and Lee Strasberg's Actor's Studio in New York, Method acting is the perfect style for the self-conscious and divided mood of the fifties. On one hand it emphasizes ensemble playing and group relationships, while at the same time it stresses each character's separate interior reality and emotional duality. In Method acting the most important element is the inner subtext which emerges, often in silences between the lines, from the character's struggle with the group and with himself, his divided nature. The most effective Method acting roles, such as Johnny in *The Wild One* or Jim Stark in *Rebel Without a Cause*, are usually characters with a subtle anxiety within them but with little external power to cope with it. Because of the pressure of this conflict, they constantly seem on the verge of breaking down, falling to pieces, or becoming violent.

Brando, Montgomery Clift, Julie Harris, Eli Wallach, Patricia Neal, Kim Hunter, Anthony Perkins, Rod Steiger, and the other Method performers who emerged in the fifties are best in divided parts based on the unresolved tension between an outer social mask and an inner reality of frustration that usually has a sexual basis. In contrast, the popular roles played by earlier actors such as Spencer Tracy, Humphrey Bogart, Katharine Hepburn, James Cagney, Bette Davis, or Fredric March seem exceptionally well-integrated and direct. Fifties audiences responded instinctively to the new Method performances not only because they were often technically superb, but because the moviegoers themselves were experiencing a similar duality, largely unacknowledged and unexpressed, within themselves and their society.

The cool, self-confident pose adopted by Brando's character in *The Wild One* disguises a person who is actually insecure and anxious—still the child who was harshly beaten by his old man—which explains why he treasures a stolen racing trophy and fights Chino to protect this popular emblem of masculine victory. Throughout the movie Johnny alternates between the roles of a rather sullen, shy boy and a brooding, menacing adult. From his first entrance leading the swarm of motorcycles, this man/boy is established as a figure of considerable sexual power which he communicates almost effortlessly to all of the other characters. His sexual magnetism, in fact, is shown to be an extremely ambiguous force— Johnny appeals to males and females alike, and while this is never openly expressed by the character, there are unmistakable signs that he needs the adoration of both sexes.

The true romantic triangle lurking just below the surface of *The Wild One* features a wholesome girl-next-door type, Kathy, and a wise-cracking hood, Chino—both of whom are in love with Johnny. He is also pursued by a slut type named Britches, but the only characters who ever break Johnny's cool and arouse his anger are Kathy and Chino. Lee Marvin's Chino, supposedly a mean, freaky counterpart to Johnny, is really his brother under the skin—a crude and somewhat comic embodiment of a hidden aspect of Johnny. Once both belonged to the same motorcycle group, until Johnny got disgusted with the childish behavior of Chino's boys and split with his own boys. But like a doppelganger, Chino follows him, hoping to reunite the old gang and crying out to him mockingly, "I love you, Johnny."

This buried and feared taboo side of Johnny's character was acknowledged later in Kenneth Anger's underground film, *Scorpio Rising*, in which Johnny appears as a flickering fantasy image on the TV set of the hero, who models himself after Brando and James Dean and leads a gang of bike boys whose entertainments include a drag party and an initiation ceremony that is explicitly homosexual. (The nearest that the hipsters in *The Wild One* ever get to this type of exhibitionistic behavior is dancing in front of the local beauty parlor with hair dryers on their heads or scaring the cop's daughter by chasing and circling her on their motorcycles.) The closeup of Brando that appears in *Scorpio Rising* emphasizes his male stud qualities—the brooding, babyish features; the dreamy, heavy-lidded eyes; and the thick, sensual lips which suddenly curl into a strange smile.

In contrast to the subversive tone of *Scorpio Rising*, Benedek's bike film is tame and respectable. The latent elements in the plot are seldom permitted to surface. Although they tease the town girls, the outlaw cyclists never engage in any graphic sex talk. All potential eroticism between Johnny and Kathy is communicated furtively in looks and disguised gestures. When Britches, a parody of the tough B-girl stereotype from earlier movies, gets drunk and makes a direct pass at Johnny, he takes a swig of her beer and rejects her with disdain, far more cruelly than he had rejected Chino.

The only sequence in *The Wild One* that comes close to realizing the sexuality implicit in the story is Kathy's long motorcycle ride with Johnny through the dark countryside. After stopping his rebels from tormenting her with their cycles, Johnny says only, "Get on," and then when they have reached their destination, a quiet spot in a park, he says, "Get off." The ride seems to release her wilder impulses and she reveals her secret desire to go away with him. But

115

Stanley Kubrick's early sixties film about a nymphet, *Lolita,* featured Sue Lyon.

Marlon Brando as Johnny, with stolen racing trophy attached to bike handlebars, in *The Wild One.*

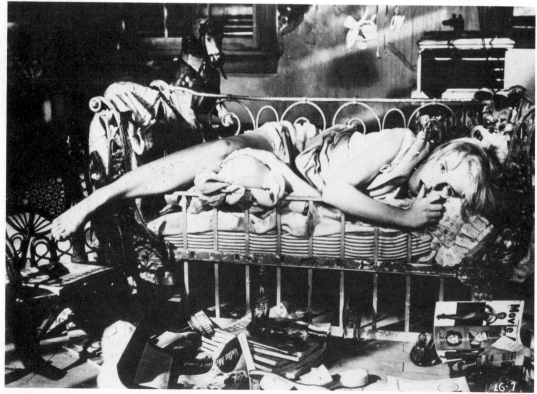

Carroll Baker as the child bride in Elia Kazan's *Baby Doll.*

Mister Rock and Roll with Lionel Hampton's band.

Mamie Van Doren dancing in *Untamed Youth*.

Elvis Presley in a mid-sixties film *Easy Come, Easy Go*.

Johnny becomes angry and insulting, causing her to run away in tears. A group of paranoid male townsfolk, led by the local bully, assume that Kathy has been assaulted and give Johnny a beating, a punishment he bears stoically until he escapes and weeps beside his bike.

As a low-angle closeup emphasizes Brando's upturned, anguished face— surely one of the most famous shots of the fifties—one might well ask why is the leader of the Black Rebels crying? Because the unjust beating by older males reminded him of his father's rough treatment? ("My old man hit harder than that," he said defiantly to the men.) Or because he wishes he had run away with Kathy to start a "normal" life? Or perhaps returned with Chino to a deviant hipster life? Or rather is Johnny weeping because he doesn't know what style of life he prefers, and wishes both the squares and the crazies would let him alone?

In the final sequences, after being exonerated of the death of the old dishwasher who was accidentally struck by his bike, Johnny receives moral counselling from a sheriff—a concession demanded by the Breen office to clarify the meaning of the movie for the audience. Finally Johnny returns to Bleeker's Cafe where Kathy is a waitress and passes his stolen racing trophy across the counter to her. Then like a mysterious, isolated, romantic hero from a western, he climbs on his cycle and roars out of Wrightsville—back to the open highway and the gang lifestyle.

While the motorcycle formula was revived many times after *The Wild One,* most notably in Roger Corman's *The Wild Angels,* the genre did not become big business until 1969 when Dennis Hopper's *Easy Rider* captured the under-twenty-five audience by presenting a story that confirmed their popular tastes and values. Like *The Wild One,* Hopper's movie pretends to be serious social criticism, while actually offering a skillfully-made escapist fantasy in the traditional Hollywood mode. Although Billy and Wyatt of *Easy Rider* are superficially freer in that they openly smoke grass, go skinny-dipping, and get laid, they are still not too far from the boys in *The Wild One* in their fundamental distrust of females and their preference for male companionship and the open road.

The villains of the formula—the paranoid, middle-aged townsfolk—have grown nastier over the years and, instead of merely giving the troublemakers a beating as they did in Benedek's film, they shotgun the heroes of *Easy Rider.* In the late sixties and seventies the final ritualistic slaughter of young male and female outlaws, beginning with *Bonnie and Clyde* and continuing through such movies as *Thieves Like Us,* becomes with repetition a plot cliché as arbitrary and phony as last-minute rescues and happy endings were to earlier movies.

After *The Wild One,* the most significant and revealing movie of the fifties is Nicholas Ray's *Rebel Without A Cause,* with James Dean, Natalie Wood, and Sal Mineo (and Dennis Hopper in a minor role). A popular box office hit in 1955, the movie used a formula that is potentially more threatening than the bike genre and made more explicit some of the latent sexual elements in *The Wild One*. Dean's extraordinary performance was a major factor in the movie's success. Starring in only three movies, *East of Eden, Giant*, and *Rebel* (he died in an auto crash one month before *Rebel* was released), Dean became a cult hero in the Brando mold but with stronger appeal to "straight" middle-class youth as well as a large homosexual following.

"This is Jim Stark, teenager from a 'good' family," states a *Rebel* poster, showing Dean in T-shirt, red jacket, and jeans and emphasizing that the character is not one of the hoods of *Blackboard Jungle* or the bikers of *The Wild One*. Because the bike genre deals with social outcasts, gypsy figures roaming the highways, it is for most members of the audience basically a safe and romantic experience. But *Rebel* and movies such as *Blue Denim, The Young Stranger, Splendor in the Grass*, and *The Graduate*, are closer to the audience's lives in their portraits of the social and sexual traumas within the American household. The middle-class family is not attacked by freaky outsiders but by its own children who no longer accept its cherished attitudes and values. Typically, in the troubled youth genre, parents and other adult figures are callously authoritarian, while the kids are portrayed as sensitive, misunderstood creatures.

Under the credits for *Rebel*, Dean falls to the sidewalk beside a mechanical monkey in a red cap. He winds up the monkey, plays with it, then puts it to bed by covering it with a newspaper—a lost child sheltering an abandoned toy. Taken to the police station for drunkenness, Dean meets two other disturbed teenagers: Sal Mineo's Plato who has been arrested for shooting some puppies with his mother's pistol and Natalie Wood's Judy, a girl in bright red lipstick and coat who was found wandering the streets. All three teenagers are stranded at the station in the middle of the night because, emotionally, they are homeless. Jim's father is a weak, indecisive fool totally dominated by his wife and her mother; Judy's father reacts with hostility whenever she approaches him for much-needed affection; and Plato's divorced parents have left his upbringing to a black maid, who is among the few likeable adults in the film.

Dawson High School, where Jim is a new student, is respectable on the surface but actually dominated by teenage gangs who amuse themselves by testing outsiders. Judy's boyfriend Buzz is a close kin to the toughs in *The Wild One*, except that he and his followers use hot rods instead of bikes. On a field trip to Griffith Planetarium, where the students are shown a film depicting the end of the world, Jim is provoked into a switchblade fight with Buzz. This encounter leads to the "chicken run," the central image of the film, a night sequence in which Jim and Buzz race in stolen autos towards a cliff's edge. The first driver to abandon his vehicle is the chicken. Judy's intense excitement, as the two cars rush past her toward the cliff, underscores the sexual implications of the contest. Jim escapes at the last minute before his car tumbles over the edge, but Buzz

119

catches his jacket sleeve in the door handle and plunges to a fiery death. Later when Jim tells his father and mother about the accident, they are afraid that this scandal may ruin their reputations and urge him not to go to the police. Like nearly all of the adults in *Rebel*, Jim's parents are more concerned with outer appearance than with the realities of their children's lives.

The rest of the action builds to the death of Plato. Like *The Wild One*, Ray's movie focuses on a sexually confused trio consisting of one female and two males—but in *Rebel* the homosexual potentiality of the males' relationship is more apparent. Plato is clearly infatuated with Jim and substitutes him for his absent father, while Jim understands and responds sympathetically to the younger boy's attention. As with Chino and Johnny, Plato and Jim may be seen as separate aspects of the same schizoid personality. Both characters are linked by their hypersensitivity, insecurity, and repressed violence. But Plato's homosexuality makes him too vulnerable and, in keeping with Hollywood's usual treatment of such characters, he is identified from the beginning as doomed. All of the other students, except for Jim and Judy, irrationally reject or torment Plato who, when frightened, steals his mother's nickel-plated .45 kept beneath her satin bed pillows.

Finally, hiding in a deserted mansion in the hills near the planetarium, Jim, Judy, and Plato act out a fantasy of the happy life they have never experienced. Jim rests his head on Judy's lap while she sings Plato to sleep with a lullaby. Their childlike dream is interrupted by Buzz's gang who try to trap Plato in an empty swimming pool. Wounding one of them, Plato flees to the planetarium, where he is eventually shot by the police when they see his gun. He dies wearing Jim's red jacket, but Jim had already emptied the weapon and shouts from the planetarium steps, "I've got the bullets." Despite a superficial reconciliation between Judy, Jim, and his parents, the overall impact of *Rebel Without a Cause* carries a sense of deep, irreconcilable conflict between the values of the older generation and the new. Plato's useless death is a bleak forecast of things to come.

Rebel spawned many lesser screen imitations in the fifties, and Sal Mineo continued to play a wayward teenager in such movies as *Crime in the Streets* and *Dino*; but one of the most offbeat and strangely memorable treatments of adolescent torment was Gene Fowler's *I Was a Teenage Werewolf*, the start of a series of low-budget horror movies aimed at exploiting the growing youth market. *Teenage Werewolf* made several million dollars in its first year, packing in young audiences across the country and enjoying a special popularity at drive-in theaters where its peculiar blend of horror and humor could perhaps best be appreciated.

Michael Landon, later to become Little Joe of the TV series *Bonanza*, plays a disturbed high school student, having problems with teachers and his girlfriend's family. But instead of turning into a switchblade-carrying delinquent, Landon becomes a victim of lycanthropy—a more direct expression of his sexual hangups and his latent hostility towards the family and society that has victimized him. His repressed tendencies released by a psychiatrist's secret treatment, he acts out impulses that normal teenagers must keep hidden. Half wolf, half adolescent (still wearing his school jacket), Landon roams the woods at night —a hairy embodiment both of adolescent frustration with the adult world and of adult paranoia about the teenage culture.

Still another interesting variation on the troubled youth formula are the numerous rock and roll movies, generally despised by adults and relished by teenagers—titles such as *Rock Around the Clock; Rock, Pretty Baby; Don't Knock the Rock; Mister Rock and Roll;* and Frank Tashlin's rock satire *The Girl Can't Help It.* Rock and roll music originated in the bold rhythm and blues music of the black music stations and most of the rock numbers in these movies featured black performers like Little Richard, Fats Domino, Chubby Checker, and Gene Vincent and his Blue Caps. Their lyrics and beat were often outrageously sexual, even though the rock and roll genre plots were generally antiseptically clean. The uninhibited musicians are usually kept on one side of the bandstand and the white teenagers on the other.

The first white male performer of the fifties to really let it all hang out was Elvis Presley, who learned his style from black rhythm and blues artists like Bo Diddley and used it to excite millions of screaming white teenagers. Although his TV and movie images were considerably toned down—chiefly by shooting above the waist—Presley's live performances were explicitly erotic, earning him the nickname "the Pelvis." His resemblance to Brando in *The Wild One* and the aggressive sexuality of his performances were a direct challenge to the repressive atmosphere of the fifties, and teenage fans responded with hysteria to the release his music seemed to offer. Yet in all of his fifties movies, such as *Love Me Tender, Jailhouse Rock, King Creole,* Presley's sensuality is muted, disguised, until finally, as critic Radley Metzger has observed, he got "wholesomed to death" and became in the next decade an acceptable object of nostalgia for middle-aged audiences.

Although made in 1961 and set in the twenties and thirties, Elia Kazan's *Splendor in the Grass,* scripted by William Inge, is essentially a fifties movie, particularly in its strong portrait of high school kids struggling in a small Kansas town against insensitive families and outmoded social customs. Warren Beatty and Natalie Wood appear as "nice" teenagers, Bud and Deanie, both driven by libidinous urges they have difficulty controlling and kept apart by selfish parents with other plans for their childrens' lives. Barbara Loden is extremely effective as Bud's sister, a naughty, exhibitionistic flapper type who taunts Deanie for her good-girl image.

When Bud is sent away to Yale by his wealthy father, Deanie remains passively at home until eventually she cracks up under the pressure of pent-up emotions. (The script doesn't explain why Bud doesn't also fall to pieces; the

121

implication is that sexual repression doesn't affect men as much as women, a standard Hollywood myth recurring in many movies.) According to writer Murray Schumach, Kazan shot a sequence in which Deanie became hysterical in the bath and raced naked down the hallway to get away from her mother. But the Production Code ruling against nudity—a ruling which was to disappear later in the decade—forced Kazan to delete the hallway dash. The final image of *Splendor in the Grass* is quiet and poignant—after having decided to marry other people (Bud is already married, Deanie will wed her doctor), the couple meet briefly for the last time, silently consider the separate directions their lives have taken because of their parents' interference and then separate forever.

John Frankenheimer's *All Fall Down*, made in 1962, offers yet another variation on youthful identity problems and sexual anguish. Written by William Inge from the novel by James Leo Herlihy, this movie features Warren Beatty as Berry-Berry, a spoiled son idolized by his parents and younger brother, Clinton, played by Brandon de Wilde. The mother and father, Angela Lansbury and Karl Malden, are extensions of the oppressive parents in fifties movies. Beatty's role is a descendant of the Brando and Dean characters, as well as the Tennessee Williams stud heroes, but he has turned sour and cynical—Berry-Berry loves only himself. The sexual tension emerges when Echo O'Brien, Eva Marie Saint, arrives in the household and attracts both brothers. Naturally, in keeping with Hollywood stereotypes, this mature woman is irresistibly drawn to the narcissistic stud who cons, mistreats, and eventually causes Echo to commit suicide. Disillusioned by his older brother's behavior, Clinton departs in search of other heroes.

Brandon de Wilde shows up again as an adolescent with an identity crisis in Martin Ritt's *Hud*, one of the most popular box office hits of the early sixties and a major transitional work pointing to movies of the seventies. Based on the Larry McMurtry novel *Horseman, Pass By*, the movie combines the troubled youth genre with the western framework. The story, which is set on a twentieth-century cattle ranch, concerns the conflict between an aging ranch owner, played by Melvyn Douglas, who looks upon the values of the new age with contempt, and his son, Hud, who feels that his father's values are impractical. McMurtry described his hero as "a gunfighter who lacks both guns and opponents," a man "whose capacities no longer fit his situation." Instead of gun or horse Paul Newman's Hud has a Cadillac which he drives around the dull little Texas town, searching for some excitement, chiefly fights, drink, and women. In *Midnight Cowboy* Joe Buck admires a poster of Hud, but never manages to achieve Newman's smooth confidence and self-control.

Patricia Neal won an Academy Award for her characterization of Alma, the housekeeper who functions both as a substitute mother figure in the Bannon home and a sexually attractive woman who arouses Hud and his nephew, Lon, the Brandon de Wilde role. Much of the movie's power derives from the subtle inter-

Barbara Loden and Warren Beatty as sister
and brother in Kazan's *Splendor in the Grass*.

Candy Clark, Charlie Martin Smith, and
Ronny Howard in George Lucas' recreation of
the early sixties *American Graffiti*.

Patricia Neal fights off the advances of
Paul Newman in *Hud*.

Elizabeth Taylor attracts young boys for her poet husband in
Joseph Mankiewicz's *Suddenly Last Summer* which won
Code approval in 1959 despite its themes of homosexuality
and cannibalism.

play of this triangle—especially from the different ways Alma deals with each male, and from her recognition of her own bruised identity, Lon's adolescent traits, and Hud's wilder reality. In contrast to Echo in *All Fall Down*, Alma is no pushover for the stud cowboy. She is, in some ways, very much like Hud—a loner toughened by her experiences, hanging on to her independence.

The ending is a bit contrived and pat: Hud's attempt to force himself upon Alma, Lon's discovery and realization that he must break loose of his uncle's influence. Lon rejects his uncle because he isn't a noble cowboy like Shane, but one point of the movie is that even if Hud had wanted to—which he didn't—he couldn't become such a heroic figure in the modern west. Yet despite all the attacks on his character and his rejection by the other characters, the movie sides with Hud and expects the audience to do likewise. The self-righteous old rancher, Homer, may appeal to the spectator's conscience, but Hud's reckless nature and gunfighter qualities speak to more basic emotions.

It is significant that George Lucas set *American Graffiti* in 1962, during John F. Kennedy's administration, for events in the following year made it painfully clear that a different era was beginning. The uptight fifties were obviously over, and we were headed into the turbulent sixties. Late in 1963 a nation of television viewers watched Kennedy's funeral in Washington, D.C., and saw Jack Ruby shoot Lee Harvey Oswald in Dallas. This was also the year of the "March on Washington" led by Martin Luther King, and the Vietnam War was beginning to appear more frequently on home TV sets. A year later the Beatles, accompanied by deafening shrieks from the studio audience, made their first appearance on the Ed Sullivan Show. The Age of Aquarius was not far away.

The next decade in Hollywood saw further re-adjustments in the studio system as more independent productions were shot in other parts of the world, the end of the traditional "glamorized" star system, the rise of new "authentic" stars, the final collapse of the censorship code, and the subsequent leap "from prudery to pornography," as Molly Haskell has described the change that occurred in the screen's treatment of sex. The over-thirty audience continued to desert movies for television, until by 1970 the major portion of the filmgoing public were urban youth between twelve and twenty-five years old.

As the Greaser Age faded, the obsessive and often disguised motifs of the fifties—rebellious youth, deviant sexuality, questioning of middle-class values and loss of faith in established institutions—came to dominate the screen in the sixties and seventies. The young alienated rebel reappeared in scores of movies, but his character underwent radical changes. His evolution can be traced through Brando, Dean, Mineo, Presley, Beatty, Newman, up through Dustin Hoffman, Dennis Hopper, Peter Fonda, Alan Arkin, Timothy Bottoms, Jeff Bridges, Ryan O'Neal, and the heroes of *Summer of '42* and *American Graffiti*. The rebel figure

125

begins as a neurotic, ambiguous, electric and potentially dangerous character and declines into softer, safer, more vulnerable and victimized types.

Later movies using the rebel character are also less apt to treat the character in a completely serious fashion as in the fifties; instead they offer a mingling of seriousness and absurdity, pain and humor, that encourages audience disengagement and laughter rather than straight identification. Arthur Penn's *Bonnie and Clyde*, which Warren Beatty starred in and produced, distances us from the Barrow gang of the Depression era and romanticizes them at the same time by using slapstick comedy techniques and Lester Flatt–Earl Scruggs music. The movie achieves a Keystone Cops hilarity, until Clyde is attacked by a butcher during a grocery holdup and then later happens to shoot a man in the face during the getaway from a bank robbery; afterwards in the car chases and gun battles the comedy is always mingled with real pain, creating an unsettling effect—the audience is not sure whether to laugh or cry—right up to the final sacrificial slaughter of Bonnie and Clyde by villainous Texas Rangers.

Aside from its zany-serious atmosphere and slow-motion massacre, the thing that sets Penn's movie apart from its predecessors—such as Fritz Lang's *You Only Live Once*, Nicholas Ray's *They Live by Night* or Joseph H. Lewis' *Gun Crazy*—is the treatment of the principal characters not as pathetic, innocent victims led astray into crime but as cute, fun-loving country kids, not overly talented or smart, who get a kick out of playing bank robbers and follow their stories in the tabloids, where their minor exploits are elevated into heroic feats admired by the Okies. Extremely conscious of his public image, Clyde always introduces himself to persons that he is about to rob. Bonnie composes a ballad for the newspapers. What the newspapers don't know, however, is that their famous gangster, in his own words, "ain't much of a lover boy" because he suffers from impotence, an ailment that is miraculously cured shortly before he is killed. His tattooed sidekick, C. W. Moss, also appears to have a sexual malady, though unfortunately it is not explored in the movie. The writers, David Newman and Robert Benton, considered making Clyde homosexual, but this condition would have been more difficult to cure and would have spoiled the "young love" image that is the basis of much of the movie's popularity.

During that same year, 1967, Mike Nichols' comedy *The Graduate*, with Dustin Hoffman, Anne Bancroft, and Katharine Ross, rose to fame and glory with another story of young love. Celebrated by many critics as a "milestone" in American film, the first movie to deal maturely with the generation gap and the realities of modern young people, *The Graduate* has become the most successful troubled youth film ever made—ranking seventh on Variety's 1975 list of All-Time Box-Office Champions, having earned nearly fifty million dollars. Based on Charles Webb's 1962 novel, it focuses on Benjamin, graduate of an eastern college, who comes home to the suburbs of Southern California where he is seduced by Mrs. Robinson, wife of his father's business partner. The situation is complicated by the fact that Benjamin falls for Mrs. Robinson's daughter, Elaine, a swinging Berkeley chick. This offbeat sexual triangle prompted critic Stanley Kauffman to praise the movie's "daring" moral stance, in accepting "the fact that a young man might have an affair with a woman and still marry her daughter."

Actually, what is most clever, as well as somewhat deceptive, about *The Graduate* is the way it manages to appear morally complex and liberated, while really taking a stance that confirms the most conventional morality. This is accomplished by making all of the adults "heavies," but particularly Mrs. Robinson who, instead of being a complicated human being, becomes a one-dimensional stereotype of the evil older woman—a fantasy figure similar to the wicked Queen in *Snow White*. Benjamin, on the other hand, is clean-cut, almost virginal, and clearly made uncomfortable by Mrs. Robinson's aggressive sexuality. "This is the sickest, most perverted thing that's ever happened to me," Benjamin says of the affair. The moral stance towards their relationship is one of strong disapproval, verging on repulsion, especially when the older woman tries to prevent Benjamin from seeing her daughter. In the end Benjamin and his long-haired princess, Elaine, get all of the audience's sympathy and adoration simply because they are young, earnest, and apparently untainted by any of Mrs. Robinson's disturbing sexual urges. As Stephen Farber and Estelle Changas have observed, Nichols' movie is "rather offensively prudish in splitting sex and love, implying that sexual relationships are sick and perverted."

The Graduate is at times an extremely funny movie, obviously the work of a skilled though conservative satirist—but it is no landmark of maturity. If it had been less escapist and truly liberated, *The Graduate* probably would not have been greeted so warmly by its public. Although still somewhat skittish and moralistic in its approach to sex, Nichols' *Carnal Knowledge*, made in 1971 from a Jules Feiffer script, is a more successful work, dealing effectively and often humorously with two males who manage to retain their adolescent sexual hang-ups and immature attitudes toward females well into adulthood. In *The Graduate* the hero seems undersexed; the heroes in *Carnal Knowledge* think of little else, constantly planning strategies in which life is treated as one big make-out contest. Ultimately the males in Nichols' movie derive more excitement from describing their sexual tactics and exploits to each other than in the sexual activities themselves.

Jonathan and Sandy are cartoonlike in their simplicity and their women are caricatures; yet this flat mode of characterization works in *Carnal Knowledge* because it is consistent with the purpose of the movie, which is about people imprisoned in rigid stereotyped attitudes and roles. Moreover, the deck isn't stacked so unfairly against one set of characters, as in *The Graduate*; instead it is stacked

127

rather heavily against *all* the characters, born losers whose carnal games bring them little fun, mostly pain and misery. Finally, when both heroes are in their forties, Jonathan treats Sandy and his new teenage "love teacher" from the Village to a slide show, with caustic commentary, of all his sexual encounters and conquests since age eleven. Titled "Ball-busters on Parade," the show horrifies Sandy and reduces his girlfriend to tears. But Jonathan quips, "What are you crying for? It's not a Lassie movie."

The frankness of *Carnal Knowledge* and many other movies that followed was made possible by a period of freedom unprecedented in the history of the film industry. Despite some problems with the MPAA classification system adopted in 1968 and the recent Supreme Court decision redefining the guidelines for obscenity, American directors today can do or say pretty much anything on the screen; yet, with some exceptions, popular movies made in Hollywood in recent years have continued with depressing regularity to rehash the fifties youth formula and the young antihero. The major exceptions have been movies like *Deliverance, Scarecrow, Papillon, The Longest Yard,* and the Academy Award winners *The French Connection, The Godfather,* and *The Sting*—all male adventure or police stories, usually treating women and sex only incidentally.

Surrounded by a vast range of potentially exciting contemporary material, many directors in the seventies have played it safe by restricting themselves almost exclusively to life as viewed from the younger side of the generation gap, either in the context of the old west (*Bad Company, Pat Garrett and Billy the Kid*), the thirties (*Paper Moon, Thieves Like Us*), the forties (*Summer of '42, Class of '44*), or the fifties (*The Last Picture Show, American Graffiti, Badlands, The Lords of Flatbush*). Except for disc jockey Wolfman Jack, a few policemen, teachers, and other minor figures, there are hardly any adults at all in Lucas' 1973 movie *American Graffiti,* a low-budget project that has become one of the most popular box office hits of recent years. It concentrates on a group of kids, mostly high school class of '62, driving their cars around the streets of Modesto, California, during one summer night.

Although based partly on the director's life, *American Graffiti* does not use a documentary tone but instead shows us a past transformed by rock and roll and beach party movies, as Lucas has acknowledged. While cruising the neon-lit streets around Mel's Drive-In Restaurant, the kids listen to a montage of commentary and banshee howls by Wolfman Jack and songs by artists like Fats Domino, Chuck Berry, the Flamingos, and the Beach Boys. Lucas and his cameraman Haskell Wexler worked out a "jukebox" style of lighting to give the movie an unreal, carnival-like atmosphere.

Like a beach party or hot rod movie, *American Graffiti* offers a very slim, uncomplicated plot structured around a few communal events—such as a sock hop and a drag race—and a cast of characters who resemble types from fifties

Anne Bancroft as Mrs. Robinson and Dustin Hoffman as troubled college youth Ben in the sixties box office hit *The Graduate.*

Faye Dunaway admires Warren Beatty's weapon in *Bonnie and Clyde.*

Thirties pop culture is emphasized on wall of young lovers' hideout in Robert Altman's Bonnie and Clyde remake *Thieves Like Us.*

movies. The ghost of James Dean haunts Big John Milner who wears a T-shirt, jeans, and boots and puts on an air of tough indifference as king drag racer. Like Brando in *The Wild One*, he gives a memento—his gearshift knob—to a female, although in Big John's case the girl is a thirteen-year old who happens to be cruising with him that night. There is also a sexy, bourbon-drinking blonde, Debbie, who thinks she looks like Sandra Dee. She teams up with a short, homely underdog, Terry the Toad, who wears white bucks and fancies himself a cool dude. The other lead couple features Steve, a clean-cut, class president type, and Laurie, head cheerleader who wants Steve to settle down and marry her. Curt, the sensitive, intellectually-inclined loner and the movie's real hero, spends his time either in romantic pursuit of a blonde in a white Thunderbird or fooling around with some local hoods called the Pharaohs, while trying to decide whether to depart in the morning for college.

Lucas obviously enjoys capturing the desperately horny mood of the cruising adolescents and their humorous graffiti, sexual slang like "snatch . . . porking . . . coping a feel" and silly pranks like shooting squirt guns from cars, jerking down Toad's pants, dangling a bra from a car or throwing a moon by pressing bare buttocks against a car window. Nearly everybody is on the make, hoping to score. Feeling high on Coke and Old Harper, Debbie and Toad make out in a field near a canal bank, while Steve tries to "go all the way" with Laurie but is pushed out of the car. Big John threatens to seduce Carol, his thirteen-year-old passenger, in order to trick her into revealing her address so he can take her home. But the sexual tension in *American Graffiti* is, like Big John's threat, essentially harmless, exploding into jokes and merriment instead of violence.

American Graffiti avoids being simple nostalgia by subtly emphasizing mortality and change—chiefly through Big John with his sense of the dangers of dragging ("All the ding-a-lings get it sooner or later," he says) and his awareness that "the whole strip is shrinking," as well as through Curt who is the only character in the movie to escape from Modesto. In the morning, as his transistor plays "Goodnight Sweetheart" and the blonde in the white T-bird cruises below on the highway, Curt heads into the future in a DC-3. There is no sudden traumatic loss of innocence as in *Rebel Without a Cause*; instead Curt experiences a gradual awakening and recognition that he must grow up, partly inspired by the Wolfman's advice to get his "ass in gear" because "there's a whole big beautiful world out there" beyond the limits of his hometown. Eventually Curt becomes a writer living in Canada. Although we learn from the brief cameos in the end that Big John was killed by a drunk driver and Toad was reported missing in action in Vietnam, the final effect of the movie, like its music, is light, upbeat, and reassuring.

American Graffiti recreates the teenage styles and the popular culture of the fifties in an unselfconscious and seemingly effortless manner. In spite of similar techniques—the use of actual locations, authentic radio shows—Robert Altman's 1974 movie *Thieves Like Us*, another Bonnie and Clyde story set in the thirties, appears stagey and artificial. The Coke bottles, pop culture, and ornaments of the era are emphasized like set pieces or road signs to remind us that we're in the thirties. The skinny, plain-looking protagonists, Bowie and Keechie, are perfect in appearance; but their "romance" lacks intensity and their lives are too pathetic and helpless.

Bowie and Keechie's first love scene is played against the background of a thirties' radio broadcast of *Romeo and Juliet*, an arty device that comments too obviously on the action and undercuts serious involvement. A later bath scene in which Keechie is briefly seen nude seems perfunctory, with no real purpose beyond emphasizing her already-established vulnerability. Typically, any interest in sex displayed by older characters is shown as somewhat unnatural; one of the older gangsters, T-Dub, is presented as a lecher, unable to keep his hands off younger women. The presence of the stereotyped dirty old man, of course, emphasizes the innocence and purity of the young lovers.

Just as the subterfuges and strategies of fifties movies are now transparent, so our own disguises, evasions, and fantasies in dealing with sexuality will be apparent, perhaps even laughable, to future movie audiences. We have moved from the neurotic, high-risk relationship to sex displayed by fifties heroes and heroines to the more casual, low-risk attitude of seventies characters, who are, like Bowie and Keechie, chiefly accommodating victims swept along helplessly by events. But in the exchange something valuable has been lost. These newer screen characters hold few surprises, are rarely spontaneously alive and compelling, and consequently we seldom care as much about their problems.

Hollywood and its audience are in the midst of a transitional period, resembling the crisis of the early fifties, when many of the accepted characters and cherished formulas no longer seem to be working. Once again, as in the fifties, a few gutsy European directors are leading the way into unexplored territory, particularly in their complex treatments of sexual identity. After having come through the rather frenziedly "liberated" late sixties and early seventies, most American directors appear to have grasped the basic techniques of the striptease but without fully understanding the essentials—the more intangible, mysterious elements that make the dance truly erotic and meaningful. This next step, creatively and imaginatively using the screen's freedom to explore the full experience of sexuality, its joys as well as pains, in characters of all types and ages, will involve considerably more risk.

Russ Meyer's *Cherry, Harry & Raquel.*

6.
The Sex Genre: Traditional and Modern Variations on the Flesh Film

WAYNE A. LOSANO

*I*N THE past, the flesh film was a comfortable genre, unassuming and predict-able. It was a very tightly constructed type, working within narrow confines. In his essay "Twenty-Six Propositions about Skin Flicks," Fred Chappell points out that the flesh film has traditionally been characterized by poverty of the imag-ination.[1] Perhaps we couldn't always guess just what would come next, but we were, for the most part, a shot or two ahead of the film. Certainly nothing occurred that we had not expected.

The films' plots, if in fact they had plots, were always extremely simplistic, never corrupted by imagination. Like the 16mm sex films now being distributed from the West Coast, about the only prologue to sexual encounters was a ringing doorbell. We knew, after all, the real reason for the telephone man's visit. Even from the beginning of the sex film, when films were always silent, inevitability was central to the plots. What else could be expected after the masked villain sneaked into the bedroom of the sleeping heroine that first time back in the early thirties classic *Masked Rape* or the villainous dentist administered ether to his desirable patient in the 1920 *Slow Fire Dentist* but that the uncourtly male would, in true melodramatic fashion, have his way with the young lady? In *Contemporary Erotic Cinema*, William Rotsler lists the classic sex film plots:

PLOT 1. A woman alone at home becomes aroused by reading or by handling some phallic-shaped object. Masturbation follows. A man arrives, is invited inside, and sexual play begins.

PLOT 2. A farm girl gets excited watching animals copulate. She then runs into a farmhand or a traveling salesman, and sexual play begins.

PLOT 3. A doctor begins examining a woman and sexual play begins.

PLOT 4. A burglar finds a girl in bed and rapes her or vice-versa.

PLOT 5. A sunbather or skinny-dipper gets caught and seduced.[2]

Rotsler's list, while not fully satisfactory, does indicate the genre's basic simplicity, although we perhaps should add the automobile-pickup plot (*Pick Up,
Nude in a White Car, Midnight Plowboy*, etc.), the costume-adventure-epic-orgy
films (*O.K. Nero, Sins of the Borgias, deSade*, etc.), and one or two other basic
formulas in order to get the full flavor of the genre. Arthur Knight and Hollis
Alpert summarize the conventions quite nicely: "When a female steps out of the
house in a stag film—whether it's a date for dinner . . . or an afternoon appointment with her doctor—she's certain to wind up in a sexual adventure."[3] (Of
course, it's not necessary that she step out of the house.) The frequent complaint
against the genre, that *everyone* in these films must "get laid, blown, fingered,
buggered, or tolled off,"[4] that there can be no *mystery*, is certainly a valid one.
Once we see a character, we know that character will play some role in the film's
sexual adventures. When the camera focuses on two women sitting alone (as in
The Animal, 1967), we know a lesbian scene will ensue; if a secretary or a nurse
appears, we know she will participate somehow. If, as in Meyer's *Vixen* or in
The Sweet Body of Deborah, a character decides to take a shower, we know he
or she will be quickly joined by a lover—a far better experience, we must agree,
that Janet Leigh had in her *Psycho* shower.

Russel Nye says that the popular audience needs predictability in its entertainment,[5] and the plots of the sex films answered this need. In its characters
also the sex film was predictable. The male characters, most often relatively
unimportant figures and easily replaced by various devices or creatures, tended
to be indistinguishable from each other. They generally fell into two types; either,
in the catalog description, "good-looking young studs, well-built and well-hung"
(romantic heroes) or aging, paunchy, hairy, and unattractive sorts (demonic
heroes). They were, say Knight and Alpert, usually "lower socioeconomic types—
pimps, drifters, and the like. . . ."[6] and unattractive men appeared regularly. The
same portly male appeared in over thirty stag films of the forties and fifties
(*Night School, Black Market, Varsity Girls*, etc.).[7] The women in the flesh films
were also predictable. We pretty much knew what they would look like and we
knew they wouldn't be able to act. They may not always have been the battered
and tattooed women Chappell describes,[8] but we suspected they weren't the
"fabulous Continental models" they were billed as. Their bored faces were heavily
made up and their preternatural bust development made them seem often of
mythic stature. Most of us fondly remember June Wilkinson (43-22-36) in *The
Playgirls and the Bell Boy*, and older fans or those who have seen Graffiti Productions' *History of the Blue Movie* (1970) will remember Candy Barr in *Smart
Alec*. Bust size, rather than acting ability, was the primary criterion for stardom.

133

Russ Meyer, in his many sexploitation films, was particularly skilled at unearthing pneumatic women for his films. Erica Gavin of *Vixen* (1968), Uschi Digart and the other women of *Cherry, Harry and Raquel* (1969), and the amazing Lorna Maitland of *Lorna* (1964) are all Meyer creations, calculated to cloud men's minds. The sex film heroine's lack of acting ability, her evident lack of involvement in the sexual machinations through which she was going, further strengthened the sense of unreality conveyed by the films. These women were clearly "professionals" in the game of sex and thus, for most of the audience, outside of the normal stream of experience and, of course, clearly recognized as evil women.

Along with their plots and characters, other aspects of the sex films were rigidly predictable. Their settings, for example, became so familiar as to seem downright homey, although most of us try to keep a better house than the films portrayed. We knew, however, that the couch they were using or that slightly sagging bed was one we had given to the Salvation Army some years before, our little touch with fantasy as it were. Although we could fantasize more exotic settings, the touches of decay evident in the one-room settings of most of the stag films placed them outside our reality in a world which merely to enter was somehow sinful. We were clearly slumming, observing an environment and a pattern of behavior much below us. Meyer's *Common Law Cabin* (1967) and *Lorna* (1964) and the many hillbilly films like *Tobacco Roady* and *Southern Comfort* vividly depict stylized poor-white Southern environments. With the old farmer's daughter jokes firm in our minds, we expect such environments to produce a variety of sexual perversions.

Watching these films, with their low settings, allowed us to keep a certain distance between ourselves and the action. We could delight in what we saw, utter the customary "tch, tch" of disapproval, and return to our own world which was untouched by such evils. I remember one film—the titles of sex films are often difficult to remember—shot entirely in a cheap motel room, a universally recognized metaphor for sexual evil. The spread which covered the room's small bed went through a marvelous metamorphosis during the course of the film. It started off well enough, clean and faded as we would expect, but each sexual encounter took its toll and by the end of the film the spread was wrinkled and stained, perhaps metaphorically reflecting the audience's experience with the film. We were able to view evil, get a bit soiled, but be cleansed by a return to our relatively pure world. In general, our experience with sex films paralleled the experience of the Victorians with their underground literature. The films provided an illicit pleasure but were sufficiently separated from everyday reality that we never lost our balance, our ability to distinguish between reality and fantasy, good and evil.

Along with unimaginative plots and familiar characters and settings, the flesh films offered correspondingly unimaginative and ordinarily sloppy cinematic techniques. All of the one-reel stag films we watched would be scratched or otherwise marred; if there was dialogue it would be out of synchronization. More often, there was simply annoying silence or, worse, an irritating voice-over narration. About ten minutes into *Love Me, Please* one begins to wish the sound would fail so the heroine's inane narrative will cease. Listening to the audience's embarrassed coughing or heavy breathing was usually preferable. Watching the films' lighting effects was always fun; the screen would now be blindingly bright, now obscured in darkness, without regard for any of the symbolic values of light and dark nor for whether the scenes depicted were interior or the rarer exterior ones. Catching a glimpse of the cameraman's shadow was, of course, a great *coup*, and trying to handle transitions between awkward editorial cuts was a continual challenge.

The content of the traditional sex films was also familiar stuff and, given the possible permutations, surprisingly predictable. There was, course, familiar heterosexual love-making in a variety of positions, and we nearly always saw the anticipated lesbian scenes complete with the expected artificial devices. Foreshadowing today's great interest in small-group dynamics, stag films such as *Pajama Game*, *Love Nest*, and *Wild Night* early featured sexual encounters among three, four, or five people. Bigger budget films—say several thousand dollars—offered orgy scenes of more or less epic scope. More ambitious films offered greater variety: *Teeny Tulip* offered a woman trying to copulate with a horse, and dogs had their roles in several stag films (e.g., *Pumping Pup*), if seldom in commercial movie houses. Fetters and fetishes added extra spice.

Until fairly recently, most of the sex shown in commercial theaters had certain strange limitations, such as a fear of showing male sex organs or actual penetration. As late as 1967, Alpert and Knight were able to complain: "The ultimate dream of most pornography fanciers—a professionally produced feature-length stag film in sound and Technicolor—probably exists only in fantasies."[9] The short stag films shown to men's smokers audiences have, of course, always been hard-core, but commercial films have customarily ranged from X-films (relatively cool films lacking sexual explicitness) to XX-films (sexploitation or simulation films).[10] Russ Meyer's films, for example, have been predominantly in the XX category (*Vixen*, *Lorna*) as were *I Am Curious—Yellow*, *Love Camp 7*, *The Godson*, *The Ribald Tales of Robin Hood*, and innumerable others. In these films there was much nudity but we saw no erections or penetration. Films such as *Last Tango in Paris*, *Camille 2000*, *deSade*, *Without a Stitch*, and Meyer's *Beyond the Valley of the Dolls* received but one X.[11]

The overall result of the limitations of these commercially shown films, and of the very private screenings of the stag films, was to increase the sense of evil experienced by the audience. We could see some real sex if we saw it in someone's basement or nudity and faked sex in a downtown theater. Lesbian love was ac-

135

ceptable in a moderate way and it opened up pleasing Freudian fantasies, but the rest was kept secret. Some of the genre's greatest artistry, in fact, resulted from its efforts to suggest but not show intercourse. In *Carmen Baby* the camera pans slowly down and up a row of colored bottles behind which Carmen and her lover are supposedly making love. This artiness, as bad as it is, is still superior to the several thousand close-ups of supposedly passion-ridden faces we were given in lieu of being shown intercourse or fellatio. With all of its readily apparent flaws, however, the faked sex had its role in heightening the sense of evil surrounding the films. If even these worldly and corrupt filmmakers refused to depict sex fully, reasoned the audience, there must be something terribly evil involved.

The result of all these genre restrictions was not surprising. The films had limited appeal to a highly specialized audience. Unconcerned with the niceties of filmmaking, this audience saw nothing wrong with flawed camerawork and faulty editing. It was there to view an evil world. This was the simple fact: the world depicted had to be presented as and was recognized to be terribly sinful. Chappell criticized the audience of the sex films for being a fearful and suspicious lot,[12] and his criticism was just. Attending sex films was a private, furtive experience. One was always uncomfortable when the theater lights went on; the immediate reaction was to glance around to discover just what strange types would attend such filth.

Things have changed now. The old audience, stereotyped into raincoat carrying old men, has been replaced by a more varied group. Young people, women, and respectable-looking middle-aged couples are appearing with increasing frequency. Film critics have recently delighted to list the respectable big names who have attended *Throat*. These same critics have hailed *Throat* as a "sociological phenomenon." Ralph Blumenthal sees it as engendering a kind of currently fashionable "porno chic." *The New York Times Magazine* has devoted an entire article to the phenomenon and *Playboy* ran a lengthy special on it (August 1973). In the *Times* article Blumenthal avers with apparent pride that members of the *Times* news staff went *en masse* to see *Throat* during their lunch hour. During the courtroom proceedings surrounding *Throat*, experts like Arthur Knight and John W. Money of Johns Hopkins University praised the film for expanding the audience's sexual horizons and producing healthier attitudes towards sex. Although *Throat* is by no means the first of the "new" flesh films—the change has been coming about for several years now—it has become the best known, perhaps the most famous sex film of all time, and the attitudes toward it reflect the more open attitudes towards the flesh film in general. In addition, *Throat* is representative of the new "type" of sex film in its highest development.

Working in a particular genre imposes certain definite limits on the artist, no matter what medium he may be working in. To be successful in the genre, the artist must observe its limits and work within them. Any variations must stay

picaresque tales along the lines of *Tom Jones*. *Whatever Happened to Miss September* is built on an imaginative idea, the search for a magazine centerfold playmate, and in true detective-story fashion traces the hero's search through multiple levels of depravity until he finds the girl.[14]

All of these changes toward greater artistry—*Throat* even has a reasonably entertaining musical score—have contributed to the death of the sex film as it was once known. Now that the films are well made, with more respectable and elaborate settings and more attractive and wholesome actresses, the experience is no longer that of descending into a new and evil world. Rather than giving us an opportunity to see how we should not live, the films set out to show us how to live more fully. A sub-genre of this new form, the sexual documentaries such as *Teenage Fantasies* and *Students*, no longer emphasizes the evils of the erotic world but tries to educate the audience so that it will be better able to participate in fulfilling love-making activities. So now we sit for an hour or more, watching fellatio or cunnilingus or various sexual positions completely removed from any sort of fictional environment, while a "doctor" lectures us on matters of technique or on the general all-around benefits of performing such acts.

The key to this new genre is not in the explicitness of the sexual acts depicted; most of them would be termed hard-core pornography but they are generally less erotic than most of the earlier sex films which practiced more restraint. Nor is the present moral climate totally responsible for the emergence of this new genre, for many things still strike us as evil. What distinguishes these films from their predecessors is their tone, their attitude toward their subject matter. *Mona* openly approaches a lad on a lighted street and asks him if he wants her to perform fellatio on him; in *The Nurses* a nurse has intercourse with a patient so that she may obtain a urine specimen after the act; in this same film another nurse has intercourse with a patient while giving him an enema; in *Dynamite* the peripatetic heroine is screwed in the back of a bouncing panel truck, seriously disrupting the following traffic; in *Meatball* the hero unfailingly gets an erection every hour and reinforcements must be brought in to spell his tiring nurse. Some contemporary "pornographic" literature has been using the same light approach—Ed Martin's *Busy Bodies* and Akbar del Piombo's *Who Pushed Paula?* are excellent examples—and the effect is to make sex just good clean fun.

A heroine who goes door to door selling sex articles for a film called *Yvonne Calling* or a hero with a perpetual erection may be good fun, but they're not good pornography. Watching a couple screw to the Pepsi theme song is not calculated to arouse an audience—erotically, anyway. Seeing an eye peering at you from a girl's vagina (*Pillow Party*) is surprising but not sexy. What we have now is irony, not eroticism. Evil is gone and laughter fills the theater. During some of the earlier efforts in the new sex film there was often some tension between the old audience which was still trying to see low people perform low acts and the new audience

Tura Satana is the heroine in Meyer's *Faster, Pussycat! Kill! Kill!*

Marie Liljedahl as Snow White in *Grimms Fairy Tales for Adults Only*, directed by Rolf Thiel.

Sister Jeanne of the Angels and Father Barre, a professional exorcist, attempt to drive out the Devil in Ken Russell's *The Devils*.

Luis Buñuel juxtaposes sex and religion in *Simon of the Desert*.

which came to enjoy the fun. Now the old audience is in danger of disappearing completely. Our experiences with these films parallels our experience with screen violence; we found we could laugh at violence, now we find we can laugh at sex. Sociologically, this is all very good and speaks well for our increasing honesty and freedom from puritanical restrictions. Artistically, however, the effect may be less positive for in adopting an ironic approach makers of flesh films have so drastically altered the nature of the genre as to produce an entirely different thing. When they do take the material seriously, the result is something like a documentary advocating freer practices and preaching the need for sexual fulfillment but totally sterilizing the film through an overly clinical treatment.

If the sex film is to continue as a viable genre it must somehow recapture its lost sense of evil. In this it could take a lesson from the Victorian underground classics and from some of the more lowly modern pornographic literature. In both forms the sense of evil is highly developed. In *Man with a Maid,* for example, the hero creates an elaborate plan to avail himself of the charms of the women he desires. His den is filled with various rigged chairs, couches, chains, and pulleys, all designed to hold a woman captive while he "has his way with her." This trap ensnares its primary target and is used successfully several more times. In the novel's final episode, the hero captures an aristocratic woman and her spoiled daughter and forces the ladies to make love to each other. Both women feel fully the evil of what they are forced to do but both succumb to their passions, thus heightening their—and the audience's—feelings of guilt.

The erotic successes of the hero of *Romance of Lust* are based on the desires of various older women to corrupt the young and seemingly innocent hero. Contemporary pornographic literature is very big on depicting the forced or partially-forced corruption of staid older women who in some way represent the establishment. Society dames, teachers, and librarians are all forced to participate in sexual activities. In *Teacher's Pet* the virginal and prudish teacher is repeatedly raped by her bosses, students, and parents of students, until her civilized defenses are destroyed. In *Piano Teacher* the "heroine" is raped by her students on the stage during the musical recital. Such common literary motifs fulfill our wildest fantasies and allow us to re-experience some of the more guilt-ridden moments of our youth.

For sex films to be successful within their intended limits, they must present themes and motifs which we can see as evil. A recent film, *Sleazy Rider* (the title is unfortunate), borders on being a truly erotic sex film. In one scene we see through the bathroom window the sheriff's daughter furtively locking the bathroom door and listening to determine if anyone is nearby. She then takes out a muscle magazine and, using the magazine's illustrations as a fantasy-stimulus, masturbates to orgasm. Of course, auto-eroticism is common in flesh films but in this scene was clearly presented as wrong (a feeling which many of us share in spite of loosening restrictions); the situation and the behavior of the character heightened the pleasure. In this same film the motorcyle gang around which the film centers breaks into the sheriff's home, ties up the sheriff, and rapes his daughter. The audience can recognize rape as evil and the girl's struggles heighten the scene's eroticism. However, the film fails to capitalize on its own depiction of evil since the daughter too quickly becomes a willing participant in the orgy following her rape. Similarly, the mother puts up no real resistance to her rape and after about a one-minute token protest she heartily joins in the orgy, thus destroying any sense of evil which could attach to her violation.

The key to an effective sex film is not the amount of flesh on display nor the graphicness of the sexual activities depicted, but rather the moral stance from which the subject is treated. A film such as Frank Perry's *Last Summer* is highly erotic in its sense of evil, and the build-up to the ultimate rape scene is highly developed. Such development and accompanying involvement with characters would also seem necessary if the sex film is to survive. The writers of erotic fiction have long been aware of the importance both of elaborate plot development and involvement with characters and of the need to create a strong sense of evil.

Sex filmmakers have, for the most part, ignored both important features of the art. They have opted for instant gratification and have thus failed to develop a truly erotic climate, and they have allowed the sense of evil to atrophy. In a recent *New York Times* interview, Luis Buñuel declared that, to him, religion and its accompanying sense of sin is necessary for the full appreciation of sex: "Sex without sin is like an egg without salt." Ken Russell's *The Devils* is our most vivid depiction of this religion/sex juxtaposition, and the sex films would do well to try to capture some of Russell's tone.

The plot of a recent big sex film, *The Devil in Miss Jones*, rests on the heroine's being given a brief life of lust to make up for being unjustly damned as a result of her suicide. Here again there is unrealized potential, a failure to develop an erotic climate, for there is no build up to the heroine's sexual encounters: she goes from total innocence to total involvement and, in the wild parade of sexual activities which follow, the "sinfulness" of her acts is lost. This particular film is, however, saved somewhat by its serious tone and by its powerful ending, strongly reminiscent of Sartre's *No Exit,* in which Miss Jones' lustful acts intensify her eternal torture.

The sex film, as we once knew it, was a private, somewhat tainted, and exclusively male experience. I would not like to see a return to the timid artificiality of earlier sex films, but some revitalization of the sense of evil and a desocialization of the genre—back to its originally private, particularly male nature[15]—seems essential if the sex film is to survive.

Alice Day is the helpless victim in late twenties film *The Gorilla*.

7

Monster Movies: A Sexual Theory

WALTER EVANS

*A*S HAS ever been the case, Dracula, Frankenstein's monster, the wolf man, King Kong and their peers remain shrouded in mystery. Why do they continue to live? Why do American adolescents—of all ages—keep Dracula and his companion monsters of the thirties and early forties alive, yet largely ignore much better formula movies of the same period, westerns (*Stagecoach*), gangster movies (*Little Caesar, Public Enemy*), and others? What is the monster formula's "secret of life"? Is this yet another of the things which "man was not meant to know"?

The formula has inspired a plethora of imaginative theories which attempt to explain the enduring popularity of these movies: contemporary social prosperity and order[1]; political decay[2]; the classic American compulsion "to translate and revalue the inherited burden of European culture"[3]; the public's need for "an acceptance of the natural order of things and an affirmation of man's ability to cope with and even prevail over the evil of life which he can never understand"[4]; the "ambiguities of repulsion and curiosity" regarding "what happens to flesh, . . . the fate of being a body"[5]; our "fear of the nonhuman"[6]; the social consequences of "deviance from the norm," particularly physical deviance[7]; and "mankind's hereditary fear of the dark."[8]

Dracula, Frankenstein's monster, King Kong, and others have been fruitfully approached as cultural symbols, but their power and appeal are finally much more fundamental than class or political consciousness, more basic than abstractions of revolt against societal restrictions, yet more specifically concerned with certain fundamental and identifiable features of human experience than such terms as *darkness* and *evil* seem to suggest. A film like *Return of the Vampire* may make timely allusions to the Nazi menace, but the classic horror movies deemphasize such nonessential material. Their power, it seems to me, is finally and essentially related to that dark fountainhead which psychically moves those masses in the American film and TV audiences who desperately struggle with the most universal and in many ways the most horrible of personal trials: the sexual traumas of adolescence. Sex has a central role in many popular formulas (Andrew Sarris has said, "There are no nonerotic genres any more"[9]), but sexuality in horror movies is uniquely tailored to the psyches of troubled adolescents, whatever their age.

Adolescents find themselves trapped in an unwilled change from a comparatively comprehensible and secure childhood to some mysterious new state which they do not understand, cannot control, and have some reason to fear. Mysterious feelings and urges begin to develop and they find themselves strangely fascinated with disturbing new physical characteristics—emerging hair, budding breasts, and others—which, given the forbidding texture of the X-rated American mentality, they associate with mystery, darkness, secrecy, and evil. Similarly, stirred from a childishly perfect state of nature King Kong is forced into danger by his desire for a beautiful young woman, a dark desire which, like the ape himself, must finally be destroyed by a hostile civilization. Also, stirred from innocence and purity (see the wolf man poem which appears below) by the full moon which has variously symbolized chastity, change, and romance for millennia, the wolf man guiltily wakes to the mystery of horrible alterations in his body, his mind, and his physical desires—alterations which are completely at odds with the formal strictures of his society. The mysterious, horrible, physical and psychological change is equally a feature of Frankenstein's monster, of Dracula's victims, the Mummy and his bride, and countless other standard monster movie characters.

The key to monster movies and the adolescents who understandably dote upon them is the theme of horrible and mysterious psychological and physical change; the most important of them is the monstrous transformation which is directly associated with secondary sexual characteristics and with the onset of aggressive erotic behavior. The wolf man, for example, sprouts a heavy coat of hair, can hardly be contained within his clothing. Comparatively innocent and asexual females become, after contact with a vampire (his kiss redly marked on their necks) or werewolf (as in Cry of the Werewolf), sexy, aggressive, seductive—literally female "vamps" and "wolves."

The transformation is less obvious, and perhaps for this reason more powerful, in King Kong (1933). Kong himself is safe while hidden deep in the prehistoric depths of Skull Island, but an unappeasable sexual desire (made explicit in the cuts restored in the film's most recent release) turns him into an enemy of civilization until, trapped on the world's hugest phallic symbol, he is destroyed.

Eddie Powell and Maggie Kimberley in
The Mummy's Shroud, a Hammer Films
updating of a thirties horror film.

Jenny Hanley is menaced by the vampire in bat form in the
Hammer Films remake *The Scars of Dracula.*

The psychological transformation of Ann Darrow (Fay Wray) is much more subtle. While alone immediately after exchanging vows of love with a tough sailor she closes her eyes and, as in a dream vision, above her appears the hideously savage face of a black native who takes possession of her in preparation for the riotous wedding to the great hairy ape. Significantly, only when civilization destroys the fearful, grossly physical beast is she finally able to marry the newly tuxedoed sailor.

As adolescence is defined as "developing from childhood to maturity" so the transformation is cinematically defined as movement from a state of innocence and purity associated with whiteness and clarity to darkness and obscurity associated with evil and threatened physical aggression. In the words of *The Wolf Man*'s gypsy:

> Even a man who is pure at heart
> And says his prayers by night
> May become a wolf when the wolfbane blooms
> And the moon is full and bright.

The monsters are generally sympathetic, in large part because, as remarked earlier, they themselves suffer the change as unwilling victims, all peace destroyed by the horrible and psychological alterations thrust upon them. Even Dracula, in a rare moment of self-revelation, is driven to comment: "To die, to be really dead. That must be glorious. . . . There are far worse things awaiting man, than death." Much suffering arises from the monster's overwhelming sense of alienation; totally an outcast, he painfully embodies the adolescent's nightmare of being hated and hunted by the society which he so desperately wishes to join.

Various aspects of the monster's attack are clearly sexual. The monster invariably prefers to attack individuals of the opposite sex, to attack them at night, and to attack them in their beds. The attack itself is specifically physical; Dracula, for instance, must be in immediate bodily contact with his victim to effect his perverted kiss; Frankenstein's monster, the wolf man, the Mummy, King Kong, have no weapons but their bodies. The aspect of the attack most disturbing to the monster, and perhaps most clearly sexual, is the choice of victim: "The werewolf instinctively seeks to kill the thing it loves best" (Dr. Yogami in *The Werewolf of London*). *Dracula*'s Mina Seward must attack her fiancé, John. The Mummy must physically possess the body of the woman in whom his spiritual bride has been reincarnated. Even more disturbing are the random threats to children scattered throughout the formula, more disturbing largely because the attacks are so perversely sexual and addressed to beings themselves soon destined for adolescence.

The effects of the attack may be directly related to adolescent sexual experimentation. The aggressor is riddled with shame, guilt, and anguish; the vic-

him, once initiated, is generally transformed into another aggressor. Regaining innocence before death seems, in the best films, almost as inconceivable as retrieving virginity. It is interesting, and perhaps significant, that the taint of vampirism and lycanthropy has an aura of sin and shame not unlike that of VD. The good doctor who traces the taint, communicable only through direct physical contact, back to the original carrier is not unlike a physician fighting VD.

Many formulaic elements of the monster movies have affinities with two central features of adolescent sexuality—masturbation and menstruation. From time immemorial underground lore has asserted that masturbation leads to feeble-mindedness or mental derangement: the monster's transformation is generally associated with madness; scientists are generally secretive recluses whose private experiments on the human body have driven them mad. Masturbation is also widely (and, of course, fallaciously) associated with "weakness of the spine,"[10] a fact which helps explain not only Fritz of *Frankenstein* but the army of feebleminded hunchbacks which pervades the formula. The wolf men, and sometimes Dracula, are identifiable (as, according to underground lore, masturbating boys may be identified) by hairy palms.

Ernest Jones explains the vampire myth largely as a reflection of a mysterious physical and psychological development which startles many adolescents—nocturnal emissions: "A nightly visit from a beautiful or frightful being, who first exhausts the sleeper with passionate embraces and then withdraws from him a vital fluid: all this can point only to a natural and common process, namely to nocturnal emissions accompanied with dreams of a more or less erotic nature. In the unconscious mind blood is commonly an equivalent for semen . . ." And the vampire's bloodletting of women who suddenly enter into full sexuality, the werewolf's bloody attacks—which occur regularly every month—are certainly related to the menstrual cycle which suddenly and mysteriously commands the body of every adolescent girl.

Monster movies characteristically involve another highly significant feature which may initially seem irrelevant to the theme of sexual change: the faintly philosophical struggle between reason and the darker emotional truths. Gypsies, superstitious peasants, and others associated with the imagination eternally triumph over smugly conventional rationalists who ignorantly deny the possible existence of walking mummies, stalking vampires, and bloodthirsty werewolves. The audience clearly sympathizes with those who realize the limits of reason, of convention, of security; for the adolescent's experiences with irrational desires, fears, urges which are incomprehensible yet clearly stronger than the barriers erected by reason or by society, are deeper and more painful than adults are likely to remember. Stubborn reason vainly struggles to deny adolescents' most private experiences, mysterious and dynamic conflicts between normal and abnormal, good and evil, known and unknown.

149

The giant ape inspects Fay Wray and removes some of her clothes in a sequence that censors forced the studio to cut from *King Kong*.

Lon Chaney carries off Esmerelda in the silent classic *The Hunchback of Notre Dame.*

Lon Chaney Jr. as the hero cursed with lycanthropy in George Waggner's *The Wolf Man.*

Fredric March alternately tortures and courts Miriam Hopkins in Rouben Mamoulian's *Dr. Jekyll and Mr. Hyde,* among the most erotic of early thirties horror movies.

Sexuality
in the Movies

Two of the most important features normally associated with monster movies are the closely related searches for the "secret of life" and "that which man was not meant to know." Monster movies unconsciously exploit the fact that most adolescents already know the "secret of life," which is, indeed, the "forbidden knowledge" of sex. The driving need to master the "forbidden knowledge" of "the secret of life," a need which seems to increase in importance as the wedding day approaches, is closely related to a major theme of monster movies: marriage.

For the adolescent audience the marriage which looms just beyond the last reel of the finer monster movies is much more than a mindless cliché wrap-up. As the monster's death necessarily precedes marriage and a happy ending, so the adolescent realizes that a kind of peace is to be obtained only with a second transformation. Only marriage can free Henry Frankenstein from his perverted compulsion for private experimentation on the human body; only marriage can save Mina Harker after her dalliance with the count. Only upon the death of adolescence, the mysterious madness which has possessed them, can they enter into a mature state where sexuality is tamed and sanctified by marriage.

Psychiatrist Anthony Storr has discussed a precursor of monster movies, fairy tales, in a similar context:

> Why is it that the stories which children enjoy are so often full of horrors? We know that from the very beginning of life the child possesses an inner world of fantasy and the fantasies of the child mind are by no means the pretty stories with which the prolific Miss Blyton regales us. They are both richer and more primitive, and the driving forces behind them are those of sexuality and the aggressive urge to power: the forces which ultimately determine the emergence of the individual as a separate entity. For, in the long process of development, the child has two main tasks to perform if he is to reach maturity. He has to prove his strength, and he has to win a mate; and in order to do this he has to overcome the obstacles of his infantile dependency upon, and his infantile erotic attachment to, his parents. . . . The typical fairy story ends with the winning of the princess just as the typical Victorian novel ends with the marriage. It is only at this point that adult sexuality begins. . . . It is not surprising that fairy stories should be both erotic and violent, or that they should appeal so powerfully to children. For the archetypal themes with which they deal mirror the contents of the childish psyche; and the same unconscious source gives origin to both the fairy tale and the fantasy life of the child.[11]

The marriage theme, and the complex interrelationship of various other formulaic elements, may perhaps be best approached through a close analysis of two seminal classics, *Frankenstein* and *Dracula*.

Two events dominate the movie *Frankenstein* (1931), creation of the monster and celebration of the marriage of Henry Frankenstein and his fiancée Elizabeth. The fact that the first endangers the second provides most of the conflict throughout the movie, conflict much richer and more powerful, perhaps even profound, when the key thematic relationship between the two is made clear: creation of life. As Frankenstein's perverse nightly experiments on the monstrous body hidden beneath the sheets are centered on the creation of life, so is the marriage, as the old Baron twice makes clear in a toast (once immediately after the monster struggles out of the old mill and begins wandering toward an incredible meeting with Henry's fiancée Elizabeth; again, after the monster is destroyed, in the last speech of the film): "Here's to a son to the House of Frankenstein!" (The line is followed by a close-up of a painfully embarrassed Henry Frankenstein.)

Frankenstein's fatuous father, whose naive declarations are often frighteningly prescient (he predicts the dancing peasants will soon be fighting; on seeing a torch in the old mill he asks if Henry is trying to burn it down), declares, when hearing of the extent to which his son's experiments are taking precedence over his fiancée: "I understand perfectly well. Must be another woman. Pretty sort of experiments they must be." Later, after receiving the burgomaster's beaming report on the village's preparations for celebration of the marriage, he again associates his son's experiments with forbidden sexuality: "There is another woman. And I'm going to find her!"

There is, of course, no other woman. The movie's horror is fundamentally based on the fact that the monster's life has come without benefit of a mother's womb. At one point Frankenstein madly and pointedly gloats over his solitary, specifically manual, achievements: "the brain of a dead man, ready to live again in a body I made with my own hands, my own hands!"

Significantly, a troubled search for the "secret of life" is what keeps Henry Frankenstein separated from his fiancée; it literally proves impossible for Henry to provide for "a son to the House of Frankenstein" before he has discovered the "secret of life." Having learned the "secret of life," he ironically discovers that its embodiment is a frightening monster horrible enough to threaten "normal" relations between himself and Elizabeth. Henry's attempts to lock the monster deep in the mill's nether regions are finally thwarted, and, in a wholly irrational and dramatically inexplicable (yet psychologically apt and profound) scene, the monster—a grotesque embodiment of Frankenstein's newly discovered sexuality—begins to move threateningly toward the innocent bride who is bedecked in the purest of white, then quite as irrationally, it withdraws. On his return Henry promises his wildly distracted fiancée that there will be no wedding "while this horrible creation of mine is still alive."

Significantly, the monster himself is pitifully sympathetic, suffering as adolescents believe only they can suffer, from unattractive physical appearance, bodies they don't understand, repulsed attempts at love, general misunderstanding. Though endowed by his single antagonistic parent with a "criminal brain," the monster is clearly guilty of little but ugliness and ignorance, and is by any reckoning less culpable than the normal human beings surrounding him. He does

153

not so much murder Fritz as attempt to defend himself against completely un-warranted torchings and beatings; he kills Dr. Valdeman only after that worthy believes he has "painlessly destroyed" the monster (a euphemism for murder) and as the doctor is preparing to dissect him; the homicide which propels his de-struction, the drowning of the little girl, is certainly the result of clumsiness and ignorance. She had taught him to sail flowers on the lake and, flowers failing, in a visual metaphor worthy of an Elizabethan courtier, the monster in his ignorant joy had certainly meant only for the girl, the only being who had ever shown him not only love, but even affection, to sail on the lake as had the flowers. His joyful lurch toward her after having sailed his flower is, beyond all doubt, the most pathetic and poignant lurch in the history of film.

The monster is, of course, finally pitilessly destroyed, and Henry is only ready for marriage when his own body is horribly battered and weakened, when he is transformed from the vigorous, courageous, inspired hero he represented early in the film to an enervated figure approaching the impotent fatuity of his father and grandfather (there is plenty of fine wine for the wedding feast, Frankenstein's grandmother would never allow grandfather to drink any), prepared to renounce abnormal life as potent as the monster in favor of creating a more normal "son to the House of Frankenstein."

The message is clear. In order to lead a normal, healthy life, Henry Franken-stein must—and can—give up dangerous private experiments on the human body in dark rooms hidden away from family and friends. He must learn to deal safely and normally with the "secret of life," however revolting, however evil, however it might seem to frighten and actually threaten pure, virgin womanhood; only then, in the enervated bosom of normality, is it possible to marry and to produce an acceptable "son to the House of Frankenstein."

Dracula's much more mature approach to womankind is clearly aimed at psyches which have overcome Henry Frankenstein's debilitating problem. *Dra-cula*, obviously enough, is a seduction fantasy vitally concerned with the condi-tions and consequences of premarital indulgence in forbidden physical relations with attractive members of the opposite sex.

Of all the movie monsters Dracula seems to be the most attractive to women, and his appeal is not difficult to understand, for he embodies the chief charac-teristics of the standard Gothic hero; tall, dark, handsome, titled, wealthy, cul-tured, attentive, mannered, with an air of command, an aura of sin and secret suffering; perhaps most important of all he is invariably impeccably dressed. With such a seductive and eligible male around it is certainly no wonder that some-where in the translation from novel to film Dr. Seward has become Mina's father and thus leaves Lucy, who also lost the two other suitors Bram Stoker allowed her, free to accept the Count's attentions. Certainly any woman can sympathize with Lucy's swift infatuation ("Laugh all you like, I think he's fascinating") and

A victim awaits the vampire in *Taste the Blood of Dracula* with Christopher Lee.

Boris Karloff's first entrance in the best known
of all horror films, *Frankenstein,* directed by
James Whale.

The vampire also enslaves men: Bela Lugosi
and Dwight Frye in Tod Browning's *Dracula.*

Mina's easy acceptance of Dracula as her friend's suitor ("Countess, I'll leave you to your count, and your ruined abbey").

Having left three wives behind in Transylvania, Dracula is obviously not one to be sated with his second English conquest (the first was an innocent flower girl, ravaged immediately before he meets Lucy and Mina), and he proceeds to seduce Mina, working a change in her which does not go unnoticed, or unappreciated, by her innocent fiancé: "Mina, you're so—like a changed girl. So wonderful—" Mina agrees that indeed she is changed, and, on the romantic terrace, alone with her fiancé beneath the moon and stars, begins, one is certain, the first physical aggression of their courtship. John is suitably impressed. "I'm so glad to see you like this!" Discovered and exposed by Professor Van Helsing, Mina can only admit that (having had relations with Dracula and thus become a Vamp) she has, indeed, suffered the proverbial fate worse than death, and shamefully alert her innocent, naive fiancé: "John, you must go away from me."

Only when John and his older, respected helpmate foil the horrible mock elopement—Dracula and Mina are rushing to the abbey, preparing to "sleep," he even carries her limp body across the abbey's threshold—only when the castrating stake destroys the seducer and with him the maid's dishonor, is Mina free to return to the honest, innocent, suitor who will accept her past, marry her in the public light of day, and make an honest woman of her.

Lucy, who has no selfless suitor to forgive her, marry her, and make an honest woman of her, is much less successful. When last seen she has become a child molester, a woman of the night who exchanges chocolate for horrible initiations.

The thematic importance of innocent victims turned monster, like Lucy and Mina, Dr. Frankenstein's creation, King Kong, the wolf man and others, points directly to one of the most commonly observed and perhaps least understood phenomena of monster movies, one which has been repeatedly noted in this paper: in those classics which are best loved and closest to true art the audience clearly identifies with the monster. Child, adult, or adolescent, in disembodied sympathetic fascination, we all watch the first Karloff monster who stumbles with adolescent clumsiness, who suffers the savage misunderstanding and rejection of both society and his creator Henry Frankenstein, and whose fumbling and innocent attempts at love with the little girl by the lakeside turn to terrible, bitter, and mysterious tragedy.

Clearly the monster offers the sexually confused adolescent a sympathetic, and at best a tragic, imitation of his life by representing a mysterious and irreversible change which forever isolates him from what he identifies as normality, security, and goodness, a change thrusting him into a world he does not understand, torturing him with desires he cannot satisfy or even admit, a world in which dark psychological and strange physical changes seem to conspire with society to destroy him.

Cliff Gorman, Reuben Greene, and Laurence Luckinbill are guests at the party in William Friedkin's *The Boys in the Band*, based on Mort Crowley's play.

8.

The Boys on the Bandwagon: Homosexuality in the Movies

GENE D. PHILLIPS

*I*N SPRING 1968 Mart Crowley's *The Boys in the Band* opened on off-Broadway and became the first successful American play to give an honest treatment of homosexuality on the stage. Two years later the film version, written and produced by Crowley, accomplished the same breakthrough on the screen. Crowley has said that he had no intention of espousing a social cause or starting a trend when he wrote *The Boys in the Band.* "Homosexuality used to be a sensational gimmick," he comments. "The big revelation in the third act was that the guy was homosexual, and then he had to go offstage and blow his brains out." This does not often happen in real life, so it does not occur in *Boys.* "If you once get over the fact that eight of the nine characters are overt homosexuals, you know the most sensational thing about it," Crowley says.

Nonetheless, theatrical producers had a great deal of trouble getting over precisely that fact when Crowley first submitted his play to them. Actors who read the script turned down the parts they were offered because they feared damaging their careers. Finally Crowley convinced both backers and performers that he had written a play of worth and it went into production. The rest is history. The play was a phenomenal success and Crowley received several offers for the film rights. Since the film medium has always been even more reticent than the theater in dealing with a topic like homosexuality, however, he ran into just as much difficulty getting assurance that the film would be faithful to the play as he had in getting the play produced in the first place.

Film producers have always feared offending the movie-going public with a story that dealt more than tangentially with homosexuality. They have been aware of the deeply rooted prejudice in America against homosexuals. In 1969, for example, a Louis Harris poll disclosed that 63 percent of the nation considers

157

homosexuals "harmful to American life," although in many cases the people interviewed were not clear as to just why they felt that this was true. The National Institute of Mental Health, in a report released the same year, commented that "homosexuality represents a major problem for our society largely because of the amount of injustice and suffering entailed in it," and that "the extreme opprobrium that our society has attached to homosexual behavior has done more social harm than good, and goes beyond what is necessary for the maintenance of public order and human decency."

In fear of the attitude of the public, therefore, movie versions of plays and novels that treated homosexuality in the past were either completely rewritten or partially revamped to obscure that aspect of the story. When William Wyler filmed Lillian Hellman's *The Children's Hour* in 1936 as *These Three*, the gossip at the girls' boarding school centered around suspicions that one of the women who ran the school was having an affair with a man, rather than with another woman as in Hellman's original. (When Wyler remade the film in 1962, however, the film medium had matured to the point that the original plot could be used.)

When Billy Wilder made *The Lost Weekend* in 1945 the hero's self-doubts about being homosexual were eliminated and the film concentrated on his alcoholism. For sheer originality, however, it was impossible to top the producers of 1947's *Crossfire*. The outcast from society who is murdered in the story is transformed from a homosexual into a Jew, giving the whole story an anti-Semitic theme which author Richard Brooks had never envisioned. (In a kind of poetic irony Brooks himself, now a film director, deleted most of the references to the homosexual nature of Perry's and Dick's relationship when he filmed Truman Capote's book *In Cold Blood*, about the two killers who murdered a Kansas family.)

Tennessee Williams has often dealt with homosexuality in his plays and it is interesting to see how this theme was allowed gradually to creep into the film versions. When *A Streetcar Named Desire* was brought to the screen in 1952, references to the traumatic experience in the past of Blanche Dubois (Vivien Leigh)—her discovery that her husband was homosexual—was thoroughly veiled. The incident not only became much more enigmatic than Williams had ever intended but became almost incomprehensible. The screen version of Williams's *Cat on a Hot Tin Roof* (1958) managed to obscure the relationship between the Paul Newman character and his old school chum in much the same way. But Williams fared much better when Gore Vidal adapted *Suddenly, Last Summer* for director Joseph Manckiewicz in 1960. This film treated homosexuality more frankly than ever before on the screen, although one suspects that the film was at pains to emphasize the hideous death of the homosexual Sebastian—who is killed and eaten by young cannibals whom he had originally goaded into sexual encounters—in order to "justify" treating such material in the first place.

Deborah Kerr, who starred in both the stage and screen versions of Robert Anderson's *Tea and Sympathy*, has told me how disappointed she was with the revisions made when the play was filmed in 1957: "They should have waited a few years to make the film. They had to obscure the idea that Tom Lee was homosexual by making the basis of the gossip about him the fact that he was somewhat effeminate. Now that homosexuality is a topic of conversation the film could be made honestly. It was not, after all, about homosexuality so much as it was about prejudice and gossip in a small college town."

Otto Preminger's *Advise and Consent* (1962) was not much of a step forward in the treatment of homosexuality on the screen, either. Don Murray played a United States senator who has guarded his homosexual past even from his wife. Both the script and direction of the film were heavy-handed. Preminger milked one scene dry, in which Murray goes to a gay bar to meet a blackmailer, but offered little insight into the plight of the Murray character. Moreover, both *Advise and Consent* and the remade *The Children's Hour*, filmed the same year, are classic examples of what Mart Crowley was talking about: in each homosexuality is used as a sensational "third-act" revelation, after which the character discovered to be homosexual must obligingly commit suicide.

In England, however, filmmakers were beginning to deal with homosexuality more understandingly and directly. Basil Dearden's *Victim!* (1961) was a frank and serious look at the social and psychological pressures on the homosexual in that country. The plot focused on the vulnerability to blackmail of anyone suspected of being homosexual. A respected barrister (Dirk Bogarde) befriends a lonely young vagrant (Peter McEnery), who in turn kills himself in a futile attempt to save the barrister's reputation.

Several other actors had turned down the role of the barrister before Bogarde accepted it—on condition that there would be no compromise in treating the story. "Otherwise, why make it?" he asked. *Victim!* became the first film ever to use the word homosexual. Moreover, it provided the sympathetic understanding for its hero lacking in films like *Advise and Consent*. Yet Bogarde recalls that while the film was being made, the cast and crew were sometimes treated as if "we were making a film which attacked the Bible. But it was an enormous and surprising hit."

When I asked the late Basil Dearden if he thought that *Victim!* had influenced audiences in their attitude toward homosexuality, he replied: "People's minds cannot be changed by a movie. Problems or points of view can be expressed but that is all. Though *Victim!* pleaded tolerance for homosexuals, I am sure it never converted a single person to the cause it espoused. While myself not being homosexual, I have many friends that are who are charming and intelligent people. Even if they weren't, I would still plead tolerance for them."

Tony Richardson's *A Taste of Honey* (1961) presented a delicately nuanced

159

story of a young girl (Rita Tushingham) who is deserted by her irresponsible mother after she has become pregnant with an illegitimate child, and is cared for by a shy homosexual (Murray Melvin) during the time of the approaching birth with the kind of consideration she never received from her mother. The story was told with a reticence that explored but did not exploit the material. The same can be said for Sidney J. Furie's *The Leather Boys* (1963) in which the hero begins to look for sympathy in an old pal when his marriage to a girl as immature as himself (played again by Rita Tushingham) begins to turn sour. What he is really doing is attempting to relive his adolescence, and the relationship begins to take on a dimension of which he is naively unaware.

A similar development overcomes Tony, a young aristocrat (James Fox), when he unwittingly allows himself to fall under the domination of the forceful personality of his servant Barrett (Dirk Bogarde) in Joseph Losey's British film *The Servant* (1963). Tony is an irresponsible and immature individual who lacks any moral convictions or realistic personal goals and Barrett resents being subservient to someone whom he considers in many ways his inferior. He therefore derives perverse pleasure from methodically reducing the weak-willed Tony through drugs and alcohol to a degraded wreck.

As the film progresses Tony gradually submits to Barrett's stronger personality and develops an emotional attachment to Barrett that he does not clearly perceive for what it is. In the key scene on the staircase Barrett strengthens his hold on Tony by threatening to leave, and Tony stands above Barrett on the stairs to block Barrett's passage up to his room to pack. Barrett pushes past him as they talk and the scene ends with Tony kneeling below Barrett on the stairs abjectly begging him to stay. Their exchange of positions on the staircase symbolically underscores the way that their respective roles of master and servant have been totally reversed.

As the film ends we see Tony once more on the staircase, groveling in a drunken stupor after Barrett has expelled Tony's former fiancée from the house for the last time. Losey photographs Tony, imprisoned as he is by his addiction to drugs and alcohol as well as by his emotional dependence on Barrett, through the bars of the bannister railing.

In America at the time it still appeared that homosexuality would remain the exclusive province of underground filmmakers like Andy Warhol's clan and Kenneth Anger. Anger had made *Fireworks* (1947) while still in high school; it was a fifteen-minute sadomasochistic fantasy climaxed by an exploding Roman candle serving as a phallic symbol. In 1966 Anger made his celebrated *Scorpio Rising*, an uncompromising look, twice as long and twice as searing as *Fireworks*, at the milieu of the homosexual motorcycle cult.

In 1967 Frank Simon filmed his brilliant documentary *The Queen*, concerning a beauty contest among homosexual transvestites at New York's Town Hall. The

Wendy Craig, Dirk Bogarde, and James Fox in Joseph Losey's *The Servant*.

master of ceremonies and contest organizer, Jack Doroshow, narrates the sixty-minute film, and his straight-forward commentary effectively reinforces the telling images of a group of young men who have retreated into a world of fantasy. "You ask a queen, 'What's your name?' " Doroshow says at one point, "And the queen says 'Monique,' and you say 'That's marvelous, darling, and what was your name before?' And the queen will look you straight in the eye and say, 'There was no name before!' "

So far, the best feature-length American underground films to deal with homosexuality are *Flesh* (1968) and *Trash* (1970), which Paul Morrissey directed under the Warhol banner.

When *Flesh* opened in one of the London cinema clubs (which are not under the jurisdiction of the British censor), it gained widespread free publicity because it was seized by the police then returned to the theater for exhibition because the censor, among other officials, refused to support a court action against it. The censor, John Trevelyan, refused to grant the film a certificate for commercial exhibition, but he later told me that he felt *Flesh* gave an insight into the life of a male hustler and his customers unmatched by any other film of its kind. The more recent *Trash* (1971) provides a similar kind of character study, and is the first such underground feature to be booked into commercial theaters in cities like New York and Chicago.

The other kind of independently produced films dealing with homosexuality is, of course, the hard-core pornography which has become increasingly more available, at least in major cities. Until the late sixties these films were mostly 8mm pictures made with all of the technical expertise of the average home movie, with no plot or dialogue, and accompanied by pop records played either on the sound track or in the projection booth.

These films consisted basically of a series of homoerotic fantasies acted out on the screen, as for example, in a film called *Pool Party*, a product of the early sixties. This movie consists of young men frolicking at poolside in their swim suits

161

for a while until they shuck their trunks and pair off for mutual sex. This particular short film simulated orgasm by showing one of the teenagers pouring foaming champagne across the thighs of his partner, another working up a soapy lather around his midsection while taking a shower. Most gay porno movies do not employ such indirection, I found while serving as a consultant to the Attorney General's committee on pornography for some years.

Thus *The Sex Garage*, a black-and-white short perhaps made about the same time as *Pool Party*, portrays sadomasochistic behavior and leather fetish graphically enough, I am told, to repel even some frequenters of gay porno houses. One of the performers makes love to his motorcycle, with his attention particularly given to its sleek rubber tires.

Since there is a limit to the sexual gymnastics that can be devised for a gay porno movie, some of their makers began in the late sixties to cast about for variety. The increasing prominence of Blacks on the screen in commercial motion pictures had its counterpart in the rise of the Black gay film, including Lancer Brooks's *Black Heat*. *The Closet*, which details the fantasies of a man undergoing a massage, attempts by the use of elaborate cinematic techniques, such as superimpositions and other types of trick photography and editing, to vary the routine presentation of sexual experiences.

Another method of producing a pornographic film distinguishable from its predecessors was the introduction of a story to motivate the sexual encounters in the movie. *A Deep Compassion* (1972) is one of these. Written and directed by Brad Kingston, this feature-length Eastman color movie concerns Rocky (Duane Fergus), an escaped convict who hides out in the mountain home of Carl, a young blind man (David Arlin). While he is being driven to Carl's remote house by two buddies, he asks the one who is not driving to join him in the back seat of the car for some sex because, he explains, he has been out of circulation for two years. Their sexual experience is intercut with occasional shots of the driver looking over his shoulder at the proceedings in order to facilitate audience identification.

Rocky is finally left alone with Carl in the mountain retreat. Before the inevitable seduction occurs, however, there is a fantasy sequence in which Carl imagines that he is loved by a handsome god of the forest. They frolic naked through a wooded glade in slow motion, photographed in gauzy soft focus, but the scene turns out simply to be an elaborate prelude to the same kind of sodomitic sequence shown earlier in the film in a more realistic context.

The only truly dramatic moment in the picture occurs when Carl hysterically smashes Rocky's skull with his cane (accompanied by music lifted from the sound track of Hitchcock's *Psycho*) after Rocky has brutally raped him, and throws himself over the mountainside. Nonetheless it is clear that whatever plot the film aspires to serves merely as a skeleton on which to hang the various extended sex scenes which in fact account for the bulk of the picture's ninety-minute running

The beauty contest in Frank Simon's
documentary *The Queen.*

Steven Arnold's *Luminous Procuress.*

Max Born on board Lica's ship in *Fellini Satyricon.*

time. *A Deep Compassion* does illustrate, however, an attempt by a maker of gay erotica to introduce some variety into his material.

More accomplished and polished than any of the underground films mentioned so far is the British movie *A Bigger Splash*, directed by Jack Hazan and shown at the 1974 Cannes and New York Film Festivals. It is a feature-length documentary about how the personal life of painter David Hockney influences his professional work. Shot over a period of four years, the picture enacts, and at times re-enacts, incidents in Hockney's private life, centering around the breakup of his five-year relationship with a younger man named Peter.

Hockney is shown from time to time brooding over sketches that he had done of Peter over the years, in an effort to finish a painting of Peter begun before their breakup. At one point we see Hockney discussing Peter with a friend and then we cut to Peter making love with a young man his own age in a fairly explicit scene. "I tried not to be melodramatic about the homosexual scenes," Hazan has told me; "I didn't mean to shock, but only to be real." Finishing the painting of Peter at long last serves as a catharsis for Hockney, who has by now gotten over the whole affair. This is betokened by his decision to destroy all of the sketches of Peter that he has been holding on to up to this point.

Hazan's film in no way touts the gay life, but does provide one of the most revealing pictures of the homosexual world yet shown on film. And the fact that its subject is a real person makes *A Bigger Splash* all the more significant.

Hollywood finally began coming to grips with homosexuality in the late sixties, but still trailed behind the British and the American underground. John Huston's *Reflections in a Golden Eye* (1967), for example, transferred Carson McCullers' tortured novel to film with all of the compassion for human frailty of a police report. McCullers' view of the human condition, as personified in the twisted lives of a middle-aged homosexual army officer and his neurotic wife (Marlon Brando and Elizabeth Taylor), was somehow mislaid between page and screen. As a result, Brando's grappling with his infatuation for a young recruit failed to evoke pity from the audience and seemed only curious and grotesque.

A more significant step in the right direction was John Flynn's *The Sergeant* (1968), which starred Rod Steiger as another older soldier infatuated with an enlisted man (John Philip Law). This time the story was told in a way that enlisted the audience's sympathy with the desperate struggles of a flawed fellow human being. Asked if he considered *The Sergeant* something of a breakthrough, the film's producer, Richard Goldstone, replied, "I felt it would open up the subject of homosexuality for more serious consideration on the screen. After all, the film is basically about loneliness. The Steiger character is a man who has been cast into a rigid mold. He reaches out for another human being, but in so doing shatters the mold which he has created for himself in terms of his personal behavior, and thus violates the whole pattern of his life. He cannot face this fact and it destroys him." Yes, true to the Hollywood formula, Steiger was required to blow his brains out upon discovering his homosexual tendencies.

Referring to the films of the past which have somehow touched upon homosexuality, one critic has noted that they served a function larger than themselves: they prepared the way for more direct attempts to penetrate the homosexual mind and milieu. Had the screen version of Frank Marcus's *The Killing of Sister George* (1968) been faithful to his seriocomic play, it might have been the milestone which *The Boys in the Band* was to become. For one thing, an explicit lesbian sex scene was included in the film which was not in the play, although *Sister George* was highly successful on the London stage without it. "Opening out" the play for the screen in other ways bloated its taut two-hour running time on the stage into two-and-a-half hours on the screen. Furthermore, the added location sequences tended to destroy the play's claustrophobic atmosphere, which was so important to picturing the closed and insulated homosexual world.

Stanley Donen's film of Charles Dyer's play *Staircase* (1969) failed on the screen for different reasons. In it Rex Harrison and Richard Burton played two aging homosexual barbers. Asked why he took the role, Harrison said, "The story is really about loneliness and human failure. These two subjects are so much a part of everyone's life that most people will not, or do not, recognize their presence. I would like to hope that in *Staircase* I can shed a little more light on these universal frailties." But the previous screen image of both superstars militated against an audience's accepting them as two miserable middle-aged queers—which is one reason Mart Crowley insisted that the film of *The Boys in the Band* use the original off-Broadway cast, none of whom would be familiar to movie audiences and who could thus submerge themselves in their roles.

The most successful American film—financially as well as artistically—to treat homosexuality before *The Boys in the Band* was made, significantly enough, by a British director: John Schlesinger. *Midnight Cowboy* (1969) tells the story of Joe Buck (Jon Voight) who comes from Texas to New York with the hope of becoming a stud for rich and lonely ladies, but winds up hustling men instead to get money to take his ailing friend Ratso Rizzo (Dustin Hoffman) to Florida for his health. Although Joe and Ratso move in a milieu inhabited by homosexuals, Schlesinger says that his point was to show how two men can have a meaningful friendship without necessarily being homosexual. Asked why he thought homosexuality was being more commonly portrayed on the screen, he replied, "It comes from what's happening all around us. Everybody does more or less what he wants to these days, and films are a reflection of that attitude; homosexuality is just one part of the whole scene. . . . I hope that I have been able to get into the film that mixture of violence, desperation, and humor that I found all along 42nd Street when we were shooting there." As far as I'm concerned, he did.

165

The Boys in the Band, however, is different from all its predecessors because it presents the homosexual in his own environment and not just as a misfit in the heterosexual world. In *Boys* there is a chance to explore the homosexual's psychological and social problems as he tries to live at peace with himself in his own world. "I got the title from those movie musicals in the 1940's where Frances Langford or Peggy Lee or somebody was always saying, 'Let's have a great big hand for the boys in the band,' " says Crowley. "It means 'men in the minority,' something like that."

The plot concerns a birthday party given for a homosexual named Harold (Leonard Frey) by his friend Michael (Kenneth Nelson) and attended by a group of friends who represent a variety of homosexual types—not stereotypes. For instance, the fact that one homosexual is Catholic, one Jewish, and another Negro indicates that homosexuality touches all groups. Michael, the Catholic, can live neither with nor without his homosexuality: "I'm one of those truly rotten Catholics who gets drunk, sins all night and goes to Mass the next morning," he says. As a matter of fact, the story ends with his going off to a midnight mass at St. Malachy's in Manhattan.

Crowley treats Michael and the others with a perfect blend of compassion and wry wit. For example, the midnight cowboy (Robert La Tourneaux), who is Harold's "birthday present" from one of the guests, is told to stand in the corner with the other gifts; underlying the scene is the pathetic situation of a young man like Joe Buck who has looks and little else and knows it. Michael's unhappiness at being homosexual drives him to make rather cruel jokes at the expense of himself and his friends, and even to try to make Alan, an old college chum from Georgetown University who happens in on the party, admit that he too is homosexual—as if adding one more member to the ranks will somehow make Michael feel less an outsider. Michael epitomizes his feelings about being homosexual in the now-famous line, "Show me a happy homosexual and I'll show you a gay corpse."

Crowley has been criticized by some homosexuals for presenting them from an unflattering angle. He counters: "The story is about self-destruction. I am talking about the self-destructive tendency in homosexuals who flagellate and demean themselves out of self-hatred because they've been so shunted aside and considered such freaks by society. . . . I hope there are happy homosexuals—they just don't happen to be at this party. Besides, Michael is too often taken as the spokesman for all the others. He is really the only truly unhappy person among the nine; all of them have complex natures and have their own feelings about being homosexual."

In transferring *The Boys in the Band* from stage to screen, director William Friedkin had the good sense to realize that the play's success stemmed not so much from merely dealing with homosexuality but from being, in his words, "well constructed, with brilliantly drawn characters, witty dialogue, and a gripping denouement. To hoke it up with unnecessary location shots, flashy photography or background music would have been wrong." Adds Crowley, "A film does not add variety to a scene by simply breaking up dialogue from the play with shots of the Seagram building and three or four other location backgrounds. The variety must come within the scene by photographing the action from different points of view."

Hence Friedkin has not attempted to "open out" the play for the screen in the manner of *Sister George,* beyond introducing each guest in his own milieu before he goes to the party. "I want the audience to be another guest at the party," he explains, "to be involved in the action, not simply observers." During the course of the party, Michael has each of the guests attempt to call someone whom they have truly loved in the past. It is noteworthy that none of the guests can complete a call outside the apartment except Alan, the sole "straight" guest, who phones his wife. (One of the other guests, Hank, talks to his companion, Larry, by calling him from the next room in the apartment.) The homosexual is locked in his own world and cannot reach the world outside which disdains and ignores him, Crowley seems to be saying. For this reason, it was very important that the film be shot almost entirely in Michael's apartment, which thus becomes a microcosm of the homosexual world.

Other indications of how far the screen has come in its treatment of homosexuality can be found in a variety of films of the seventies ranging from *The Music Lovers* and *Entertaining Mr. Sloane* to *Death in Venice* and *Sunday, Bloody Sunday.* In the British screen adaptation of Joe Orton's play *Entertaining Mr. Sloane* (1970) Peter McEnery, who played the shy homosexual in *Victim!,* enacts the title role of a young man who trades on his attractiveness to a middle-aged brother and sister named Kath and Ed (Beryl Reid and Harry Andrews) to secure free room and board. Like all of the work of Orton's short career, this is black comedy and has been played as such in the film. The acting is broad, the costumes and decor suitably outlandish, because the characters are more grotesques than human beings, and as a result the movie is at times irresistibly funny.

It looks for a while as if Sloane will rule the household as Kath and Ed both vie for his affections until, in a fit of rage, Sloane murders their meddling father. That puts them in a position to blackmail him into staying on under their mutual domination indefinitely: they make an arrangement whereby they shall take turns "entertaining Mr. Sloane." *Sloane* was the first feature film of British TV director Douglas Hickox and, like Friedkin, he has concentrated more on rendering the play on the screen in the spirit in which it was written than in enlarging the canvas against which the action is played. He and his cast achieved ensemble acting of a high order, as did Friedkin and his actors in *Boys in the Band,* and

167

Jon Voight and Dustin Hoffman in
John Schlesinger's *Midnight Cowboy.*

Frederick Combs prepares for the party in
The Boys in the Band.

Richard Chamberlain as Tschaikovsky and Christopher Gable as Shilovsky in Russell's *The Music Lovers.*

Peter Finch treats the illness of his lover Murray Head in Schlesinger's *Sunday, Bloody Sunday.*

one shudders to think what could have happened to this material in the hands of an unsubtle and heavy-handed director.

A serious attempt to explore the homosexual mentality was made by Ken Russell in *The Music Lovers* (1971), a film about the composer Peter Tschaikovsky's conflict with his homosexuality. As in Russell's biographies of composers for BBC-TV, he has drawn a definite connection between the man's life and his music. "The Russians have never admitted that Tschaikovsky was homosexual," says Russell. "Yet he said himself that his inner conflicts were there in his music and this was one of his conflicts. His *Sixth Symphony* is tortured and tragic. In one scene in the film Tschaikovsky (Richard Chamberlain) is shown in bed with the rich Vladimir Shilovsky (Christopher Gable) whose possessiveness helped push Tschaikovsky into thoughts of marriage. The composer, Russell points out, had always longed to have a family, and so he married Nina (Glenda Jackson), a neurotic nymphomaniac who was infatuated with him; the marriage, of course, was a disaster. Russell's is the first film of Tschaikovsky's life and work that deals with this aspect of his personality.

In *Death in Venice* (1971), based on Thomas Mann's novella, the Italian film maker Luchino Visconti explored a somewhat similar terrain. Visconti's earlier pictures had occasionally and tangentially dealt with homosexuality. For example in *The Damned* (1969) the director had used sexual perversion as a metaphor for the overall breakdown of morality in Nazi Germany in the thirties, climaxed in the film by the Night of the Long Knives in which one faction of Nazi troopers systematically annihilates another while the latter is engaged in a drunken homosexual orgy. With *Death in Venice*, however, Visconti made a much more subtle symbolic use of a homosexual theme.

The movie deals with Gustav Aschenbach (Dirk Bogarde), an aging musician in turn-of-the-century Venice who becomes obsessed with a golden-haired young man with whom he never exchanges a single word. Ultimately the dying Aschenbach sees the lad as a projection of his own desolate longings for ideal beauty and friendship. As one critic noted, that this is also an indication of latent homosexuality is not really the point. What Visconti is getting at through the artist's figure is the universal problem of relating the life of the mind to that of the body; or, in other words, it is the tension between spirit and flesh which torments Aschenbach. And Visconti wisely does not try to resolve this tension in the film. He rather chooses to present it for our consideration—and our sympathy, especially in the scene in which the hapless old man garishly paints his face and dyes his hair in a pathetic attempt to close the age gap between himself and the boy whom he idolizes.

John Schlesinger's *Sunday, Bloody Sunday* (1971) also turns on the love of an older man for a younger man. Daniel Hirsch (Peter Finch), a Jewish doctor, is involved with Bob Elkin (Murray Head); but so, he soon discovers, is Alex

Greville (Glenda Jackson), a divorcee. "Bob represents those young people today whose lives consist in having an experience and then taking the nearest exit to some other experience," Schlesinger comments. "Their whole lives are filled with exits. I wanted a young actor to play Bob, to make it clear that it is not so much a question of Bob's being bisexual but of his being somehow unformed. He can switch experiences on and off, just as he switches on and off between Alex and Daniel." Indeed, whenever a conflict arises with one of them, he takes refuge in the other.

Schlesinger treats Daniel's homosexuality in a very matter-of-fact way. "*Sunday, Bloody Sunday* is not about the sexuality of these people," he explains. "It asks the audience to accept them as they are. I am tired of homosexuals being portrayed in films as either hysterical or funny. This is the first film I know of that asks you to accept the homosexual characters as people. There is no special pleading. I didn't want to preach in the film that we must be tolerant of others, but rather to imply the kind of acceptance I mean."

"I suppose the film shocked some people," Schlesinger adds, "but I didn't set out to shock anybody. The scene in which Murray and Peter were shown greeting each other with a kiss is a case in point. Both of them were totally involved in their parts and they were certainly less shocked by the kiss than the technicians on the set were."

Inevitably the irresponsible and uncommitted Bob gets bored with his life in London and takes a plane for America, leading to the final scene in the picture in which Daniel is spending a lonely Sunday afternoon trying to learn Italian from a record, as he prepares for a trip to Italy that he was originally supposed to take with Bob. Daniel is sitting in the patient's chair in his office; suddenly he looks across the desk into the camera as if he were asking a doctor for advice. He confesses that he lives a lonely life and wonders what to do about it:

"I want his company and people say, what's half a loaf—you are well shot of him; and I say, I know that, but I miss him, that's all. . . . All my life I've been looking for someone courageous and resourceful, not like myself. He wasn't it; but we were *something*." Originally, Schlesinger notes, Daniel finished the speech by saying that no one has any right to call him to account; "but that line was dropped because, as I said, I wanted to avoid special pleading."

Serious films like *Sunday, Bloody Sunday, The Boys in the Band,* and some of the other movies which have been discussed present homosexuality not as a curiosity but as part of the human condition; perhaps there will be more like them in the future now that the motion picture industry has treated such problems with frankness and integrity. Hopefully, a lot of boys will not jump on the bandwagon merely to exploit the subject. For worthwhile treatments have a universal value: as a character in a recent Broadway play said about homosexuals: "They are sad and mixed up—like the rest of us."

171

Prostitutes and a customer in Fellini's *Roma*.

9.
Sexuality in Contemporary European Film

LESTER KEYSER

It is the powerful impact of these brightly-lit images moving in black space and artificial time, their affinity to trance and the subconscious, and their ability to influence masses and jump boundaries, that has forever made the cinema an appropriate target of the repressive forces in society—censors, traditionalists, the state.

Amos Vogel, *Film as a Subversive Art*

LARGELY because they were free of the restraints of the large corporate studio, an institution liable to puritanism and conservatism, and unbridled by archaic, self-righteous production codes, European filmmakers, from the very inception of cinema, have generally been more daring and sophisticated in their explorations of human sexuality. In America, nudity, illicit sex, perversion, and even scenes of passion were all excluded from the screen in the mid-thirties by an unprecedented self-imposed censorship. Individual artists were under no such constraints on the continent, and the markedly different conditions are apparent in their films. One good example is *Ecstasy*, a film by Gustav Machaty, released in 1933 in Czechoslovakia, which not only featured Hedy Lamarr in the nude, but centered as its title suggests on her emerging sexual consciousness, making eroticism its principal focus.

Machaty was not, of course, alone in his probings of the erotic impulse. The German expressionists, the French surrealists, and even the Russian formalists all gave sex a prominent place in their works. *The Cabinet of Dr. Caligari* is, for all

172

its theatrical devices, a Gothic thriller, full of repressed sexuality, rape, and murder. Its suggestive sets highlight the thin line between sanity and insanity, between the normal and abnormal, and are not far from the stylistics of von Sternberg, whose *The Blue Angel* introduced Lola (Marlene Dietrich) to a world every bit as mesmerized by her sexual charms as the professor (Emil Jannings) she victimized. A few years earlier in G. W. Pabst's *Pandora's Box*, Louise Brooks played Lulu, a similarly hypnotic figure whose sexuality destroyed an older male.

When Dali and Buñuel first sliced open the human eye in *Un Chien Andalou*, they also opened the world of cinematic vision to the regions of the unconscious. Their "desperate call for murder" was a cry for a new freedom in cinema, a freedom from the conventions of narrative structure and a freedom from visual taboos. Even Eisenstein, the most intellectual pioneer in world cinema, was not deaf to this call; he went to Paris, then Hollywood, and finally Mexico in his quest for a fuller, more engaging and humane cinema. Though never completed and carelessly edited by others into three separate works, his *Que Viva Mexico!* remains, as Parker Tyler notes in his *Classics of the Foreign Film*, the world's "sole abortive and indisputable classic to date."[1] In *Que Viva Mexico!* Eisenstein began probing both the dark and light sides of human life, pinpointing the social and sexual repression permeating peasant life.

Free to range among all social strata and physical phenomena, European filmmakers rejected the genres common to American films, the westerns, the gangster epics, and the lavish musicals, in favor of more individualistic visions of reality, more probing dissections of modern life. The more bizarre reaches of human behavior became common fare on European screens. Few viewers will forget, for example, the terrifyingly realistic picture of a child molester Fritz Lang presented in *M*, the lush treatment of lesbianism Leontine Sagan offered in *Mädchen in Uniform*, or the dark musings on superstition and sexuality Carl Dreyer limned in his *Day of Wrath*.

European filmmakers seemed especially preoccupied with the tension between mind and body, between the animal and the civilized. The modern European consciousness had obviously been formed by the discoveries of Darwin, Freud, and Marx. European filmmakers, working in the most modern of all arts, were struggling to reconcile man's animal heritage, his subconscious drives, and his need for social structures. The apotheosis of this theme comes in the work of Jean Renoir. In his *Rules of the Game*, the natural proclivities of his characters are always at odds with the cherished norms of society. The madcap antics at the masquerade party are constantly played off against the need for decorum, the need for a social hierarchy. Jealousy, infidelity, and even murder are all eventually hidden behind a thin veneer of civilization. Characters controlled by more fundamental and primitive impulses hypocritically give assent to long-standing traditions of class and honor: they pay lip service to the rules of the game, which are,

173

as the film shows, grand illusions. The film was unpopular when first released in 1939; only after the Second World War was its validity recognized.

Many of these serious European films were, because of the language barrier and the extreme differences in approach and content, virtually unknown to the mass audience in America. If the films were shown at all, it was usually in cosmopolitan areas or on arthouse circuits, or perhaps in an enlightened museum. Not until 1960 did a major European film capture the imagination of the American viewing public and generate long lines at box offices. Ironically, this landmark film countered American innocence with continental experience, indeed Old World decadence, in as dramatic a confrontation as Daisy Miller's visit to the Coliseum. The new title on the neighborhood marquee came from Rome not Hollywood, and in it, Federico Fellini took a sharp look at La Dolce Vita, using his camera, he declared, to put a thermometer to a sick world. La Dolce Vita did more, however, than measure the sad changes modern life had wrought in sexuality, or indicate the symptoms of the modern malaise. La Dolce Vita revolutionized modern cinema, forcing films around the world to deal with adult themes in a serious manner. La Dolce Vita launched the so-called "swinging sixties" at the same time it brought film art to international status. For all these reasons, it is easy to agree with Andrew Sarris that "it could be argued that in . . . social impact, La Dolce Vita is the most important film ever made."[2]

Like so many of his predecessors in European cinema, Fellini examines in La Dolce Vita the seemingly ineluctable chasm between man's sexuality and his social milieu. His protagonist Marcello (Marcello Mastroianni) is a talented man in search of a context; Marcello longs for communication, for meaningful sensual and intellectual involvement, but finds himself in a universe that seems to negate the possibility of total involvement. La Dolce Vita is in essence a chronicle of Marcello's unsuccessful search for something more in life. He never finds the added dimension he seeks, but resigns himself to life in a desolate wasteland where sex is an opiate, a desperate and meaningless attempt to escape all-encompassing ennui.

La Dolce Vita opens with a stunning shot of a helicopter carrying a statue of Christ. The visual shock, the ironic incongruity of the key symbol of ancient values being transported by modern technology, immediately suggests Fellini's concern with the displacement of higher values in modern life. Fellini's hero is a journalist who parlays the scandalous escapades of the upper class into a comfortable livelihood; the once revered savant, the writer, has been reduced to a purveyor of modern gossip in tabloid newspapers. Marcello's gossip column is in fact the chronicle of an aimless generation cut loose from transcendent values and incapable of real carnal satisfaction.

Marcello has numerous sexual adventures in La Dolce Vita, but all his escapades leave a taste of ashes rather than providing sweet emancipation from cares.

Emil Jannings and Marlene Dietrich in von
Sternberg's *The Blue Angel.*

Conrad Veidt kidnaps Lil Dagover in Robert
Weine's *The Cabinet of Dr. Caligari.*

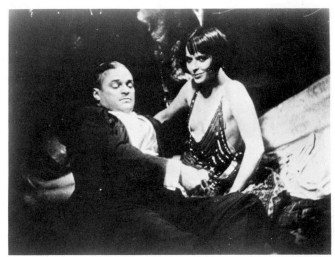

Fritz Kortner and Louise Brooks as Lulu in
G. W. Pabst's *Pandora's Box.*

Brigitte Helm in Pabst's *L'Atlantide.*

Marcello's fleeting liaison with Anouk Aimée highlights the confusion of material goods and satisfaction which haunts capitalist society. They make love in a prostitute's quarters, but the wealthy heiress cannot escape her nymphomania. This careless amour leads Marcello's unstable mistress (Yvonne Furneaux) to attempt a jealous suicide. She seems caught in the dilemma of liberated sex; freedom from responsibility is too much for her to bear. Escaping from both these women, Marcello has a tempestuous night on the town with a famous American movie star (Anita Ekberg), but the glamor fades with the dawn. In the light of day, he is as lonely and lost as ever.

Fellini's startling picture of a world devoid of feeling set the tone for many European films in the early sixties. In most of them sex is seen as just another blind alley, a futile outlet for energy in an enervating world. In 1961, for example, Michelangelo Antonioni screened *L'Avventura* at Cannes, announcing his creation of a cinema about the new man—an individual who finds all his aspirations crushed in the Copernican universe, a nightmarish galaxy where human beings are no longer central and the earth is only a small speck in a seemingly infinite expanse. All sense of teleology is gone in *L'Avventura*; the viewer is confronted with what Antonioni describes as "a detective story back to front."[3] The basic plot involves a search for Anna (Lea Massari) by her lover Sandro (Gabriele Ferzetti) and her girl friend Claudia (Monica Vitti). During the search Sandro and Claudia become lovers, and they never find Anna. Eventually Sandro cheats on Claudia, but she forgives him. At the end of the film, Sandro and Claudia are reconciled to the fickleness of their emotions and the casualness of their relationship. In a world seemingly governed by chance, they feel no responsibility to any orders or rules; instead, they accept their desires.

Antonioni's presentation of the search in *L'Avventura* emphasizes the bleakness of the island landscape and the isolation of the characters. Their sexual encounter provides the only alternative to solitude and lonely quest. Sandro and Claudia move in a vale of shadows; sex offers them a transient respite from all-encompassing mystery.

A similarly bleak and highly abstract view of human sexuality dominates *Last Year at Marienbad*, a stylized and ambiguous film directed by Alain Resnais which caused a sensation in Europe in 1961. Resnais filmed *Last Year at Marienbad* entirely at the Nymphenburg in Bavaria, using ceaseless tracking shots through ornate corridors, repetitious narration, and complex, almost architectural, arrangements of characters to transform Alain Robbe-Grillet's screenplay into cinematic poetry.

For all its emphasis on the corridors of memory and the relativity of time and perception, *Last Year at Marienbad* is basically a love story concerning a married woman (Delphine Seyrig), her husband (Sacha Pitoeff), and a would-be lover (Giorgio Albertazzi). The dehumanization of these characters, their utter lack of emotion, is suggested by their lack of names; in the screenplay, they are identified only as A, M, and X. The world in which they move is still and silent; they seem lost in an overpowering hotel. Resnais has indicated that the very size of the rooms in which his characters move was a conscious use of psychoanalytic imagery; the rooms are large, he notes, to "indicate a tendency to narcissism."[4] Throughout the film, M's memory of the last year is constantly contradicted by the physical reality documented on screen. His fantasy of a love affair is clearly at odds with reality. M is locked in his illusory memories, trapped by his own narcissism; he is an isolated pawn in a world he cannot comprehend and cannot escape.

The icy detachment of *Last Year at Marienbad* provided a definitive and unforgettable portrait of the ennui, sexual boredom, and alienation in modern life. European filmmakers were fascinated, however, by the possibilities inherent in the triangular relationship of A, X, and M. Love triangles were, of course, a staple of literature and cinema, but the new young filmmakers did not accept the normal focus in such narratives: the resolution of the triangle in a traditional pairing. Instead they explored the dynamics of the triangle, concentrating their attention on the evolving sexual code it entailed. The apparent failure of normal relationships forced filmmakers to study new patterns of sexuality.

Perhaps the most famous ménage à trois in the history of cinema appears in François Truffaut's *Jules and Jim*. Truffaut, the *enfant terrible* of the *Cahiers* group, treats his principals with tender affection in a film as notable for its lyricism as its sexual candor. At the center of the film is Kathe, stunningly portrayed by Jeanne Moreau, an immensely vibrant character, mysterious, forceful, capricious, and highly desirable. She is the great temptress, who seduces both Jules (Oskar Werner) and Jim (Henri Serre), two youthful chums. Kathe first marries Jules, but when the relationship fails, she marries Jim; the three then live happily together for a while. Jim decides to leave, but Kathe cannot stand the idea. She drives a car off a bridge, killing both Jim and herself, leaving Jules to mourn his lover and his friend.

Truffaut's tragic idyll is most notable for its sparkling *joie de vivre*. When Kathe, Jules, and Jim are together, the screen seems incandescent with passion. Their bicycle trips, picnics, and frenetic wanderings around Paris have a charm and an excitement far removed from the dreary despair of *L'Avventura* and *La Dolce Vita*. Life as Jules, Jim, and Kathe live it is vibrant and vital; their sexual relationships are life-giving and meaningful. When the trio is together, Kathe is happy: she chooses death rather than the dissolution of the triangle.

Jean-Luc Godard's vision of the love triangle in *Le Mépris (Contempt)*, released a year after *Jules and Jim*, is not so rosy as that of his colleague on the *Cahiers* staff. Once again the woman of the triangle, Camille Javal (Brigitte Bardot), is all-important; Bardot seems to be playing herself, the international sex

177

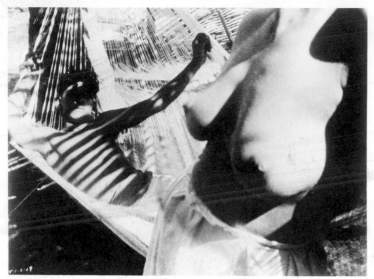

Peasants in Eisenstein's *Que Viva Mexico!*

Marcello Mastroianni in Fellini's *La Dolce Vita*.

Monica Vitti and Gabriele Ferzetti in Michelangelo Antonioni's *L'Avventura*.

Delphine Seyrig and Giorgio Albertazzi in Alain Resnais' *Last Year at Marienbad.*

Oskar Werner and Jeanne Moreau in François Truffaut's *Jules and Jim.*

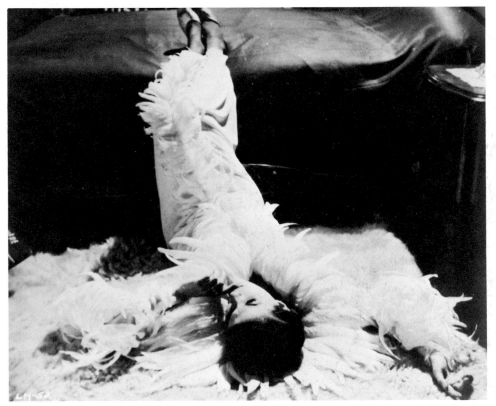

Delphine Seyrig in Alain Resnais' *Last Year* at *Marienbad.*

kitten and symbol of the sensual life. Camille's husband Paul (Michael Piccoli), who is working on a film based on *The Odyssey*, cannot satisfy her; she feels only contempt for him. But the American film producer Jeremy Prokosch (Jack Palance) she runs away with also fails her. She decides to leave them both, but just as she asserts her freedom, she too dies in a car accident.

Camille's sexuality seems to be destroyed by relationships which try to contain her free spirit. Both Jeremy and Paul are too possessive; they want to reduce everything to a simple compact, an eternal pair. Camille is less interested in control and seems much more in tune with the flow of life. The triangle is, to her, a natural thing. Her life deals in triangles. The men cannot handle the conflict, however, as they search for lost ideals. Their attempt to recapture the classic ideal of *The Odyssey*, their dependence on Fritz Lang, the old master, to direct their efforts, and their inability to cope with the female aptly named Camille, suggest their detachment from modern realities. Their failures as lovers reflect their inadequacies as thinkers and as artists. Yet ideas and ideals have become so central for them that more basic, amorphous emotions are beyond them.

One year later, the brilliant young Polish director, Roman Polanski, dealt with the same primitive drives, again in the context of a triangle, in his *Knife in the Water*. In Polanski's work, coscripted by Jerzy Skolimowski, almost all pretense of civility is gone. The film portrays an almost Oedipal conflict between the cynical married man Andrzej (Leo Niemczyk) and a young hitchhiker (Zygmunt Melanowicz) for the attention of Andrzej's wife Christine (Jolante Umecka). Cut off from civilization on a yacht, the men reenact a veritable totem feast. The tension is palpable as Andrzej and the young man constantly taunt each other, compete in petty games, and finally fight over trivial objects. In the background constantly is the real prize, Christine, whose provocative bathing attire creates an aura of pervasive sexuality.

The emerging emphasis on the battle of the sexes, on the ritualistic combat intrinsic in the mating game, led European filmmakers into even bleaker visions of dominance and submission as the key elements in human sexuality. The conflict involved, of course, not only heterosexual love, but relations between individuals of the same sex. Ingmar Bergman, for example, scandalized European audiences in 1963 with his somber story of two sisters, *The Silence*. Viewers were so disturbed by this picture of human sexuality that Bergman was deluged with hate mail and received a number of threats on his life.

The Silence is a critical film in the history of sexuality on screen; it pictures a universe almost beyond emotions, beyond sexuality, but still haunted by the physical vestiges of the old drives. Susan Sontag clarifies this phenomenon in her essay "The Aesthetic of Silence." Words, she writes, are key links to the past, the building blocks of memory; to destroy continuity, she asserts, is to go "to the end of each emotion or thought. And after the end, what supervenes (for a while) is silence."[5]

Bergman's two sisters, Ester (Ingrid Thulin) and Anna (Gunnel Lindblom) have been traveling in a foreign city. What they intended, Ester reveals, was "a lovely pleasure trip to the most beautiful place on earth." Instead they find they cannot escape their natures and are lost in a city where they cannot fathom the language. The two sisters almost seem opposite facets of one personality, Ester the mind, and Anna the body. Ester is a scholar, a linguist, who cannot control her lesbian urges; she spends her time locked in the hotel, wracked by a terrible cough, constantly eating and smoking. To allay her sexual tension, she masturbates, but still finds no peace. Anna is young and voluptuous. Her nudity in the bath is a constant temptation to Ester. Yet Anna can find no meaningful release for her energy; she makes love with a man in the hotel, but the act has no meaning. Eventually she leaves Ester dying in the foreign city, and continues her journey to a distant home with her son, Johan.

Bergman's portrait of the two women, neither of whom can find wholeness or integrity in their lives, makes their sexual drives seem a cruel cosmic joke. Ester and Anna cannot satisfy each other, and they cannot find release in the alien world they inhabit. Inevitably, they hate themselves and each other. As they try to satisfy their needs, they find themselves tearing at each other. Anna's body is both a temptation and a reproach to Ester; Ester's civility and culture, a cruel comment on Anna's vulgarity.

Bergman had originally intended The Silence as a study of two men. In England, Joseph Losey, a displaced American, stayed with masculine characters in his own involved study of dominance and subservience in sexual relationships. Based on a powerful screenplay by Harold Pinter, Losey's The Servant introduces still another level to the fray: his film is as much about the conflict of social classes in England as it is about the topsy-turvy affair of the master (James Fox) and the butler who eventually dominates him (Dirk Bogarde). Sex became a perfect metaphor for Losey; the seesawing of power in the homosexual liaison of Fox and Bogarde was his mirror of the similar lack of stability in English society. The individual's drive for power vis-à-vis his mate became a paradigm in The Servant for the larger power politics so central in a decade of revolution and upheaval.

Many European films in the late sixties develop Losey's theme, using repressed sexuality and a drive for more liberated relationships as an emblem of a similar political quest for more responsive institutions, for greater involvement in the process of government. In 1968, for example, Lindsay Anderson focusses on the collapse of the class system in England exacerbated by a youthful revolt. Set entirely in a boy's school, Lindsay's film If is an ironic commentary on the values encapsulized in Kipling's poem of the same name. His hero, Mick (Malcolm

Jean-Luc Godard's *Weekend* with
Mireille Darc.

Ingrid Thulin and Gunnel Lindblom in Bergman's *The Silence*.

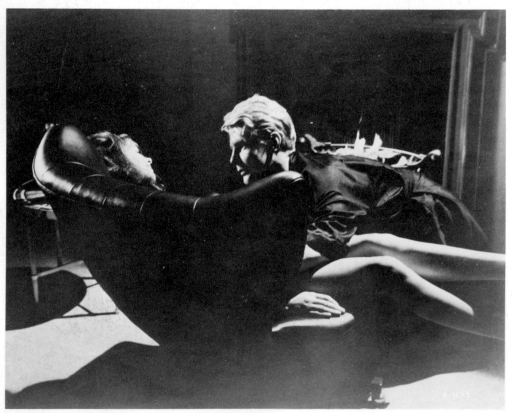

Sarah Miles and James Fox in Joseph Losey's *The Servant*.

Lea Massari and Benoit Ferreux in Louis
Malle's *Murmur of the Heart*.

Dirk Bogarde and Charlotte Rampling in Liliana Cavani's
The Night Porter.

Dusan Makavejev's *WR: Mysteries of the Organism.*

Jean-Louis Trintignant and Stefania Sandrelli in Bernardo Bertolucci's *The Conformist.*

Charlotte Rampling and Dirk Bogarde in Liliana Cavani's *The Night Porter.*

Sophia Loren in Vittorio De Sica's *Yesterday, Today and Tomorrow.*

McDowell), is the victim of an outmoded and repressive Victorian education. He and his colleagues find all their natural drives frustrated in a closed universe where sex is suppressed or sublimated. When the boys act up, they are beaten savagely or humiliated under cold showers. Away from the masters, however, their primitive urges find release in the rhythms of the "Missa Luba" and in impassioned affairs with a local waitress (Christine Noonan). Finally, the breach between the system and its servants becomes irremediable and the boys turn on the masters in an orgiastic guerilla attack. All their fantasies explode in a cathartic battle. Lindsay's sympathies are obviously with Mick and his girl. Commenting on the many images of repressed sexuality in the film, the images of physicals, masturbation, and forbidden pinups, and of a frustrated wife's nude walk through the boys' dormitory, Lindsay argued that his vision of the school was a vision of an institution "that frustrates the natural instincts in the body;" given this context, the boys' revolt is, Lindsay feels, "a pure violent expression of sex."[6]

The dichotomy between restrictive institutions and liberated sexuality is the central thesis of Dusan Makavejev's kaleidoscopic ode to Wilhelm Reich, *WR: Mysteries of the Organism*. Makavejev began research on his film in 1969 and shot most of the footage in 1970. Completed, the film was banned in Yugoslavia. There is good reason for a totalitarian state to look askance at Makavejev's art. Beginning with the theories of a man who died in an American prison because he would not deny his beliefs, Makavejev explores not only the concept of a vital force Reich felt man must rediscover to be free, but stops along the way to document the rise of hard-core pornography in America, to lambaste the failure of the Russian revolution to free people from a possessive, capitalistic attitude to sex, and to urge the development of a new freer sexual consciousness that would topple all institutions. *WR: Mysteries of the Organism* is revolutionary both in technique and in content. Makavejev rejects a traditional narrative mode; rather, he presents a collage of striking images. Viewers must supply the connections; their visceral responses to juxtaposed images of Stalin at Christmas, of transvestites in a lower East Side gallery, of groupies plaster-casting penises, and of Reichian therapy sessions, are the substance of the film. If a viewer is free enough to allow his thoughts to wander outside traditional structures, he has taken the first step to the freedom both Reich and Makavejev extol.

Makavejev's call for freedom and a liberated sexuality is hammered home by his refusal to turn the camera away from scenes rarely treated in earlier cinema. Nudity pervades the film, with every intimate detail of the sex act in plain view; the film is also crowded with images of the outer reaches of sexuality, epitomized in the presence of Jim Buckley, the editor of *Screw* magazine, whose erect penis becomes a work of art. It is no wonder that Amos Vogel calls the film "one of the most important subversive masterpieces" in modern cinema.[7] Makavejev not only calls for liberation; he leads cinema to new freedom by his example.

The movement towards a new permissiveness is undoubtedly the major revolution in European film of the seventies. Fellini's image of a sick world had, young filmmakers felt, begged the question. How could one talk about sickness, they asked, when man is only obeying his most fundamental drives? Instead of castigating man for some mysterious fall from grace, the new generation of filmmakers preached a gospel of acceptance in their films. Sexuality became their new desideratum, the one contact man had with Nature and the cosmic in a world where institutions had gone astray.

It is hard to overestimate the dimensions of this shift in attitudes towards sexuality. In the new European cinema, all the old taboos were broken and the guilt associated with sexual promiscuity rejected. Even incest, once the horror of every society, could not withstand the new tide of freedom. In *The Murmur of the Heart*, a delightful comedy by Louis Malle, the sexual education of fourteen-year-old Laurent (Benoit Ferreux) includes an interlude with his mother Clara (Lea Massari). The act is presented as a positive, indeed lovely and touching, moment in his life. Neither mother nor son is traumatized; they accept their sexual episode as a part of life, a stage in a natural cycle. They are beyond taking the conventions of the society in which they move seriously. Sex, in *The Murmur of the Heart*, seems one of those private things humans have to gird themselves against the insanity around them. Malle's family would have enjoyed themselves at the very parties that bored Fellini's Marcello. They can accept their own irrelevance in the cosmic scheme by holding on to simple pleasures.

Sex as a refuge from the absurdity of everyday life is an even more explicit theme in Bernardo Bertolucci's *Last Tango in Paris*. Alienated from everything around them, Paul (Marlon Brando) and Jeanne (Maria Schneider) set up an apartment in Paris where they can satisfy their innermost desires, free from problems of identity and position in the larger world. In the apartment, they work out the dynamics of dominance and subservience in an increasingly unconventional series of erotic acts. Outside, they are plagued by relatives, lovers, material concerns, politics, and religion. In the apartment, they really live; it is their dream world. When the ideal fails, the result is death.

Last Tango in Paris inverts all the values of the Judeo-Christian tradition. Sex emerges as the positive pole of human life, whereas civilization, restraint, and self-control are viewed as negative traits. A similar inversion is evident in Stanley Kubrick's *A Clockwork Orange*, a film based on Anthony Burgess' celebrated novel. The novel was a cautionary tale about the dangers of behavior modification in modern society; government could, it shows, reduce its citizens to little wind-up automatons. Kubrick is not as concerned, however, with the problem of free will. His presentation of Alex (Malcolm McDowell) emphasizes instead the vitality of the young hoodlum. Though Alex is a sadist who finds joy in brutality and destruction, he is still shown as more likeable than the shallow, hypocritical

187

zombies who try to remold him. Sex is so plasticized in Alex's world that his blood and guts approach, his savage rapes and brutal actions, seem alternatives to a total lack of feeling, a deadly clinical detachment. Kubrick's sympathy for Alex shocked the normally tolerant and sophisticated Pauline Kael, who published a lengthy tirade accusing the director of "sucking up to the thugs in the audience."[8] As usual, Kael's interpretation of the film is a good one. Like many other European filmmakers, Kubrick is willing to accept any expression of sexuality as more desirable than any social restraint.

Pauline Kael was not, of course, the only one shocked by *A Clockwork Orange*. The progressive trend in European films, the self-conscious espousal of a new permissiveness, has disoriented many cinema-goers. With each new assault on traditional values, a furor has erupted. Fellini was soundly denounced for the decadence of *La Dolce Vita*; Makavejev's *WR: Mysteries of the Organism* was banned in many countries; and Bertolucci's *Last Tango in Paris* inspired innumerable law suits. Liliana Cavani's most recent effort, *The Night Porter*, continues the tradition. *The Night Porter* was confiscated in Italy and condemned by the Church, yet audiences all over the world are lining up to see Cavani's operatic depiction of a sadomasochistic love affair.

The Night Porter is a graphic film; director Cavani forces her audience to see all that sadism entails. In the concentration camp where Max (Dirk Bogarde) first meets Lucia (Charlotte Rampling), the depicting of humiliation and torture is relentless. The audience sees Max abusing the nude Lucia, cutting her arm only to lick the wound, forcing objects up her vagina, and teaching her the pleasures of fellatio in chains. Years later, when Max and Lucia meet in Vienna, it is clear that they both enjoyed their bizarre actions and they voluntarily relive their old games.

Max's one attempt at explaining his strange infatuation is ambiguous and disjointed: "It all seems lost . . . something happens . . . ghosts take shape in the mind . . . this phantom with a voice and a body." Max, now a hotel porter who wants to live as a churchmouse, obviously thought his fascist days, those twisted days in the camps when prisoners were his playthings, were all gone—sad, unexpected aberrations in a more orderly universe. Then Lucia reappears and the old itch comes back. The "ghosts" form in his mind and the phantom is once again incarnate. Lucia can no more explain her obsession than Max can. When she is discovered chained in the apartment where she and Max hide from the world, she can only purr that "Nothing is changed . . . there is no cure . . . Max is more than the past . . . I'm alright here . . . I'm here of my own free will." Both she and Max eventually die rather than give up their obsession. Perverse as their world may seem to outsiders, they are the Romeo and Juliet of Cavani's film, star-crossed lovers destroyed by forces larger than themselves.

Cavani's *The Night Porter* may be the most daring recent film but its willing-

Georgina Hale dances with her lovers in Nazi attire in a
fantasy sequence from Ken Russell's *Mahler*.

The violent conclusion of Lindsay Anderson's *IF*.

ness to explore seemingly bizarre sexual relationships exemplifies a healthy new freedom in European cinema, a willingness to take chances in the quest for insight. Young directors like Rainer Werner Fassbinder, West Germany's most prolific film genius, are not afraid to tackle seemingly impossible subjects. His latest work, *Angst Essen Seele Auf Ali*, concerns a love affair between a sixty-year-old French cleaning woman (Brigitte Mira) and a young Moroccan emigrant (El Hedi Ben Salem). In this unlikely liaison, Fassbinder isolates some universal themes about xenophobia, prejudice, and the abiding humanity which binds old and young together. He does so without skirting any of the sexual problems Ali faces in a love affair with a woman twice his age. Fassbinder and most of the newest talents on the European film scene have come to see sexuality in a new perspective. These new directors are creating a mature cinema which treats the immense range of sexual experiences as part of human life. They are neither obsessed by sex nor fearful of it. Their expanded vision augurs well for the future of European films.

PART THREE

Contemporary Landmarks

10.
I Am Curious —Yellow: A Practical Education

DAVID S. LENFEST

Lena Nyman and Börje Ahlstedt in *I am Curious—Yellow.*

VILGOT SJOMAN's *I Am Curious—Yellow,* which was the focus of the late sixties' most important censorship battle, brought consternation and public outcry from a range of people as ostensibly diverse as the U.S. Customs Service and Rex Reed, all of whom deplored it as the worst in pornography and bad taste. Some critics found the film simply dull, while others praised the honesty and candidness of the sexual sequences which, though simulated, were franker and more explicitly visualized than anything previously seen in a 35mm feature for general release.

When *I Am Curious—Yellow* was brought to trial at the U.S. District Court in New York on obscenity charges on May 20, 1968, among the witnesses on its behalf were Norman Mailer, Stanley Kauffmann, Hollis Alpert, John Simon, and the Swedish director. Discussing the ground-breaking aspects of the film, Simon stated, "I feel that it makes a genuine artistic and moral contribution by being honest about sex, by showing the enjoyment to be derived from it as well as the problems it raises, by showing its relationship to other aspects of the human personality, and the social and even political situation of the world."[1]

The representatives of the government, however, seemed most upset by the film's reunion scene when Börje Ahlstedt, the male protagonist, goes to the country to find Lena Nyman, the female lead. In the enthusiasm of their greeting they kiss each other's genitals. Although Börje and Lena do not have oral intercourse, the mere suggestion seemed to bother the government more than any of the other sexual hijinks in the film—making love on the balcony of the palace, for instance, or in a tree. The central point of contention appeared to be the shock caused by oral contact with the sexual organs. Hard-core 16mm pornography had

shown real oral intercourse for some ti[...]
witnesses testified, *I Am Curious—Yello*[...]
its execution. Nonetheless, Sjöman's na[...]
the reunion scene, was the major cause o[...]
as it contributed to its controversial repu[...]

After Grove Press won a landmark[...]
Appeals, *I Am Curious—Yellow* was su[...]
seemed to be well liked by a wide spectru[...]
much of the earlier critical scorn and le[...]
target, while its defenders at the trial were largely correct in their views. Although
the trial occurred in 1968, the film did not premiere in New York until March 10,
1969. This time span enfolds the 1968 Democratic Convention in Chicago, an
event that is generally considered to be a watershed of political consciousness for
young activists and college students. I would like to suggest that much of the
appeal of *I Am Curious—Yellow* stems from its heroine's being just the kind of
person who came to Chicago to demonstrate and who learned that power politics
is much more intransigent than he or she thought.

The form of the film was different from the usual American product as was
much of its content. The primary thematic material revolves around Lena Nyman's
search for identity in the political sphere and in her emotional involvement with
her latest lover Börje. These episodes are, however, interspersed with Lena seen
as a young actress working with her director, Vilgot Sjöman. She is shown with
him at the beginning of the film going to his apartment and later at a reading by
Yevtushenko; periodically throughout the film, Sjöman interjects himself or a
view of his camera crew into the action. The film ends with Sjöman at his Steen-
beck editing table showing rushes to a new young actress and with Lena and Börje
embracing in a descending elevator. The action of the plot is interrupted steadily
by the director reminding the audience that they are watching a film. This examination will first consider the primary plot and content, Lena's practical education, and then the film's formal characteristics.

Lena Nyman explores her own political consciousness and that of her coun-
trymen first by surveying a random group of people about their class consciousness. "Do you think that Swedish society has a class system?" She discovers that
most people have virtually no class awareness and consequently no awareness
that working class people are not treated fairly. After an interview with Olaf
Palme, then minister of transport, shots from an interview with Martin Luther
King introduce the concept of nonviolent resistance. Two primary radical social
goals are thereby brought forward for consideration. These are followed by Lena
opening her own institute, which serves as a forum where she may explore her
social environment and her self. A direct confrontation with members of the

upper middle class returning from holiday   and with a physician establishes her commitment to this practical educa

The confrontation sequence is followed by   ction to her father who
works in a frame shop, and who, we later find out,   efly in Spain against
Franco. Börje is brought home by her father and the   romantic involvement of the film begins. It is important that Lena and   make love in
her "institute" because that physical location establishes th   ip between
her love life and her other interests. The room contains a pic   nco and
a blackboard listing the number of days since her father "chick   n the
Spanish Civil War," which shows a typical disillusionment of th   th
the actions of their elders. At the same time, her father's participa
war implicitly gives Lena a social focus and direction. The room contains
of concentration camps, and her file of lovers—twenty-three to be exact, alth
she says the first nineteen were "no fun." She later tells us that she could
imagine herself beautiful with the first nineteen, and that she only achieved some
measure of self-esteem after those encounters. Here, again, Lena is paradigmatic
of what young women have learned of themselves since the women's movement
has taken hold, or what others have learned independently from time immemorial;
that you must love yourself before you can love others. Her twenty-three lovers
are a record of struggle with the self, while her social concerns represent her attempt to broaden her understanding of the social system she inhabits.

In a comic moment after their first love-making, Börje and Lena bicycle off
at dawn and make love seated on a balustrade of the palace. Again, the themes of
political and sexual exploration are joined. Lena then interviews the King, who is
retiring, asking him what it feels like to be the last king. (Another touch of humor
is Börje's close resemblance to the crown prince.) Börje's middle class outlook
begins to emerge more strongly than in his earlier conversation with Lena, and
their different social views are shown to be further apart than they seemed at
first. Throughout the "fictional" level of the film Lena's socialist and lower class
sympathies differ sharply from Börje's middle class inclinations. He is found not
to be honest with her about his other women; she rides a bicycle to the country
to meditate, while he drives out in an MG from the shop where he works as a car
salesman. They are a typical young couple, finding that their differing social
positions cause personal clashes.

Lena pickets the American embassy and has an unsatisfactory interview with
Yevtushenko, in whom she had placed much faith. In a talk with her father, she
discovers that Börje has had a child with Marie. She decides to leave for the
country, but first has another of her socialist fantasies: the country has gone
over fully to a policy of nonviolent resistance, and the TV shows a training program for new recruits who practice lying down in front of a train. Following that,
Börje starts a fight with Lena's friend, Magnus, at her institute and in a typical

195

parallel illustrating their social differences Lena is seen meditating before a picture of Martin Luther King and a broken shotgun. Later, she reads a manual of variant sexual positions, and then converses with some natives in a difficult dialect. All this emphasizes Lena's social differences with Börje. At last, he drives up to find her.

They meet in joyous sexual reunion in the scene that earned the film its lurid reputation. (Some people in 1968 and 1969 seemed to see the scene as involving oral intercourse rather than the gentle fondling that actually is shown, but, by 1973 at least, Linda Lovelace had dramatically established the difference.) After their reunion they go sightseeing in the neighborhood and their dialogue points again to the divergence in their social views. Lena talks about the deserted village and the plight of the people, while Börje talks about commercial success as a car salesman. Their conflict continues while they wash Börje's MG, and there is a comic and sexual resolution in the water. They return to the village of Rumskalla, where they were sightseeing, and climb into a tree reputed to be the largest in Europe. There they make love in full view (as we find out later) of a group of singing fundamentalist Christians, thus mocking a solemn group of their elders while they experiment sexually. As they did in the scene on the balustrade of the palace, they again demonstrate their independence.

The major emotional break between the two occurs when Lena opens the trunk of Börje's car and discovers faded roses and a hair dryer intended for Madeleine (the third woman he is known to be involved with). They fight seriously, make love, and fall asleep; Lena awakens to the sound of Börje's departing car. She is angry that he cannot be honest about his other affairs, and he is angry that she is always prying into his life. Lena then dreams of tying her twenty-three lovers to a tree, shooting Börje, and then castrating him. Again, she is a typical young person in her anger and frustration at the lack of success in her love relationship. This excursion into violent Freudian fantasy is balanced by a fantasy in which Martin Luther King becomes the voice of her conscience as she remonstrates with herself for losing her nonviolent resolution. That scene is followed by a TV spot announcing Sweden's adoption of nonviolence as a national defense posture. She breaks down in tears at her inability to live up to her ideal. She goes home to destroy her "institute," gouging the eyes out of the portrait of Franco, as she does. Thus she is shown to have broken with her home and with the symbiotic relationship with her father. Her brief excursion into the politics of nonviolence and the life of the working class has evenly balanced her middle class background. The fictional core of the film ends when she and Börje go their own way after being treated for the crabs at a hospital. Thus we are to conclude that she is free of the infection of her promiscuous love making.

The story of Lena, the young woman seeking emotional and political integrity, occupies most of the film, but it is qualified throughout by the appearance

Lena's fantasy of binding her past lovers
to a tree.

Lena interviews citizens on the streets
of Stockholm.

Lena and Börje.

of the director or of the camera crew (when Lena and Börje fight at her retreat). At the beginning of the film the audience is shown Lena, the young actress, collaborating with her director in shaping the film; at the end Sjöman has ended his relationship with her and is shown to be interested in another actress, while Lena and Börje, as actors and co-workers, descend in the elevator kissing each other. The interruptions of the fabric of the fiction seem to owe much less to the French cinéma verité than they do to the ideological parent of the whole school, Brecht. Brecht has commented on the relationship of life to art:

> Reality, however complete, has to be altered by being turned into art, so that it can be seen to be alterable and be treated as such.[2]

In theory, at least, this idea explains many of Sjöman's interruptions in the film. For example, before Lena and Börje have their climactic fight at her retreat the image is strongly established of the couple naked and asleep on the floor of an otherwise empty house. The audience witnesses two people truly naked to each other: the barren surroundings emphasize the final emptiness of their affair. Sjöman cuts to the film crew, who are embarrassed by the fight going on inside the house. The audience is reminded that this is a film (art), but that it takes place within and influences reality. If the presence and reactions of the film crew can be said to represent life (as opposed to the art of the fictional story) then Sjöman demonstrates art affecting life. This particular interruption is the most effective in the film since it is placed at the emotional climax of the fictional relationship. The ending of the film—Börje and Lena descending and embracing in the elevator—cycles the viewer back to reality and argues for the truth of the drama just presented.

In a strictly linear argument it can be said against the film that the final interruption simply negates the concept of integrity that the main character was searching for. In its defense, it seems that the contrast between art and life, and their interrelation, can be defended again as Brecht did:

> Freedom comes with the principle of contradiction, which is continually active and vocal in us all.[3]

When the audience is reminded continually that it is watching art, a dialectic is established within the film that leads to questioning its truth, its applicability to life as the viewer knows it.

Given its political concerns and its interest in the consciousness of young people in 1968–1969 it seems fair to think of the film in comparison with two of its contemporaries, Haskell Wexler's *Medium Cool* and Mike Grey's *American Revolution II*. The first is a straight fiction film showing a young reporter's reaction to the Democratic convention in 1968 and his involvement with a woman who lives in the slums with her son. The story centers on the political consciousness of its principals, but it remains a fiction. The second is a pure documentary treatment of the alignment of the Black Panther Party, the Young Lords (a Puerto Rican group), and a group of poor, white, Southern, radicals living in Chicago, who called themselves The Young Patriots. It, too, deals with political consciousness as the various political groups react to the 1968 Democratic convention and to their own attempt to create a coherent political unit. Sjöman's film is comparable on the issue of political consciousness, and it stands directly between the two, as it combines fictional elements with the documentary style of the intrusion of the making of the film. It would seem that the long-term appeal of the film owed more to its approach to these issues than to its reputation as pornography.

The sexuality of the film is finally far less important than the proposition that Lena is a young woman searching after her own integrity in political and romantic matters. Her own sexual experience is seen as part and parcel of her total development as a person, and in both the fictional and the "realistic" segments of the film she is seen to grow from her experiences. Two comments from Thomas Levin, a psychiatrist, at the trial emphasize the meaning of Lena's experience in the film:

> In both of these areas the young woman seeks through ritual . . . to establish a fundamental truth: Who she is in relationship to other people, people close to her, and her society. . . .
> That ritual . . . was, a reception over and over again in order to elicit a fundamental common response.

Dr. Levin's perception that the film is ritual seems ultimately correct when Lena's search and struggle are seen as a paradigm for initiation into contemporary society and when her experience is bracketed with those of other young people during and after the 1968 Democratic convention. It may indeed be the case that those who opposed the film on the grounds of its sexual content realized at some level its true significance and found that dimension to be much more threatening than the simple sexuality portrayed. In any case, when Lena's actions and problems are perceived as ritual they can at the same time be perceived as a different and practical education.

Jon Voight and Dustin Hoffman in *Midnight Cowboy*.

11

Midnight Cowboy

FOSTER HIRSCH

IN 1969, Hollywood discovered the underground. *Easy Rider, Alice's Restaurant, Medium Cool,* and *Midnight Cowboy* were the box office hits of the year. Rebellious youth and the sounds of the counterculture suddenly became bankable, and the studios rushed into production a spate of films that tried to snare the market that *Easy Rider* had tapped so spectacularly.

Hollywood's social consciousness didn't pay off; by the time they were released, the youth movies seemed dated, historical relics rather than up-to-the-minute snapshots. Trying to cash in on what promised to be a profitable trend rather than treating serious social themes seriously, the films didn't fool the vast public that had gone to see Dennis Hopper's landmark road movie.

Midnight Cowboy was grouped with the other hip movies, but its concerns weren't really social, and its two forlorn protagonists hardly qualified as counter-culture heroes. Beneath its vividly depicted world of urban rot, *Midnight Cowboy* was in fact an old-fashioned romance, *Camille* updated to the pestilential big city and enacted by two men, a male hustler substituting for the dying courtesan and his fifth-rate pimp corresponding to the doting Armand. (Only this time, it's the admirer rather than the prostitute who dies.) Because it was the first time, though, that the general moviegoing public had glimpsed the twilight world of the male hustler, the old story seemed new, modern, daring—hence, the film's reputation as one of the with-it pictures of its time.

The lurid 42nd Street trappings that framed the story of the male friends were revolutionary for a big-budget major studio film. *Midnight Cowboy* is set in Andy Warhol territory. For the first time, the residents of the Chelsea Hotel, the hustlers, the pimps, the winos, the kooky, strung-out party people, and the kinky losers that crowded films like *Bike Boy* and *My Hustler* surfaced aboveground. John Schlesinger's tour of the urban underbelly takes place on the same streets as Warhol's self-titillating campy escapades. Only this time the big city weirdos are cleaned up a little for mass consumption, and there's no self-parody. No one in *Midnight Cowboy* is putting us on; unlike the Warhol floor shows, Schlesinger's film is played "straight."

Female prostitutes have been recurrent figures in popular movies, but the notion of a man who sells his body has always seemed subversive. (It still does. Joe Buck didn't make male whores respectable; producers weren't drawn to his type even after the enormous success of *Midnight Cowboy*.) In 1969, Joe Buck and the grimy, dank world he moved through were startling, and even James Leo Herlihy, who wrote the novel, was surprised that the film was as frank as it was and as faithful to the spirit of his own work.

Prestige movies had never before explored the American lower depths in quite this way. The flophouse hotels, the grungy bars, the abandoned tenements supply most of the backgrounds for Joe Buck's sexual odyssey. But the cowboy's quest to conquer the women of Manhattan also takes him to penthouse apartments and luxury hotels, and Joe is an outsider in both worlds. To him, as well as to Schlesinger, the city is hard, alien, corrupt. New York on film had seldom looked so grim and plague-ridden before, and part of the film's tension—its challenge for mass audiences—was in its depiction of the American Big City as a desolate and nightmarish wasteland.

It wasn't only the settings that introduced a new level of realism in American movies—Joe's sexual encounters were franker and more open variations on the figure of the muscular male who had wandered disguised through some of the work of the fifties. Tennessee Williams' studs, William Inge's beautiful male animal in *Picnic*, actors like Brando and James Dean and Paul Newman were all testaments to the almost magical power of the sexually potent male. Inge's and Williams' heroes, though, satisfied and soothed and "saved" women, and their obvious appeal to homosexuals (their creation, in fact, by homosexual writers) was discreetly overlooked. The fifties weren't ready to consider what William Holden, stripped to the waist, his muscles rippling, might have been able to do for some of the frustrated men of that small, tight Kansas town.

Joe was the first big-time movie hero whose emphatic sexual presence was acknowledged as possible salvation for men as well as women. Joe Buck, cowboy from the sticks, was a more direct embodiment of the homosexual dream hero than any of Tennessee Williams' sultry male models. Joe is the ideal figure in a certain kind of homosexual fantasy: he's the butch fag, a particular sort of homosexual's dream of what a real man is really like. The supreme manly man, the perfect stud, Joe is in fact the exact counterpart to the midnight cowboy who is presented as the birthday gift to Harold in *The Boys in the Band*. As Joe sadly discovers, his cowboy image turns on men more readily than women. His naive, country boy dream of servicing all the hungry ladies in the big city turns sour when he learns that it's the men who are more likely to come on to him.

Joe's two encounters with males were, of course, the real reason for the film's X-rating: Main Street audiences had never seen anything like the sex in the balcony scene, in which a frightened student goes down on Joe, or Joe's "date" with a nervous nelly mama's boy.

Identifying masculinity with rugged cowboys, Joe is horrified by the idea of men sleeping with other men, and he never once confronts his own possible latent homosexuality. Admiring his own physique, looking appreciatively at the poster of Paul Newman which seems to be one of his most favored possessions, Joe might well graduate to enjoyment of other men in the flesh. But he can't get beyond worshipping Newman from afar; for Joe (as, perhaps, for most of his audience), being queer is still the disease that dare not speak its name.

The character's fear of exploring his own sexuality is shared by the director and screenwriter, and the reticence stamps the movie as distinctly pre–Gay Lib, a tentative rather than full-scale confrontation with the subject of masculine self-definition. *Midnight Cowboy* is a genuine landmark in the treatment of sexuality on film, but it is not a totally liberated treatment of the city at night. It's a movie that can't help raising the consciousness of its audience, and at the same time it's a picture that needs its own consciousness raised. Schlesinger peeks into, but he doesn't completely open, the closet.

The movie shares its hero's skittishness about being gay. It presents homosexuals as crazy (the religious huckster pimp with his stable of boys); as guilt-ridden (the boy in the theater vomits in the john after his encounter with Joe, so disgusted is he by his desires); as prissy (the aging mama's boy). The homosexuals are cartoons, and their world is presented as loathsome, intolerably isolated—as, indeed, the perfect complement to the neon soullessness and the gritty impersonality of 42nd Street.

Since the twilight world of gay men is presented as so foul and soul-denying, it's no wonder that Joe doesn't want to admit any possible similarity to the men he services. The most shocking and most unexamined moment in the film is the character's gratuitous cruelty to the older effeminate man who has picked him up. Why does Joe react so ferociously? Is it because he sees in the man a distorted and ugly part of himself? Is he, in lashing out at the helpless and pitiful man, denying something in his own nature? To dismiss Joe's violence as simply a healthy heterosexual male's disgust with an effeminate male is to neglect suggestions that the movie has thrown out about Joe all along.

The friendship between Joe and the street-wise Ratso who takes him in is possible because it's based on a denial of homosexual attraction. Joe and Ratso are manly buddies who've decided to set up house together for the sake of con-

venience. It isn't until the last scene, after Ratso dies on the bus, that Joe is able
to express his feelings for his friend physically. Protectively, he puts his arm
around his dead buddy, cradling him—a gesture he was not capable of when Ratso
was alive. The two outcasts play at being he-men. When there's tension between
them, Ratso accuses Joe of being a fag. At his harshest, the city-smart Ratso tells
the green country boy that, up here in New York, his cowboy getup is strictly
"fag stuff."

The two characters don't necessarily have explicitly homosexual feelings
for each other. But the possibility does scare them; they set limits to the way they
relate to each other. Like Brick in *Cat on a Hot Tin Roof*, they seem to want to
prove to themselves that men can have a deep feeling for each other without
being homosexuals. Of course male friendship can be deep without being physical;
but the movie never acknowledges that it can be physical without being impure.

Joe and Ratso are just good buddies, then. They're each other's best friend,
and each other's only friend. Neither one is successful with women—Ratso because, unshaven, crippled, louse-ridden, he's unfit for normal heterosexual romance, Joe because—well, because why? Joe doesn't make it as a stud for women,
and the movie never lets us know the real reason. Are Joe's difficulties with women
connected to the traumatically concluded affair with his home town girl friend?
The girl back home was clearly the town tramp, and the movie fleetingly suggests that both she and Joe were raped by a gang. Their relationship, at any rate, is
presented as something impure, and the memory of its sordid outcome is a recurrent nightmare to Joe.

Joe's two encounters with women customers are played for laughs. The episode with Sylvia Miles is decidedly anti-romance; neither character is interested
in post-coital commitments. And the after-party shack-up with Brenda Vaccarro
is ignited only when the sad-eyed career girl accuses Joe of being a fag.

Joe has fond memories of his grandmother, but his one really pure relationship is with the bum who befriends him. Male friendships are not uncommon in
American films: consider the Howard Hawks films that celebrate male comrade-
ship and competence. Butch Cassidy and The Sundance Kid paid more attention
to each other than they did to Etta Place. In *Easy Rider*, Dennis Hopper and
Peter Fonda were soulmates as well as traveling companions; women were rele-
gated to incidental and virtually anonymous sex objects. The buddies on the road
or the he-men in adventure genre has included a phobic repugnance to the possibility of sex between two men. In *Deliverance*, a vigorously defensive man's man
of a movie, sexual expression is foisted on half-wit hicks; the sexual feeling that
might have existed between Burt Reynolds and Jon Voight is thus transposed to
characters who are obviously perverts, unmistakable social misfits. More sensitive
than the other American films depicting nonphysical male "romance," *Midnight
Cowboy* yet contains the suggestion that sex between Joe and Ratso would be an

203

outrage on their masculinity. And behind that notion is the filmmakers' clear belief that the mass public was not ready in 1969 (is it now?) to accept a male love story in the full sense.

Midnight Cowboy went further than any studio film had gone before in portraying a male friendship—but it didn't go far enough. Sweetening the pill, the film made it easy for the general public to accept the legitimacy of the poor guys' feelings for each other. Both characters are presented as so forlorn and pitiable, so basically decent despite their hapless existences—and they're so persuasively and appealingly played by Dustin Hoffman and Jon Voight—that it's easy to like them and even to accept them at the same time that the movie asks us to condescend to them. Bypassing any suggestion of deviation, the movie turns a male love story into an audience-pleasing sentimental weepie that's good for as many tears as *Love Story*. Because it soothes a mass sensibility rather than challenging audience preconceptions, *Midnight Cowboy* is finally an agreeable movie, humane, compassionate, cathartic even—but not totally honest. It gives the audience what it can handle, and no more.

For all its comparative frankness, the movie is as protective and as posed in its depiction of 42nd Street and hippie culture as in its treatment of homosexuality. For all its groundbreaking hard-headedness, Schlesinger's tour of the city's low life has decidedly false notes. The cowboy hustlers lounging seductively against the movie posters are too neat, their stances too posed; reality is being rearranged for picturesque effect. The madwoman in the grim cafeteria is also too orchestrated an effect, as is the drunk sprawled in front of Tiffany's. The women on the bus at the end, preoccupied with their hair and their eye make-up even in the presence of death, are also a too blatant touch. A foreigner, Schlesinger works overtime trying to capture American callousness.

The biggest stylistic blunder is the director's handling of the hip psychedelic party. The freaks seem paraded, placed on display, to give the folks in Kansas a glimpse of big city dissipation. Oddly enough, the presence of Viva, who comes from Warhol's stable and who is, presumably, the real thing, emphasizes the artifice of the movie's strictly Hollywood style version of Warholian decadence. Viva is clearly uncomfortable; an alien presence, she remains detached, as if to say that this is all a masquerade, a put-on, for the folks back home.

Fast, impersonal sex, pot, psychedelic visions—the film tries to capture the freaky Warhol world by means of quick editing and garish color. The result is merely visual chic, already outdated by 1969. It's an outsider's view of the East Village sex and drug scene—it's *The New York Times* rather than *Rolling Stone* that's doing the story. Even so, the psychedelic light show that Schlesinger offers in place of a deeper and truer delineation of the late sixties freak scene was undoubtedly an introduction for the mass public.

Along with the country, Schlesinger matured. A scant three years after *Mid-*

Voight with Sylvia Miles.

Brenda Vaccaro and Voight.

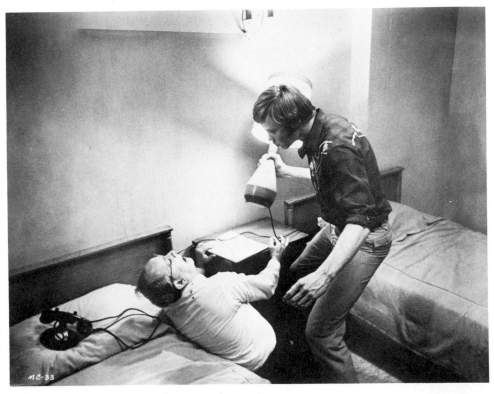

Joe Buck reacts violently to the aging conventioneer who attempts to seduce him.

night Cowboy, he dealt openly with the forbidden subject; Sunday, Bloody Sunday is the most humane and sensitive treatment yet of homosexuality in the movies. A mature man and a mature woman share a young bisexual male. The male love relationship is presented directly; the men kiss, they speak frankly about their feelings for each other. There are no secrets—the rivals know about each other's existence. The doctor isn't a stereotype; if anything, he's the equivalent of the Sidney Poitier character in Guess Who's Coming to Dinner?—a representative of a minority group who's the best possible spokesman for his people. Like Poitier, Peter Finch is a man of great dignity and achievement. He's so unfailingly sensitive and articulate, in fact, so completely free of stereotype, that audiences felt that he's too good for his rather callow young lover, just as viewers felt Poitier was far superior to the innocuous white girl he wanted to marry.

The homosexual milieu in Sunday, Bloody Sunday exists side by side with straight society. Peter Finch's heartaches are no different in kind or degree from those of Glenda Jackson. Being gay in this movie doesn't mean being hysterical or suicidal (like the campy Boys in the Band); it doesn't mean inevitable isolation, though perhaps, the film suggests, it requires greater compromise and flexibility.

A more sober view of the gay world than Midnight Cowboy, Sunday, Bloody Sunday is made in a mature style. Schlesinger avoids the hectic intercutting, the razzle-dazzle montage, that gives Midnight Cowboy a slick, disfiguring facade. Perhaps because he was uneasy with some of the undertones of Herlihy's material, Schlesinger relied on visual flash that obscures the story line and character motivation, especially in the jumbled flashbacks. Taking homosexuality out of the slums, Sunday, Bloody Sunday shows greater confidence and control. The director doesn't need to hide behind a gimmicky, elliptical style. He tells his story in an altogether unadorned manner, and the lean, taut technique is the perfect medium for Penelope Gilliatt's no-nonsense screenplay. Here, Schlesinger has made the kind of movie that can change people's minds; the film instructs and improves as it entertains.

Sunday, Bloody Sunday is the breakthrough, landmark movie that Midnight Cowboy threatens to be and never quite is. It's true, though, that audiences responded more animatedly to the earlier movie, although, finally, it isn't as probing or as humane as Gilliatt's study. People with no particular interest in the subject were deeply drawn to Midnight Cowboy's two protagonists, identifying with the characters' loneliness, their touching, childlike devotion to each other, their sad, brave attempts to fight the city, their romantic dream of escape to the Florida sun and a life that would give the warmth and the dignity that the northern jungle so mercilessly denied. Dustin Hoffman, as the tubercular, dopey, failed con man, and Jon Voight, as the big, dumb, good-natured kid from the provinces, are matchless. The work of true actors submerging their own personalities into those of their characters, their performances are surely two of the most moving in the history of American films. Their humanity gives the movie its surprisingly universal appeal and helps to thwart possible audience phobia. Through the performances of Hoffman and Voight, the movie signals its audience that the story is about real people like you and me rather than an account of two unsavory homosexuals.

Midnight Cowboy cleans up and tones down its John Rechy–*City of Night* milieu. Instead of a hustler driven compulsively to impersonal sex, we're offered a scared naive cowboy who craves affection and friendship. As a portrayal of a part of the gay subculture, Schlesinger's is obviously an easier vision to take than Rechy's, but the movie finally seems evasive on the always loaded and troublesome subject of American notions of masculinity.

A movie with terrific audience empathy, *Midnight Cowboy* deservedly won the Academy Award for Best Picture of the Year. But perhaps it would not have been so wildly loved if it had fully explored all the implications of its material.

Jack Nicholson, Candice Bergen, and Arthur Garfunkel in *Carnal Knowledge*.

12.

Carnal Knowledge

RICHARD McGUINNESS

ULES FEIFFER, who wrote the script for Mike Nichols's 1971 film *Carnal Knowledge*, has said that he meant it as a sexual history of his own generation, a generation in which men of all political and ethical stripes shared some complicity in the Playboy Bunny aesthetic. To show the immorality, as well as the sheer unworkability of the sexual expectations and exploitation of those times, Feiffer and Nichols included highly selected scenes from the lives of the two American male heroes, from their college years in the late forties through the beginning of their middle age in the late sixties. All of this is presented from so elevated and respectably "artistic" a viewpoint, however, that one would have expected few complaints about it. Surprisingly, following rumored pre-issue studio doubts about it, *Carnal Knowledge* opened to a good deal of suspicious and hostile reaction from the public.

One sort of reaction came from sophisticated film-goers who honestly thought the male sexual behavior in the film was so selectively chosen as to make the men two-dimensional and overly obsessed with "tits" and such. The way that the dialogue rings true seemed to make it all the more necessary for this part of the public to put the film down.

Missed by them, however, was the film's strong moral slant on its characters. Though the terse selection of damning material might well be said to be distorted, it is distorted for the most exemplary of ends. In isolating the characters from all cultural context and support for their childish behavior toward the opposite sex, the film emphasizes their culpability toward women, passing a judgment on them that leaves no room for any alibi that "everybody else was acting—or wanted to act—that way."

The strangest bedfellow for these more sophisticated complaints was the decision of a local censorship board in Albany, Georgia, to ban *Carnal Knowledge* outright for "lewdness" under the 1973 Supreme Court obscenity ruling. The high-court ruling, which seemed to give each locality's censors the power to decide for themselves what constitutes obscenity, seemed also potentially to mangle the chances for nationwide distribution of many Hollywood products. Although the Albany banning of *Carnal Knowledge* was eventually reversed by the Supreme Court, many film organizations have joined forces and are appealing for further clarification of the obscenity ruling.

One can easily speculate about the superficial reasons for anyone's banning *Carnal Knowledge* and come up with isolated items like the title, which makes it sound like a porno flick, and the naive, mostly verbal explicitness (plus, one expects, such essentially nonerotic details as the first on-screen unsheathing of a condom in a major American movie). These things were perhaps enough to create visions for the censors of Hollywood turning out high-class exploitation products ever after. However, primitive reactions often have some truth in them, and part of the Georgians' adverse response to this moral and dour view of sexuality from New York City may have been the instinctive perception that the film, in essential ways, has a peculiarly American odor of obscenity about it; that is, it flirts deliberately with areas that until the last few years were unmentionable except among men in private. But again, Nichols-Feiffer have highly moral reasons: the film promotes the idea that it is in the unmentionable, censorable areas of life that humanity's worst impulses are liable to flourish. In that light, the repressive Georgia decision is particularly lamentable.

The unhealthy, backroom-sex mentality and its function in male heterosexual relationships are explored in unprecedented though antiseptic detail here through the life-long friendship between the two main characters—Sandy, played by Arthur Garfunkel, and Jonathan, by Jack Nicholson. Though they are different in essential ways, the tie between them is reinforced over the years by their ritualistic advice-giving and commiseration in sexual matters. Sandy is prone to relationships with women in which affection and equal understanding are supposed to play a large part, while Jonathan seems more advanced and adult by American standards because he eschews his friend's soft-headed idealism and instead concentrates without distraction on more down-to-earth sexual maneuvering. But though they are opposites in many ways, they are still bound together by their shared sexual mythology. Jonathan is the active purveyor of the ideal of the sexual hunt, while Sandy accepts it and distorts it in his own schmucky way.

Jonathan's unspecified New York-style profession seems to be something like an investment analyst, but throughout the film his appearance remains that of a concupiscent Midwesterner—a traveling salesman—and he perpetually pollutes Sandy's sedate, thoughtful nature (Sandy becomes a doctor) with his own search for excitement. Eventually, one can't help noticing that Jonathan's relationship with Sandy resembles that which the media—and American culture generally —have to the American male: Jonathan is the serpentlike advocate of idealized sex, and manipulates this mirage of carnal adventuring as a way of selling himself and making Sandy dependent on him.

To show how unworkable is the sexual hunt mentality when practiced in the real world, Nichols uses the sort of film technique—coldly shot scenes with few cuts—that suggests the all-seeing eye of the psychiatrist. Many of the scenes are composed entirely of a single shot, and characters are constrained and edgy within an unchanging frame. This technique has sophisticated visual antecedents in Andy Warhol movies and the formal, comic-strip constrictions of a Jules Feiffer cartoon. However, the profoundest source for *Carnal Knowledge's* stiff, chilly camera is the quasi-sexual exploitation movie of yesteryear; but instead of our being trapped with two flatly nonperforming actors, *Carnal Knowledge's* pseudo-uninventive technique cages us for long periods with the horny, forlorn characters and their self-defeating behavior.

In a one-shot scene characterized by particular technical meagerness, Sandy and Susan, played sensibly and warmly by Candice Bergen, are standing in a stylized grove of a thousand or so skinny trees. Chastely dressed, they face one another and move very little. Slow-moving, somewhat-considerate Sandy wants to put his hand on Susan's breast (mostly in order to have something substantive to report back to college roommate Jonathan), and the dialogue revolves almost entirely about this problem. While the scene evinces the old-time exploitation movie's stingy reluctance to satisfy one's high sexual expectations of it, the Feiffer dialogue, filled with telling barbs at male self-deception, monopolizes our attention.

It is in these early scenes that the characters have the most mannered and self-conscious words to speak; but the verbal style works, suggesting collegians of an earlier era trying desperately to be honest while unconsciously persisting in selfish behavior ("Why are you doing it, then?" she asks in reference to his hand on her breast. "Because it's what I should be doing at this stage in our relationship," he answers guilelessly, meaning, too, that Jonathan will scorn him if he returns to the dorm with nothing to tell).

Even though the dialogue is funny, it is also too dry and concise to leave much room for belief in the reality of the characters; therefore, the sex—the explicitness of the hand on the breast—is the only element of the scene that actually unifies it or gives it any juice. Not much juice, really, just enough to keep the crowd's attention from wandering. Here, as in the rest of the movie, the sex isn't really sexual. Like the characters, it is treated clinically, either as an academic topic for cinematic discussion or for dramatic emphasis. Used in such a calculating and detached way, the sex, perversely, tends to come across, if not as pornography, then as a sure indication that this is a movie with its mind in the gutter; otherwise, why would the chaste and antiseptic handling be necessary? The same kid-gloves treatment dominated in thirties and forties movies with such hot subjects as white slavery and teenage prostitution.

Adding to the film's feeling of antiseptic sleaziness, is the device in the college scenes where the older actors are obviously impersonating innocent types much younger than themselves. This gives the naive self-deceptions of the college kids the feeling of older corruption and, indeed, suggests a subjective sense of how the characters are experiencing their first sex: with the assumption that corruption is a definitive byproduct of sexual experience. Sex wouldn't be sex without it.

Consistent with the amoral, male-supremacist sensibility *Carnal Knowledge* treats, the script is brutally elliptical in its treatment of its women. For instance, though Susan is Sandy's wife for a good part of the film, her actual role in the movie ends with the college years, as if her only real importance to Jonathan and Sandy had been as a sexual experimental animal. The effect of her disappearance after all the scenes in which Mike Nichols had directed her so sensitively is one of cruelty and unfairness to her, almost akin to Janet Leigh's abrupt exit in *Psycho*. There the dual sides of Norman Bates's personality played cat and mouse with the woman until she was killed; here, after navigating for a while the perilous Scylla-and-Charybdis narrows between sexy, egotistical Jonathan and thoughtful, dull Sandy, Susan ends up dead, too, having ceased, from the male genital viewpoint, to be of any account.

There is an important sense, though, in which Susan lives on. Characteristic of Feiffer's best creations, she is both highly individualized while at the same time managing to attain the status of a universal type, in this case, the Whole Woman; and as a whole woman, she isn't allowed very long in the male universe. Therefore, out of some sort of spiritual mitosis connected with survival, she splits neatly into the two oppressed archetypes encountered later in the film—Ann-Margret's cowlike sex-object, who controls by being passive; and Cynthia O'Neal's vigilant professional woman, who frankly needs men for support and sex while asserting her conditions and rights in every situation. The Woman is going to be around for a long time, these two types seem to say, and if you don't want her to be whole, men, then you'll have to cope with the distortions created by your narrow sexual use of her.

Despite their psychic depredations on women, though, the men in *Carnal Knowledge* are tolerable because their sexually manipulative behavior stems so plainly from feelings of powerlessness. It is sad and amusing that no matter how badly their relationships with women are going, Jonathan and Sandy can always retire to the kitchen for more tired tit-talk; and as they get older, this sort of reversion to boyhood bonds becomes an increasingly painful admission of their failure in pursuing sexual mirages.

211

Further, and partly as a consequence of their being well-mannered and so-phisticated New Yorkers, no matter how unfortunate Jonathan's influence seems to be and no matter how self-satisfied and epigrammatic the acrimony he expresses about women in private to Sandy, he is constitutionally incapable of being directly mean, violent, or vengeful to them. In nonfucking situations, he even promotes a kind of pragmatic camaraderie with his bedmates.

In his relationship with Bobbie, the ideal sex-object played overweight and increasingly passive by Ann-Margret, we get some idea of his inhibitions about expressing hostility to women directly. At the beginning of their affair, he and Bobbie act like sophisticates, aging kids who know how to enjoy themselves with-out guilt. Jonathan is even able to report to Sandy that before the Bobbie thing, he had begun to have trouble staying hard; but now, with her, he finds sex just the way it used to be. Without warning, though, she begins to grow passive and miserable. She wants to get married, and Jonathan, having admitted that he wants to hold onto Bobbie at any cost as the price of a continued erection, allows her to pursue institutional channels for her passivity—marriage and, presumably, babies.

His difficulties in expressing his loathing for her nonfucking instincts are exposed in an earlier scene in which she has just pressured him about marriage again. Cross-cutting, so rarely used by Nichols in *Carnal Knowledge*'s dialogue scenes, here gives his wildly indirect expression of frustration at her the feeling of a tempest in a teapot. In literally half the shots, he is strictly isolated with his own feelings, as if he has a stage all to himself. Jonathan rages, but he doesn't hit or hurt her. He gets into side issues involving her sleeping, her inertia, her not clean-ing up, but his attack is not to the point somehow. And the reason has much to do with the fact that Jonathan is a liberal.

He is a gallant and a liberal and has rejected the obvious male-brute role; but his need for Bobbie to be a sex-object is not lessened; therefore, out of pity for him and in appreciation for his graciously having given up caveman rights over her, maternal Bobbie is expected tactfully to recognize his sexual needs and *make herself* powerless and a sex-object.

The scene ends when Jonathan, in sheer frustration at Bobbie's horribly un-feeling suggestion that they trade in their love nest for marriage, throws the un-made sheets up in the air and they fall back on his head; but being part of the chilly Nichols vision, the moment isn't very funny. Neither, on the contrary, has the scene come close to tragedy. As in the rest of the film, Jonathan's self-deceiv-ing timorousness has avoided tragic implications and consequences. Though he spends the entire movie talking to his fellow like a sexist pig, so to speak, when he is in the presence of women, Jonathan goes around in the perpetual spiritual stoop of the well-meaning liberal.

Just as it's hard to feel cleansed by any of Jonathan's confused self-assertions, it would also be pretty hard, even for people in Georgia, to get off on the sex-

Garfunkel and Bergen.

Ann-Margret and Nicholson.

Garfunkel and new girlfriend Carol Kane
watch Jonathan's slide show.

object Ann-Margret plays here. The film is so bent on giving us uncomfortable perceptions of this distorted woman that at times we almost feel our noses obscenely rubbed in Nichols's directorial perceptions. In Bobbie's first scene, she is sitting at a revolving nightclub table having her first date with Jonathan; she has an impish look of fun on her womanly face, and her breasts are stuffed so tightly into her lowcut dress that a disconcerting vein—like some needful vulnerability—stands out on one of them. Later that night, when Jonathan buries his face in her still needfully constrained breasts, she stands there passively, without touching him, yet accepting in a motherly way his desire for her mammaries. It is a startling, sobering regression for both of them from the tired, smart pre-sex repartee they had exchanged in the cab.

Much later in their relationship, after a long-winded Warhol-type shot of her, thinking, Bobbie suggests the idea of their shacking up together. Jonathan tries to avoid the question while still giving Mama an answer that will satisfy her. Disgusted with his evasiveness, Bobbie calls him a "prick" in the tiny, sex-object voice so well-cultivated by Ann-Margret. As with the vein on her breast, a feeling of bad taste, even obscenity, comes not from the vulgar word but from our sense of her unnaturally inadequate range of expression. Once only, after sex, does Bobbie have the full-blown laughter of a woman. Otherwise, lust, sorrow, misery, and expectations of joy all seem necessarily to be filtered through the most cruel and unusual of self-limitations.

The film's cynicism is total, however, for it also assiduously puts down the women and world of Jonathan's better half, Sandy. Though the Nichols-Feiffer view of him is not as acerbic as toward Jonathan—it is at times almost gentle—we get the feeling that he, too, in his unassuming way, is also muffing life. In his search for wife or mistress with whom he can be equal after leaving Susan, he connects with a hatchet-faced professional Cindy, with whom he eventually admits getting little pleasure; and at the end of the film, when it is the late sixties and he has grown paunchy, Sandy ends up with someone he considers truly "real": a painted, pointy-faced waif from the Village. She, too, seems to be more of a poorly fabricated approximation of some badly worked-out ideal—even a fetish object (she is old enough to be Sandy's daughter, Jonathan points out helpfully)—than someone with whom he could enjoy sex or life.

But the filmmakers' objectivity toward Sandy seems more the result of their self-conscious impartiality, a kind of artistic reverse "equal-time" policy toward the opposite aspects of male sexuality, than it does a convincing condemnation of the equal-and-loving sort of human relationship. The real cause of Sandy's caricature relationships with women seems to be less Sandy than, again, Jonathan, the instigator of sexual dissatisfaction, the proponent of the kind of sex—carnal knowledge, in fact—extraneous to the individuality of the sex partners and which is sought for its own sake. With Jonathan around all the time, it is impossible for

Sandy to forget that his sexual needs are perhaps not fulfilled, or to enter deeply and unselfconsciously into the kinds of relationships he prefers. One wishes throughout *Carnal Knowledge* that Sandy would stop seeing Jonathan and work things out for himself, but he never does.

This is one of the lessons of the film, though—that Jonathan and Sandy are inseparable, two sides of the same personality: the American—or human—male (again, the Feiffer stylization supports this kind of generality). It is as if, the film seems to instruct, humanitarian love must always be tied to and corrupted by the carnal, and carnal love must in turn ever be frustrated by the humanitarian-liberal.

Though the Biblical phrasing of the title does encourage speculation at these lofty levels, the film's moral vision is most believable when, consistent with Feiffer's earlier cited comment, it seems to apply to a particular generation of Americans, a generation oppressed and oppressing within the framework of unique societal conditions. In this context, the unprecedentedly vicious analysis of sex role playing in *Carnal Knowledge* can serve as a negative model against which succeeding generations can test themselves. It would be less helpful—and, indeed, true—to apply to human, or male, sexuality as a whole the shriveling judgment that the film passes.

13

Deep Throat: Hard to Swallow

ELLEN WILLIS

*I*T GETS harder and harder to find someone who will say a good word for pornography. Angry feminists, chagrined liberals, Henry Miller and Pauline Réage fans, all agree that this is not what we meant, not what we meant at all, while the legions who never wanted to let the genie out of the bottle in the first place feel both outraged and vindicated. Die-hard (so to speak) porn liberationists like Al Goldstein of *Screw* are embarrassments to what is left of the hip subculture that spawned them—as out of date as skirts up to the thighs or inspirational speeches hailing groupies as the vanguard of the cultural revolution. Yet in spite of this ecumenical disapproval, pornography may well be the characteristic mass art form of this decade. What could be a better icon of the Nixon years than a fiftyish, balding businessman in suit and tie, briefcase on lap, hands chastely folded over briefcase (I checked), watching with solemn absorption a pair of larger-than-life genitals copulating in close-up to the strains of—was it really "Stars and Stripes Forever," or am I making that up?

The ironies may be painful, but they are hardly surprising. The revolt against Victorian morality has always had its left and right wings. On the one hand it has been part of a continuing historical process, the economic and social emancipation of women; more narrowly, it has both reflected and facilitated the shift from a production-centered (hence austere) to a consumption-centered (and hedonistic) capitalism. At this point the feminist version of the sexual revolution has been incorporated into the broader program of the women's movement, while the consumerist version has ended up on 42nd Street, which is as American as cherry pie and as masculine as chewing tobacco.

For men, the most obvious drawback of traditional morality was the sexual

216

filth
indecency
obscenity
smut

Sexuality
in the Movies

scarcity—actual and psychic— created by the enforced abstinence of women and the taboo on public acknowledgment of sexuality. Sex was an illicit commodity, and whether or not a sexual transaction involved money, its price almost always included hypocrisy; the "respectable" man who consorted with prostitutes and collected pornography, the adolescent boy who seduced "nice girls" with phony declarations of love (or tried desperately to seduce them), the husband who secretly wished his wife would act like his fantasies of a whore, all paid in the same coin. Men have typically defined sexual liberation as freedom from these black market conditions: the liberated woman is free to be available; the liberated man is free to reject false gentility and euphemistic romanticism and express his erotic fantasies frankly and openly; by extension, the liberated entrepreneur is free to cater to those fantasies on a mass scale.

Understandably, women are not thrilled with this connection of sexual freedom. In a misogynist culture where male sexuality tends to be confused with dominance and corrupted by overt or covert sadism—read any one of the endless spew of male confessional novels that have come out of the closet (or the bathroom) since Portnoy's notorious liver-fuck—its potential is frightening. Nor have men allowed themselves or each other to push their "liberation" to its logical extreme (that is, fascism). The sexual revolution has simply institutionalized a more advanced form of hypocrisy: instead of saying one thing and doing another, the game is to say and do the same thing but feel another, or not feel at all. Of course this is no news. Everybody knows it—"everybody" being middle-class intellectuals and bohemians and their feminist wives and girl friends. Which is exactly what's so embarrassing about pornography. As an ideology the fuck-it-and-suck-it phase of the sexual revolution may be passé; as a mentality it is nonetheless big business.

Like all popular culture, pornography is shaped by its social setting, and the relaxation of the obscenity laws has not only brought it out in the open but has inspired new genres, chief of which is the X-rated movie. Partly because of the logistics of movie-going, which is a communal rather than a private experience, and partly because the movie industry has only recently thrown off censorship of the crudest and most anachronistic sort, porn movies have retained an air of semi-respectability, fuzzing the line between liberated art and out-and-out smut. They turn up at art houses, where they are known as "erotic films"; they occasionally get reviewed; in time of need a stray professor or two can be induced to testify to their redeeming social value. If there is such a thing as establishment porn, these movies are it. They apotheosize the middle-American swinger's ethic: sex is impersonal recreation, neither sacred nor dangerous; above all, it has no necessary connection to any human emotion, even the most elemental lust, frustration, or fulfillment.

While pornography has never been known for its emotional subtlety, this

217

ultradeadpan style is distinctively contemporary; watching a "documentary" history of stag films that came out some time ago, I was struck by the difference between the earliest clips, which were amusingly, whimsically naughty, and later sequences, which contained progressively less warmth and humor and more mechanical sex. Traditional pornographers reveled in the breaking of taboos, the liberation of perverse and antisocial impulses. Today's porn is based on the conceit that taboos are outdated, that the sexual revolution has made us free and innocent —a fiction that can be maintained, even for the time span of a movie, only at the cost of an aggressive assault on all feeling.

Since the image on the screen is so inescapably *there*, imposing strict limits on the spectator's imagination, film is an ideal medium for this assault. Not only do most porn movies fail to build tension or portray people and situations in a way that might involve the viewer; they use a variety of techniques to actively discourage involvement. Clinical close-ups of sexual acts and organs, reminiscent of the Brobdingnagians, are one such ploy; a Brechtian disjunction between visual image and soundtrack is another. The first commercial porn movies often presented themselves as documentaries about sex education, the history of sexual mores, pornographic film making, and so on—a device that had an important formal function as well as the obvious legal one. Narrators' pedantic voices would superimpose themselves on orgy scenes, calling our attention to the grainy texture of the film; blank-faced young girls would explain in a bored monotone why they acted in porn movies—"It's the bread, really, . . . I guess I dig it sometimes. . . . It's hard work, actually"—while in the background, but still on camera, another actress fellated a colleague with the businesslike competence of a plaster-caster.

These days the narrators' voices have mostly given way to music, which generally sounds as if it were composed by a Chamber of Commerce committee just returned from a performance of *Hair*. Sexual partners in porn movies rarely make noise, and I've never heard one talk sex talk; most often they perform silently, like fish in an aquarium. When there is dialogue, its purpose is generally to break the mood rather than heighten it. In the opening scene of *Deep Throat*, for instance, the heroine enters her apartment and is cheerfully greeted by her roommate, who just happens to have a man's head buried in her crotch. He looks up to see what's happening, but roomie firmly guides his head back down to business. Then she lights a cigarette and says, "Mind if I smoke while you're eating?"—a line that just might be the definitive statement of the porn aesthetic.

Throat is the first porn movie to become a cultural event. Besides being a huge moneymaker, it has been widely acclaimed as an artistic triumph. Allegedly, *Throat* is "different," the porn movie everybody has been waiting for—the one that has a plot and characters and humor and taste and really gets it on. It has been playing at "legitimate" movie theaters around the country, and in New York, during its run at the New Mature World, the *Post* reported that lots of women

218

were going to see it, with other women, yet—an unprecedented phenomenon. When the managers of the World were charged with obscenity, Arthur Knight, film critic for *Saturday Review* and professor at the University of Southern California, testified for the defense, praising the movie for its concern with female sexual gratification and its socially valuable message that "the so-called missionary position is not the only way to have sex." He also liked the photography.

There is something decidedly creepy about all this fanfare, which—Professor Knight's remark about the missionary position excepted—has no discernible relation to what's actually on the screen. I suspect a lot of ambivalent libertarians of hedging by badmouthing porn in general while rallying around an "exception," but that they should pick *Throat* for the honor suggests that they have been missing the point all along.

True, *Throat* has certain peculiarities that distinguish it from the average porn flick. It may not have a plot, but it should get some sort of award for the most grotesque premise: the heroine's clitoris is in her throat. It's not hard to figure out how *that* fantasy got started; needless to say, I couldn't identify with it, though I did feel like gagging during a couple of scenes. Or am I being too literal? Is *Throat* really a comment on the psychology of oral fixation? (It does have one of those socially redeeming blurbs at the beginning, about Freud's stages of psychosexual development and the use of suggestion in curing sexual hangups.) Is that what the bit with the doctor blowing bubbles is all about? And near the end, when Linda Lovelace shaves her pubic hair to the accompaniment of science fiction music and the Old Spice theme, does that represent a ceremonial transition to the genital stage?

Linda is fresh-and-freckle-faced, comes on like a cut-rate Viva, sighs, "There must be more to life than screwing around," gets genuinely upset about her predicament, and hangs around for the entire movie, all of which I guess makes her a character, at least by porno standards. *Throat* also boasts lots of moronic jokes. (Linda to doctor, who is making light of her problem: "Suppose your balls were in your ear!" Doctor: "Then I could hear myself coming.") What all this means is that in ten years I may dig *Throat* as an artifact, but for now I find it witless, exploitative, and about as erotic as a tonsillectomy.

The last point is really the crucial one: movies like *Throat* don't turn me on, which is, after all, what they are supposed to do. On the contrary, I find them a sexual depressant, partly because they are so unimaginative, partly because they objectify women's bodies and pay little attention to men's—American men are *so* touchy about you-know-what—but mostly because they deliberately and perversely destroy any semblance of an atmosphere in which my sexual fantasies could flourish. Furthermore, I truly can't comprehend why they excite other people—a failure of empathy that leads straight into the thickets of sexual polarization. I know there are men who don't respond to these movies, and I'm sure it's possible to find a woman here or there who does. Still, the fact remains that their audience is overwhelmingly male—the *Post* notwithstanding, I counted exactly three other women in the *Throat* audience, all of them with men—and that most men seem to be susceptible even when, like the letter writer who complained to the *Times* that *Teenage Fantasies* was erotically arousing but spiritually degrading, they hate themselves afterward.

My attempts to interrogate male friends on the subject have never elicited very satisfying answers ("I don't know . . . it's sexy, that's all. . . . I like cunts"). I suppose I shouldn't be so mystified; "everybody" knows that men divorce sex from emotion because they can't afford to face their real emotions about women. Nevertheless it baffles and angers me that men can get off on all those bodies methodically humping away, their faces sweatless and passionless, their consummation so automatic they never get a chance to experience desire.

I've often had fantasies about making my own porn epic for a female audience, a movie that would go beyond gymnastics to explore the psychological and sensual nuances of sex—the power of sexual tension and suspense; the conflict of need and guilt, attraction and fear; the texture of skin; the minutiae of gesture and touch and facial expression that can create an intense erotic ambiance with a minimum of action. Not incidentally, the few porn movies I've seen that deal with these aspects of the erotic were made by gay men. A classic underground example is Jean Genet's *Un Chant d'Amour,* an unbearably romantic and arty movie that nevertheless had a strong effect on me when I saw it in 1964. Aside from a few masturbation scenes, the sex is almost entirely in the minds of the characters (prison inmates and a guard); the overriding mood is frustration. Yet it is exactly this thwarted energy that makes *Chant* exciting. It works on two levels: it is serious anguish, and it is also a tease. Either way, Genet makes the point that sex is a head trip as much as it is anything else. Similarly, in Wakefield Poole's currently popular *Bijou* the coming-out process is presented—again too romantically for my taste—as a kind of psychedelic theater in which the hero discovers his various sexual personalities and accepts the male body in all its aspects.

Women have no pornographic tradition, and at the moment it doesn't look as if anybody's about to start one. The New York Erotic Film Festival recently scheduled an evening of movies by women, but they turned out to be more about self than about sex, which pretty much sums up a lot of women's priorities right now. I enjoyed them; in the middle of the whole dying culture of swingerism they radiated life. Still, I was disappointed that no one had made my movie. Maybe next year.

14

Last Tango in Paris: The Skull Beneath the Skin Flick

JACK FISHER

Marlon Brando and Maria Schneider in the tango palace.

CRITICS and commentators have hailed (or damned) the erotic elements of *Last Tango in Paris* so strongly that film audiences, unused to fine distinctions between "erotic" and "pornographic," may be understandably disappointed to discover that the film is not essentially about sex. To expect to see Brando constantly scoring is to be unprepared for five-sixths of the movie's running time and for the rather mysterious relationships between its many characters, who would be unnecessary in even a medium hard-core film.

True, Bernado Bertolucci has captured the aura of human sexuality very well in those parts of the film where he set out to do so; but *Last Tango* is chiefly concerned with the attempts of a number of people to alter the reality of their lives and the lives of those around them. Their attempts fail, and their failures lead them to confront the presence of death in their lives.

These attempts to make changes in their lives and the recognition of death as an aftermath of love tie the film firmly to the tradition of "Grand Romance." As in other Romantic works, the first meeting of the lovers is marked by "bolt of lightning" recognition. Their social situation is hostile to their alliance. Both are committed to somebody else (Paul is committed to a dead woman, which is perfectly typical of the Romantic syndrome—see the Brontes). They occupy a never-never place where their love can be consummated away from the world. Their affair is the "too perfect to last" variety. In fact, with a few important differences, *Last Tango* is a variation of *Camille* or *One Way Passage.*

The most important difference is the amount of overt sexuality—very little for a skin flick but a lot for a Romance. Equally important is the number of people involved. No mere two- or three-sided affair, the action is expanded to include

221

Marcel and, as a living presence, Rosa, in addition to Paul, Jeanne, and Tom. In order to understand what is going on, we must keep in mind this five-sided rela tionship: while going with Tom, Jeanne becomes involved with Paul, who was married to Rosa, who was sleeping with Marcel. The pattern then has Paul as the connecting link between two sets of people, each of whom has a further and complicating relationship with someone else. The role of Paul is central to the entire schemata. We can begin by examining how he relates to Jeanne and to his dead wife Rosa—two women who are in many ways similar.

There is no question of Paul's worldly or archetypal identity. He is the ani- mal, the stud, the Heathcliff-like demon lover. He represents, as he says of himself, "the best fucking around." Furthermore, he is a man of some mystery, whose background includes exotic places and romantic occupations—correspondent in Tokyo, revolutionary in South America. He is for Jeanne (and Rosa) the Romantic Stranger with awesome sexual power.

He is also a rather banal, irresponsible bum who, when he isn't practicing his craft of humping, seems rather childlike, childish, and dull. Quiet, he projects a dark and somewhat dangerous quality. But he is not bright enough to stay quiet all the time and when he talks, even in Brando's seductive tones, there emerges an adolescent masking his lack of maturity in virility. The two sides of Paul, suggested at the beginning by Francis Bacon's title pictures, are the cause of all the trouble for everybody.

When Jeanne meets Paul, she is swept off her social stances. Her relationship with the filmmaker Tom has been typically youthful and uncontrollably exuber- ant. They are raucous children together, practicing mod arts of making movies and pretending to be the people in the film. They also live a life of respectable young bourgeoisie: they go together but they don't sleep together. Paul fills in all that Tom has neglected. Jeanne is a child, but she is also a sensual woman. She has grown up in stuffy surroundings, dominated by a forbidding father. Paul provides sex, mystery, and not only domination but domination from a man almost her father's age. She responds enthusiastically but, interestingly, she does not respond completely. She goes ahead with Tom and his movie and their life. Despite Paul's gifts, she agrees to marry Tom.

The situation with Rosa was much the same. Rosa also came from a bourgeois background. When she met Paul the first time, she too succumbed to him sexually. Unlike Jeanne, she married him and the mysteries began. She took a lover, Marcel, who was very different from Paul, if not his opposite.

The repeated actions by Rosa and Jeanne suggest not only an affinity between them but a continuing deficiency in Paul. Whatever he has is not enough to keep them from hedging their commitments to him. One keeps a boy friend, the other takes one. The problem seems to be the perennial conflict between romance and reality. Paul is both demon and dullard.

Instead of resigning themselves to the problem, however, Rosa and, to a lesser extent, Jeanne try to do something about it. They begin to change the nature of reality, and they share this action with everyone else in the film. A minor character like Marcel makes a rather pedestrian attempt to alter the physical reality of his years by means of a secret chinning bar. For the major characters, the changing of reality is more obvious and more consequential and comprises the major action of the film.

Tom spends his entire film life creating a fantasy Jeanne who will conform to his own inner vision. His Jeanne will be very like Ava Gardner when she loved Mickey Rooney. This is appropriate, for Tom seems to want to be Andy Hardy when he was in love with Polly Benedict. Pursuing these changes, Tom rigs the facts of his movie. Then, confusing the real Jeanne with the creation of his ostensibly true documentary film, Tom begins to rig the facts of their real life as well. The imaginary Jeanne is quotable, Hollywood-zany alive, and despite being ultramod, she is pure. She is extravagant yet tender; hard-boiled, yet romantic. When he directs Jeanne to the point that she conforms to his vision, he proposes to her. Their marriage is to be an endless cinéma-verité, with him filming her—and thus correcting her—the rest of their lives. Jeanne is reluctant, then compliant; but when her compliance releases the buried Mickey Rooney in Tom, turning *him* into a Hollywood zany, she flees back to Paul.

For Paul, the battered survivor of a world he never imagined, the impulse to change things is just as pronounced as it is with Tom. In fact, except for extraneous details, Paul's changes are exactly like Tom's. He invents a world, he puts Jeanne into the world, and then he directs her as thoroughly as Tom has. He tells her what she can say, how she can react, what she can show. He involves her in the same kind of fictional cinéma-verité as Tom, but where Tom's film is pregenital Hollywood, Paul's "cinema" is post-permissive pornie. Where Tom's world is talk to create the illusion of emotion, Paul's world is all action to show the inadequacies of talk. Tom builds a world of Romance—the anticipation of Love. Paul builds a world of Lust—the denial of Love. They both assault Jeanne's mind and sensibilities to change her, and when Paul has created an illusion of a girl who corresponds to his vision, he proposes to her exactly as Tom has done. Of course, Paul does not propose marriage, which would be appropriate to Tom's world, but rather a kind of solemnization of their gypsy life in the apartment.

Jeanne, the object of the movie making, also wants to change things. To understand some of her motives, we must first look at Jeanne's soul sister, Rosa. They share much, these two, the dead and last loves of Paul.

Put most simply, Rosa is looking for the perfect man and, failing to find him, sets about creating him. The perfect man, as a famous woman once said, is all brains above the waist and all peasant below. We have no doubts about Paul's peasant parts, but above the waist he isn't much. He resembles another Brando

223

role, Stanley Kowalski, if he had attended a lesser Community College for a year: full of memory without understanding. Rosa, undeterred, looks further and finds Paul's complement: Marcel. She then attempts to congeal the two lovers into one —same bathrobes, same whiskey. It doesn't work very well. Marcel is meticulous, conscientious, and quasi-intellectual, but his physicality and ardor are limited. Even stimulated by Jack Daniels, he is no raving beast. After one frustrating session of "making love without passion" she leaps from the bed and begins tearing at the wall paper. At the obvious level, her action is a simple attempt at change— to make Marcel's room white like Paul's. At a deeper level, however, it is the first sign of destructive violence, the desperation which attends her inability to change the world. The men are separate, and she begins to accept it. Marcel is boring in bed, Paul is boring everywhere else. Her experiment is a failure, and in another tearing burst of violence, she slashes her throat with a stranger's razor.

Jeanne is Rosa's spiritual and social heiress, with two differences. Unlike Rosa, who had the age and experience to become the manipulator of her affairs, Jeanne is essentially manipulated at this stage. The other important difference is that Jeanne starts out with a Marcel-like partner and supplements him with Paul. She, too, is trying to build the perfect man, and naturally encounters the same problems as Rosa. But because she is young and extroverted, Jeanne's destructiveness spills over onto others rather than turning inward.

Like Rosa, Jeanne tries to organize her life by changing her surroundings. Instead of repainting a room, however, Jeanne begins tentatively by bringing a record and player to the empty apartment. By this gift she begins, one must assume from the scenes in her mother's apartment and father's house, the process of stuffing the room with object-respectability. Objects equate with stability, and the bringing of objects suggests an attempt to stabilize her relationship with Paul. Jeanne's panic when the furniture is removed not only reveals the extent of her Full-Room-Equals-Secure-Room ideas, but further links her with Rosa's panic as she began to realize the futility of change.

The action of changing reality is a constant in the film, and produces a corollary: the search of the past. This obsession with the past, which all of the characters share, is apparently an attempt to understand reality as a preface to altering it—the searching of roots for the purpose of making change meaningful.

It is surprising how many people in *Last Tango* are either actively or passively reviewing their own past or someone else's. Some of them collect the past rather neutrally—Marcel collects clippings for some unspecified job. Jeanne's mother strokes a pair of old boots and receives "strange shivers" of memory. Some search the past for explanations, as Rosa's mother ransacks her cupboards. Some collect the past for mysterious purposes never entirely explained, as Rosa collected objects left by guests—or ex-lovers. And some, like Jeanne, Tom, and

Paul and Jeanne meet in the apartment on
the Rue Jules Verne.

Paul worry memories of the past for unspecified purposes. Whatever the reason, the result is to provide us with tantalizing insights into the reality of the people searching and searched.

Characteristically, Tom, the voyeur, does not search his own past but Jeanne's. He seems to take her reality as a measure of his own—the Rooney-Gardner fantasy—and is defining himself intentionally through Jeanne. By very carefully selecting the material in her life, he is creating a reality he can assume. Like most cinéma-verité directors he is not searching for reality by the random assemblage of "facts," but is attempting to document a reality he has already decided upon. With her reality established, his, by reflection, will be established also.

Jeanne remembers her past, as she seems to do everything, in a way satisfying to her audience. She can remember her father as a God and not the racist that she criticizes Olympia for being. She can remember the piano-playing cousin for Paul, the sensualist, as her first sex partner, her fellow masturbator (a role, incidentally, that Paul will assume in the Tango Palace). She can remember the same cousin for Tom, the romantic, as a "first love" who did "beautiful playing."

As she works her way back through the past for Tom's film, she reveals herself as a residual child used to being told what to do and what to believe. She also reiterates her kinship to Rosa in the random objects she has collected and saved. What emerges from this managed past is a kind of litmus paper–doll, totally responsive, and totally unequipped for the kind of memories she will have to deal with after Paul's death.

Paul's concern with the past is a surprise, since presumably he creates his fictional world to erect a barrier against the past. Nevertheless, he spends an inordinate amount of time shuffling through his real and imagined past. It is from his memories that we begin to sense the narrow suffocating limits of his personality. From his whole life he can think of only two pleasant memories: an old man drooling in his pipe and a dog trying to catch rabbits in the tall grass. The rest is negative: drunken parents, humiliation, vagrant wanderings, sexual liaisons which begin with cowshit covered shoes and proceed only to an enlarged prostate and a "nail." (The use of this very special term for gonorrhea, and the existence of the dead wife, recall O'Neill's drummer Hickey in *The Iceman Cometh*, a play also concerned with reality and illusion and the intrusion of death.)

After understanding the complementary actions of remembering and changing, we are ready to explore the final major action in the film, the recognition of and reaction to death. In a sense this is a continuation of the discovery and changing of life reality. Death is the discovery of the unchangeable reality.

When we begin to talk of death in *Last Tango*, the five-sided pattern shrinks, because death involves sexuality and neither concerns Tom. Like his brother photographer named Tom in *Blow Up, he* is a trivial person because his life has no sense of mortality. But when *Blow Up* Tom discovers death among his shots, he at least attempts to deal with it, while *Tango* Tom comes no closer than the grave of a romanticized dog. Tom is so committed to the ersatz life of his camera that when the issues become basic ones, he hasn't the depth perceptions to confront them.

In this he is like one of the people directly involved with death. Marcel, who has many of the biases of a Tom grown middle-aged, simply shows confusion and some embarrassment at Rosa's suicide. Like other people before him who are unable to understand death and whisper of conspiracies, Marcel is suspicious, wondering if Rosa really killed herself. Beyond that he is as helpless as Tom will be.

Paul and Jeanne are the principals in the death ritual, Jeanne unknowingly, Paul intentionally. His answer to Rosa's death is to assert the only kind of life force he understands. Like the participants in rural parts of ancient Ireland who made love at the wake, Paul is screwing in honor of the corpse and as a challenge to it.

The association of death and sex is not unique to this film. Eighteenth century literature has many descriptions of orgasms as "dying" and the "little death." What is unique here is the pronounced anality of the sex and its reflection in the visual imagery of the film.

The sodomy scene in *Last Tango* is the most shocking in the film. I am sure many of the moral objections to the film originate here. If the moment existed by itself and for itself, the objections would at least be understandable. But the scene is part of an entire pattern summed up in Paul's statement about looking up the ass of death to the womb of fear. There are many bare asses in the film and each time one is shown, there is an association with death: the little boys shitting in Jeanne's "jungle" who epitomize the death of the house and the life the house provided; the showing of Paul's bare ass in the Tango palace, where the love affair has died amidst questions of his wife's death.

There are also the scenes in which the ass or reference to the ass is an emblem for some new stage of relationship, and therefore the death of the previous condition. The appearance of the dead rat on the bed and Paul's threat to save "the asshole" for Jeanne after he has eaten the rest are all part of Paul's education of Jeanne. He is teaching her that "sacred and profane are the same thing," that sex is of the body and nothing else. Reality, as being taught, consists of smells, filth, and fluids, and not the tidy definitions she has learned in her *Larousse.* The dictionary supplied descriptions and dimensions, while the teacher Paul supplies the consequences and conditions. For him, sex and shit are virtually synonymous.

This motif of "education" is very pronounced in the two anal sex scenes. In the first, the butter scene, Jeanne is being taught several lessons, only one of

227

them related to Paul's lust. She is being dominated and therefore being taught her role in their affair. This involves humiliation and pain, part of the reality of a sexual connection. And she is forced to repeat a strange catechism about the corruption of youngsters' minds by the family and by teachers. This at the moment when she is being corrupted by her teacher! Without either of them being conscious of it, she is being instructed in mortality—the nature of the flesh—which is the first step in the recognition of death.

The second scene, in which she sodomizes him, is a sort of graduation thesis. Following his declaration about the ass of death and while she inflicts pain on him, he recites a virtual catalog of degradation. In this scene death is no longer merely the implied lesson. She is now confronted, in the image of the dead pig, with the direct connection between sex and death that is in Paul's consciousness. When she has learned this, Paul is satisfied that she knows how the world is: she knows reality and has become a suitable consort for him.

With this bestial preparation and the MGM worldview she has learned from Tom, she is ready to confront the facts of Rosa's death, the death of her affair, and the death of her lover. That Jeanne reacts as she does is traceable directly to the reality she has learned.

The cinematography of the sodomy sequence is a good point to begin consideration of the way Bertolucci visualizes this myth of reality and death. After a series of clinical closeups, short shots of Jeanne, Paul applying the butter, etc., the camera dollies away to an overhead long shot that depersonalizes the action. The shot is reminiscent of the way Arthur Penn handles the death of Buck in *Bonnie and Clyde*—the combination of macro/micro shots that pinpoints the individual human emotion and then in the long shot reviews the action calmly. The ritual of man and his environment—the flesh haiku.

The close-up and dolly shot are old-fashioned techniques of film, and they are characteristic of Bertolucci's general approach in *Last Tango*. There is very little modern tricky camera work and editing: no jitter cuts, no freeze frames, or lingering lap-dissolves. Bertolucci seems to rely on impeccably composed shots; clean, efficient sequences; and authoritative editing, without mucking about with eccentricities. It is the straightforwardness of the shooting that gives the film its particular feeling and effect. Bertolucci seems both romantic and business-like, and he achieves a unique combination of voluptuousness and vérité. There is little of the brooding camera work typical of many directors today. Bertolucci is a tracker rather than a brooder—a Renoir rather than a Bergman. He has a penchant for shooting an object and then slowly panning to a person, but primarily he is a shot-sequence-cut director.

The importance of the shot cannot be exaggerated. It is the integer of attitude that not only provides what we see but forces us to see in a particular way, as the shots in the apartment will illustrate.

The problem is to represent a place that is strange, almost alien to the outside world. The place must house Paul's mad experiment with altered reality; at the same time, it has to represent a place of passion and incipient emotion. The realization by Bertolucci and his set designer captures these qualities perfectly. The place is empty but not stripped, spacious but contained, light but not blinding, used but not condemned. Then Bertolucci and his cameraman transform the physical world into an emotional attitude. Through light that is high intensity and golden, the camera moves with deliberate, almost dignified tracking. While the ratty condition of the place is openly presented, our apprehension of it is positively conditioned. Bertolucci emphasizes the light, the airiness, the size very subtly, until the place becomes not only special in itself but a marked contrast to the dark over-stuffed interiors of the hotel and of the country house.

This contrast suggests something about the natural deceptiveness of the cinematography. The filming seems to be straightforward realism, but more is being presented than realism demands. Three shots reveal strong instances of Bertolucci's expressionistic-realistic technique. The first shot involves a sign which comments on the shot. (This is a persistent technique in the film: the street sign, "Rue Jules Verne," locates the apartment house and suggests that it is a place of fantasy; the use of the life preserver marked "L'Atalante" establishes a connection with the Jean Vigo film about romance and reality.) In the shot, Paul returns to his room and finds the door open. On the door is printed "PRIVE," and inside the room Rosa's mother is ransacking Rosa's cupboards. Instantly the shot and the sign signify that at least part of the film is involved with the invasion of privacy by the outside world—the villain of all romances. A few minutes later the statement is reiterated with the shot of Paul closing the doors of the prying neighbors.

The next shot comes late in the film. Paul and Jeanne have left the Tango palace, and he is chasing her in the street. The camera dollies to an overhead long shot to reveal their separation by the street traffic—an echo of the scene in which the subway train separated Jeanne and Tom. In that scene, because Paul from the beginning had been visually associated with trains, the appearance of the train suggests Paul as the separating agent. In the street scene, the separation motif is recalled by means of the intruding outside world, specifically the mechanical outside world, the automotive equivalent of the mechanical people in the dance hall. In addition, the angle of the shot, the overhead long shot, recalls the sodomy scene and suggests a relationship between that connection and this separation.

The third shot I want to discuss is the final one in the film, in which Paul lies on the balcony to the right of the screen. The camera dollies back to reveal Jeanne

229

in the left screen. The retreating camera makes a specific comment. If there were single shots—one on him, one on her, one on him, etc.— we would understand their relationship in a cause and effect dynamic. By the dollying back to reveal the total scene, we are presented with a reproduction, with changed figures, of the red and blue title pictures. In the titles, the red left screen suggested sensuality, the blue right screen suggested pensiveness. When the pictures are recalled, Jeanne occupies the red screen and Paul the blue, with the colors as well as positions repeated. (In Visconti's *The Damned*, there is a dichotomy of red-orange and blue-grey, each color representing a whole spectrum of emotions and forces. By the end of that film the opposing colors are united into a vital death force. In *Last Tango*, the colors remain separated; and whatever meaning they have accrued remains opposed.) The most obvious meanings in the shot are that the blue is death, and the red is the sensual excuses to avoid death—which is the action of the film.

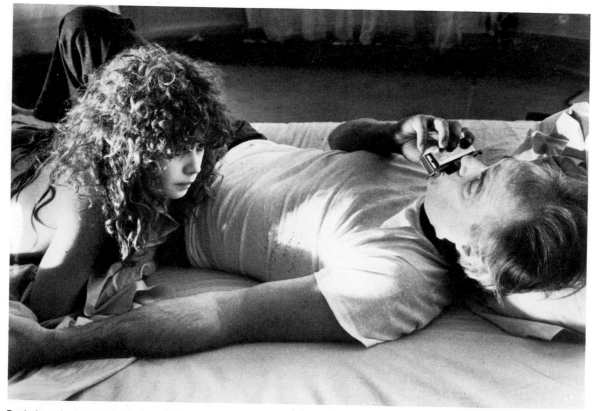

Paul plays the harmonica and recalls his childhood on a farm.

The sequence is a series of shots at one point in time and space, which maintains a consistent point of view. Bertolucci uses his sequences with remarkable efficiency. By arrangement and perfect composition of the shots within the sequence, he articulates precise aspects of his total statement. Each of the apartment sequences, for example, is different not only in story material but in the visual attitude which in turn complicates the thematic information. The accumulation of these sequences develops and refracts the original scene of sexual attraction and consummation. By packing the sequences with details, something is said about the nature of the developing relationship which is far more than a report on two people making out.

The two sequences which I want to examine briefly have the tight efficiency and burgeoning detail of the others, and also relate obviously and directly to the reality—death action. The first is really two sequences: the funeral room and the incident of the whore and her customer. In the funeral room Paul begins to talk to the corpse. As with Jeanne, he is arranging the reality of the situation to conform to his acceptance of it. He simply dismisses Rosa's death for the moment and treats her as if she were alive. The pretense goes so far that he removes her make-up because that isn't the way the living Rosa is supposed to look. There is a knock on the door in the lobby, and Paul goes downstairs after informing the corpse where he is going.

The new sequence begins with the whore and her customer at the door. The whore is a friend of Rosa's and her macabre appearance—the aged face plastered with make-up—instantly states a relationship with the made-up corpse who didn't wear make-up. The customer leaves and Paul chases him through empty, desolate streets. When Paul corners him, the man excuses himself with a story about his wife being "enough for him until she developed a disease"—again, an instant reminder of Paul's situation, which accounts in part for his violence. He punches the man and illogically calls him a faggot as an excuse for violence, in still another action of changing reality to conform to his emotional need of the moment. Paul then walks away in the early morning light which is a strange combination of the warm golds of sex and the blue whites of death. He passes a sign which says "La Bohéme." As the earlier sign shots have made comments, this sign makes a comment not only on the sequence at hand, but on the whole film. Here in the threatening dawn, a defeated man walks back to a flop house to his waxen-dead wife and her decayed friend, to explain the loss of a sale of flesh. This is the reality of La Bohéme, the romantic land of exuberant loves without responsibilities, of happy whores who never charge customers, of deaths that are beautiful and ennobling—the romantic dream which disguises (changes) a life filled with pain, confusion, exploitation, and defeat.

The other sequence, in the Tango palace, worries this same view of reality with ruthless precision and ties up the different threads of the action. The fluorescent blue-white light immediately suggests the suicide room, where Paul's other love affair died. The suggestion is reenforced by everything that happens in the sequence, when Bertolucci suddenly begins to work with unabashed expressionism. The rituals of the Tango are stiffened to a Byzantine kind of dehumanization. Social man is pictured as a precisely grotesque dance contestant. All human connection is reduced to a matter of technique. All emotion is practiced and performed.

Into this arena of created life, the two lovers drag the exhausted remains of their created love. The collision between the two creations reveals reality: the world is whirling manikins, and a bum and his bimbo haven't got a chance. The sequence concludes with a final attempt by the lovers to escape. They slump into a dark corner and defy the world by a parody of love—jacking off before they go to look for their own special razor.

Most of the statement of this sequence has been accomplished by purely cinematic means. The words are important, but we know beforehand what will be said. The important message is delivered by brilliant shots and jarring cuts, which establish a revealing montage between lovers and dancers. The result is a distillation of the real meaning of the entire film: a myth of reality and death with man disguising his mortality with practiced rituals of escape. A film, in short, that seems to be a skin flick but is really a study that probes nerves, sinews and essences.

Last Tango belongs not with the works of Russ Meyer but rather, curiously, with the works of the seventeenth century dramatist John Webster, of whom T. S. Eliot said, "Webster was much possessed by death/He saw the skull beneath the skin." What Eliot meant was not that other Elizabethan dramatists avoided death in their works but that Webster more than others, saw all actions—including his rather kinky views of sex—as a prelude to dying.

Webster was not a popular playwright. His audiences, who expected heroics and death full of purpose, were disappointed with his nihilistic slaughters. And so will many people be disappointed with Bertolucci's death flick. Even sexually liberated audiences will find small comfort in an erotic film which suggests that love, at best, is a creation to feed our evasive fantasies and that reminds us that flesh provides only a momentary respite from the knowledge we are dying.

Liv Ullmann in *Cries and Whispers*.

15.
Sexuality in Film: Reconsiderations after Seeing *Cries and Whispers*

DAVID R. SLAVITT

THE POIGNANT situation in which films are goaded on to new heights—or depths—of candor and boldness by obvious external forces, mostly the competition from television and its old movies at no cost to viewers, while the Supreme Court backs and fills and invokes capricious and restrictive "local standards," is fascinating, particularly since the whole point of the MPAA rating system was to fight local censors and vigilantes of the public morals. That rating system had grievous faults, but it worked a lot better than what we seem to have now. Until the recent decision, nobody fought very hard about an R film. *Carnal Knowledge* with its R rating was subsequently declared obscene by the Supreme Court of the State of Georgia.

Both the decision of the Georgia court and the preceding enabling decision of the United States Supreme Court are unfortunate, but neither is surprising. In fact, what they do is to fulfil in the courts and in our society at large an old Arabic belief—that any man who gazes into a vagina will go blind. All those triple-feature, 16mm split-beaver festivals have brought us to this regrettable condition.

It would be easy to blame the courts, and they are indeed entitled to their fair share of contempt and blame. But films, which is to say filmmakers and film audiences, have earned their share as well. (I've stopped here, and have reread the foregoing sentence several times, surprised at myself; it sounds like the beginning of a tirade against filth and dirt from one of those Citizens for Decent Literature screwballs. From me? I wrote that?)

Yes. And the reason is that the skin flick misses the point. It does not arouse interest or attention, or, after a while, anything else. I once watched six hours of

233

skin flicks, four at a time, projected in a huge, meaty montage on the wall of a church basement as a desensitizing experiment in a sexuality workshop I was writing about, and it *was* desensitizing. The trouble with *Last Tango in Paris* is related, I think, to the skin flick's trouble, and to the troubles of a good many contemporary novels: the study of sexuality *in isolation* is a strategic and procedural disaster. Two people in a room who don't know anything about each other and don't want to know, and Bertolucci wants us to care about them? Why should we care more than they do themselves? Why should we invest a feeling of connection they are unwilling to show to one another?

I don't mean to suggest that *Last Tango in Paris* is a skin flick, even though the box office prices try to make that dubious claim. It is a serious film, but wrong. The measure of its error is probably Ingmar Bergman's *Cries and Whispers*, which is also the best film I've seen in a couple of years. The issues it raises, moreover, are of greatest importance in any number of ways—from the legal and public to the personal and intimate. Questions of public morality finally touch, or at least ought to touch, upon questions of private morality. Mostly, of course, they don't, because any given person is likely to be himself confused about what he thinks and feels (and thinks he ought to feel) about his own sexual behavior, and a consensus of confusion is not likely to be very much clearer than any of the contributing individual muddles. *Cries and Whispers* is, among other things, a compassionate recognition of the difficulties any human being is bound to have in working out, not anything so grand as a consistent position or a coherent view, but, more modestly, a way of living, of staggering through.

Intelligently, and in great contrast with Bertolucci's pseudo-scientific atomism, Bergman gives us two sisters, Karin and Maria, who have come to their old family mansion for a death watch as their sister Agnes dwindles and dies, and he sets up between them a statement of rich simplicity about the relation between sensuality and authenticity. It is a paradigm of relational ethics in its clarity, and not only does it work in the film, it may also be true generally—that sexuality is an appetite without ethical concerns; that Maria's sexuality necessarily involves her treating other people as objects, lying to them as often as with them; and that Karin's unwillingness to say things she does not mean or to hear them said to her necessarily involves her withdrawal from the sexual arena.

The situation is nothing less than tragic, in that two competing and contradictory virtues are brought together by the death of the sister, and therefore they not only confront one another, but do so in the presence of—and in the light of—mortality. An eternal triangle, then, of love, truth, and death, and yet to describe the film this way is partly to betray it, for the arid geometry of meanings arises from acutely observed subtleties of flesh. Anyone who has seen the film will remember the mouths of the three women, as eloquent in repose as when they move in speech: the wet, full lips of Liv Ullmann (Maria), almost always slightly parted and frequently curved about an index finger or the ball of a thumb; the dry, fevered lips, cracked and swollen, of Harriet Andersson (Agnes); the severe, carefully painted, too precisely outlined lips of Ingrid Thulin (Karin) In a film full of tight head shots, in which faces virtually bulge from the screen and are held to long dissolves into flat red, such details burn themselves into the retinas in such a way as to overpower not only the desire but almost the capacity to make the abstract connections. The impact is like a blow that dulls sensation, and only in the tingle of the mind and nerves after the initial trauma has been survived do the connections and the relationships construct themselves for us.

There are, in fact, two sets of questions. The one has to do with the tension between Karin and Maria, between authenticity and sexuality. The other, related but independent, has to do with faith and sophistication, the simple faith of the servant, Anna, who can pray for the angels to protect the soul of her dead daughter (and then, wonderfully, munch an apple with a gusto that is somehow touching), and the sophistication of the parson who comes to pray over Agnes after her death, and constructs one of those conditional prayers ("If there is a God, and if he speaks our language . . .") more disturbing than comforting. These two polarities cross at Agnes, who is in pain, who suffers, gets a little better, suffers again in a scene of terrible power, and then dies. But they also connect intellectually, in that sophistication and faith are suggested as competing and contradictory virtues in a tension analogous to that between love and truth.

Again, I find myself displeased with the tone of such a formulation, which seems altogether too remote. *Cries and Whispers* is a movie of great immediacy, and the connections are entirely implicit. They are, indeed, even personal. Most of the time, biographical criticism of films is impossible because of the collective process of a movie's happening. Bergman's situation is different, because he has his repertory company of actors and his secure relationship with Svensk Filmindustri. He is, moreover, the producer as well as the director, and he wrote the screenplay. It is not wholly irrelevant, then, to cite a couple of sentences from Bergman's introduction to *Four Screenplays of Ingmar Bergman* (Simon and Schuster, 1960): "A child who is born and brought up in a vicarage acquires an early familiarity with life and death behind the scenes. Father performed funerals, marriages, baptisms, gave advice and prepared sermons. The devil was an early acquaintance, and in the child's mind there was a need to personify him. This is where my magic lantern came in. It consisted of a small metal box with a carbide lamp—I can still remember the smell of the hot metal—and colored glass slides: Red Riding Hood and the Wolf, and all the others. And the Wolf was the Devil, without horns but with a tail and a gaping red mouth, strangely real yet incomprehensible, a picture of wickedness and temptation on the flowered wall of the nursery."

More than ten years have passed since Bergman wrote that, and he does not need devils so much any more. The cries and whispers are painful and nervous enough without devils, for we can torment ourselves. The magic lantern remains, however, and appears in *Cries and Whispers* in a scene remembered from childhood, an occasion that should have been one of connection and instead was one of deep isolation. But the point is not to dissect each scene. I am only trying to suggest that the materials of the film are not so awesome and majuscule as they must seem in analysis, but altogether concrete, private, and fleshly.

The motion of the film is in fact quite simple, a process of accretion in which the sequences function like stanzas in a poem, establishing connections forward and back of increasing complexity and strength. The method is much more flexible and much richer in possibility than are the conventions of straightforward narrative. The disciplines are, if anything, even more strict, and the economies are entirely amazing. There is some narrative movement, of course. Agnes dies. Maria talks with Karin and tries to establish some degree of closeness, tries to touch her shoulder, touch her cheek, but Karin recoils from the touch and from the act of faith such a touching would, for her, require. There is a show of hostility on Karin's part, and Maria is rebuffed, but finally there is a moment of meeting, a peculiar scene of the two heads in a tight frame, talking intimately, touching, communing. We have no idea what they are talking about and it does not matter. On the sound track, there is only a passage of a Bach sonata for unaccompanied cello (the cello is the one stringed instrument with the range of the human voice). The conclusion of this line, and very nearly the conclusion of the film, involves the betrayal of that communion by Maria, exactly as Karin expected. It meant nothing, or almost nothing, was not what Maria truly felt but only what she might have liked to feel. Or, if Maria did feel anything, loyalty, commitment, fidelity had no part in the feeling. And these were the very qualities which Karin demanded and failed to find, not only in Maria, but in her own husband, and, presumably, in anyone.

There are defects on both sides. Maria is anatomized for us by David, the doctor, a man with whom she once had an affair, as the two of them stand looking into a mirror and he describes to her the changes he sees—the way the eyes which used to look straight forward now glance sideways in calculation and circumspection, the way the line of the mouth has hardened, the way the almost invisible furrows of the brow and the wrinkles around the eyes show selfishness and cunning. And we have seen Maria's character in its effect on her husband, Joakim who, after the discovery of her infidelity, goes into his study and plunges a knife into his belly in an attempt to kill himself—which fails, and he cries out to her, "Help me, help me," wonderfully unclear about whether the help he wants is in living or dying. (In any event, she turns away from him.)

If Maria's sensuality without sincerity wounds others, Karin's insistence on authenticity and fidelity to the exclusion of sexuality is self-wounding. In a se-

Ingrid Thulin and Ullmann.

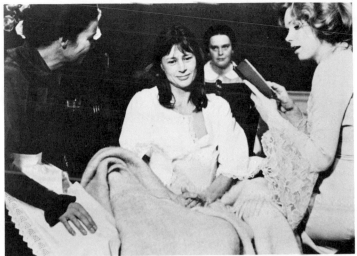

The three sisters: Ingrid Thulin, Harriet Andersson, and Liv Ullmann, with servant Kari Sylwan in background.

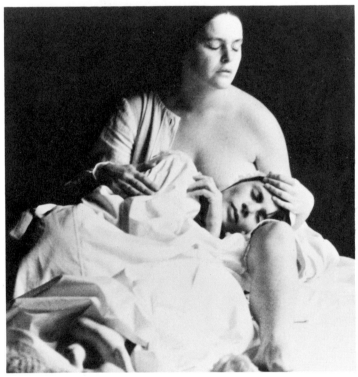

Kari Sylwan comforts Harriet Andersson.

Erland Josephson discusses Ullmann's image in the mirror.

quence which is by now famous, Karin acts out in the most literal way possible the metaphor about someone being wounded in their sex. Inserting a jagged shard of a wine glass into herself, enduring the pain, and then, in the bedroom, smearing the blood of the wound across her face, noting the look of horror on her fastidious husband's face, and—terribly, honestly—smiling at him.

The death of Agnes is the occasion for the moment of connection between the two sisters. Agnes, herself, is not established as having any kind of connection with men. She has not been married and, apparently, has contrived to avoid the entire dilemma of love and truth. Or it may be that the dilemma simply no longer applies and that as she confronts the prospect of dying she has begun the process of retreat common among terminally sick people, a withdrawal from the connections with other people. She does a watercolor of a rose and she makes entries in her diary, but if she has memories of the kind of turbulence that is playing about her in the lives of her sisters, they do not surface. Indeed, the movie ends with Anna, the servant, reading from the diary, a recollection of a day outdoors, almost certainly one of Agnes's last days of health and happiness. She sees the scene incorrectly, rejoicing in a community and a harmony which we know to have been most seriously flawed. It is an irony of considerable proportion, for she speaks with the authority of the dead, and the scene on the screen is in fact harmonious and joyful, with the three sisters dressed in white and sitting on a swing that Anna moves back and forth. And for that moment it perhaps was true: they were happy.

We can remember back to Karin's self-mutilation and her words, definite, clear, and underscored three times: "It is nothing but a tissue of lies. It is all a tissue of lies. A tissue of lies." And we can recognize that this, too, is a lie, but a helpful, a necessary lie. A kind of dream, perhaps? But we must be careful, assaying various kinds of reality. There is a truth in dreams, in fantasies, and even in superstitions. Without any difference whatever, Bergman veers off into alternative realities of such kinds, and while he makes clear that he is maneuvering, he does not assign any label to these divergent experiences, allowing us as much mystery as the characters themselves may experience. The two characterizing sequences, for example, the moment in which Maria's husband stabs himself and the moment in which Karin wounds herself, are each introduced by a narrator, intruding his voice and putting the events upon the screen at some intellectual distance. Other sequences are introduced or concluded with those long freezes and then slow fades into red. One such sequence is the very peculiar calling out of the dead Agnes for comfort, for someone to keep her company for a little as she faces the vast emptiness and loneliness of death. Agnes calls out and Anna, the servant, comes to the bedroom in which she is laid out. The deceased asks for Karin, whom Anna calls —but Karin refuses to have anything to do with Agnes, explaining, quite correctly if coldly, that she has her own life to lead. Agnes then sends for Maria, who comes in and is moved by her dead sister's plea, approaches the bed, touches the body, nearly kisses it, and then recoils. The corpse clings to her, its arm around her neck. She struggles and as she backs away, the corpse drags itself after her, falling out of bed. Finally Anna herself gets into bed with the dead woman and cradles her in a composition that recalls an earlier frame when she comforted Agnes, and perhaps the Pietà as well.

The succession of the three visitors to the corpse has a folktale quality, and is perhaps Anna's vision of what is happening and how she fits, or ought to fit, into the complicated constellation. It is a puzzling sequence in some ways, and one might like to avoid it, for its meaning is perhaps darker than anything else in the film. If Anna's vision is in some way correct, and if her private truth laps against the truths of the two sisters, then one must conclude that the balance between love and truth is not only important in and of itself, but also critical for the soul, which is what the psyche used to be before therapists cannibalized the word.

All these connections are waiting to be made, to be explored in any light and in any person's vision. That Ingmar Bergman has made such a statement is not surprising. Fellini's attack is in many ways comparable, even though the style and the vision are quite different. But compared with these meditative, bold, intelligent, and humane enterprises, the exclusions of Bertolucci seem absurd and diminished. There is no challenge in isolating sexuality, in cutting away the heart and the mind to leave only the quivering genitals. Hard-core porn does that, and because it cannot afford to do anything more, it bores us. Otherwise, if it admitted characters of some complexity or some intelligence, we should very quickly become interested in other aspects of the lives proposed for our consideration—and then it wouldn't be hard-core.

What is remarkable is not the torrent of sex films of the past five years or so. Fashions in film establish themselves in the wake of any single success and there are inevitable imitations and embroideries. And the coincidence of the Court's move toward liberality (now, apparently, reversed) with the success of *I Am Curious—Yellow* was irresistible. What is striking, however, is the foolishness and the cowardice of all those movies. By reducing people to masturbatory fantasies, by retreating from any contamination with the complexities and ambiguities of living, the makers of all those movies about stewardesses and cheerleaders and swingers have (ho-ho) muffed a great opportunity. The reaction, and the present situation, may be deplorable, but they are all too understandable.

What is most regrettable is that sexuality is not only fascinating but actually interesting. There are intelligent and profound statements to be made about human sexuality. *Cries and Whispers* is one such statement. But the mindless assertions on display in theaters in the combat zones and the tenderloins provide a better case for the moralists than they deserve—or at least they provide the appearance of a case. In fact the discriminating principle is not sexuality at all; but there is no way in a democracy to apply the appropriate standard, which is one of intelligence and taste. Stupid sex, like stupid violence, offends us. Stupidity is offensive. Stupidity is dangerous, harmful to the morals of tender minds, inimical to the public good in all ways. But there is just no way to suppress it—certainly not so long as it remains in the majority, on the bench, in the studios, in theater audiences, and among the public at large.

NOTES

1. Screen Sexuality: Flesh, Feathers, and Fantasies

JOHN BAXTER, an Australian-born writer who lives in England, is the author of numerous books, including *Hollywood in the Thirties, Science Fiction in the Cinema, Cinema of Josef von Sternberg,* and *An Appalling Talent: Ken Russell.* A frequent lecturer at London's National Film Theatre, he has been a juror in many European film festivals.

2. A History of Censorship of the American Film

ARTHUR LENNIG teaches film at State University of New York at Albany and is the author of several books, among them *Film Notes, Classics of the Film, The Sound Film,* and most recently *The Count: The Life and Films of Bela "Dracula" Lugosi.* His latest project is a critical biography of D. W. Griffith.

1. Terry Ramsaye, *A Million and One Nights* (New York City: Simon and Schuster, 1926), 399.

2. Jeremy Collier, *A Short View of the Profaneness and Immorality of the English Stage* (London: Birt and Trye, 1738), 1.

3. Ibid., 3.

4. Ibid., 5.

5. Lewis Jacobs, *The Rise of the American Film* (New York City: Harcourt Brace, 1939), 62.

6. John S. Sumner, "The Sewer on the Stage," *Theatre Magazine,* December 1923, 9.

7. Ruth A. Ingles, *Freedom of the Movies* (Chicago: University of Chicago Press, 1947), 79.

8. *Los Angeles Times,* November 19, 1924.

9. Morris L. Ernst and Pare Lorentz, *The Private Life of the Movie* (New York City: Jonathan Cape and Harrison Smith, 1930), 84.

10. Ibid., 11–12.

11. Ibid., 30.

12. Ibid., 38.

13. Henry James Forman, *Our Movie Made Children* (New York City: Macmillan Company, 1933), 36.

14. Ibid., 91.

15. Ibid., 51.

16. Ibid., 46.

17. Ibid., 151.

18. *Freedom of the Movies,* 123.

19. *New York Times,* October 2, 1933.

20. Pope Pius XI, "Vigilanti Cura," *New York Times,* July 3, 1936.

21. *Film and Television Daily,* October 31, 1969.

22. Ibid., December 3, 1969.

23. Ibid., November 11, 1969.

24. *New York Times,* March 2, 1973.

25. *Variety*, January 9, 1974.

26. Andrew Sarris, *The Village Voice*, March 20, 1969.

3. The Contemporary Movie Rating System in America

EVELYN RENOLD is managing editor of *Coast* magazine in Los Angeles and has written for the *Los Angeles Times* and other publications. In 1971 she was an intern on the MPAA Ratings Board.

4. Sex, Morality, and the Movies

LAWRENCE BECKER teaches philosophy and religion at Hollins College, Virginia, and is a frequent contributor to leading philosophical journals and to *The Film Journal*. He has recently published a book entitled *On Justifying Moral Judgments*.

5. Troubled Sexuality in the Popular Hollywood Feature

THOMAS R. ATKINS is chairman of the Theatre Arts department of Hollins College, Virginia, and editor-publisher of *The Film Journal*. His work has appeared in *Sight and Sound* and many other periodicals, and he is general editor of a new series of film books to be published by Simon and Schuster.

6. The Sex Genre: Traditional and Modern Variations

WAYNE A. LOSANO teaches film and technical communication at Rensselaer Polytechnic Institute in Troy, New York. His articles have appeared in periodicals like the *Journal of Popular Culture*, the *Journal of Technical Writing and Communication*, and *The Film Journal*.

1. Fred Chappell, "Twenty-Six Propositions about Skin Flicks," in *Man and the Movies*, W. R. Robinson, ed. (Baton Rouge: Louisiana State University Press, 1967), 57.

2. William Rotsler, *Contemporary Erotic Cinema* (New York: Ballantine, 1973), 28–29.

3. Arthur Knight and Hollis Alpert, "The History of Sex in Cinema: part 17, The Stag Film," in *Playboy*, November 1967, 170.

4. Maurice Yacowar, "Beyond the Fringe and Up the Pompous: Sex the Funny Prophet," unpublished paper delivered at the National Popular Culture Convention, May 1973.

5. Russel Nye, *The Unembarrassed Muse* (New York: Dial Press, 1970), 4.

6. Knight and Alpert, 176.

7. Ibid., 178.

8. Chappell, 57–58.

9. Knight and Alpert, 186.

10. Rotsler, 251.

11. *Without a Stitch* (1970) was, amazingly, able to "show" simultaneous anal and vaginal penetration without revealing even a hint of the male organs involved.

12. Chappell, 59.

13. Bruce Williamson, "Porno Chic" in *Playboy*, August 1973, 136.

14. Jim Mitchell, who with his brother was one of the pioneers of the hard-core films, complains that these plots "detract from the fucking, which after all is what hardcore is about." George Csicsery, *The Sex Industry* (Signet, 1973), 168.

15. Ellen Willis gives suggestions for a sex film for women in her article on *Throat* elsewhere in this book, and some of my students have developed believable cases for *The Devil in Miss Jones* being a "woman's film."

7. Monster Movies: A Sexual Theory

WALTER EVANS teaches in the English department at Augusta College, Georgia, and has published essays in the *Kansas Quarterly*, the *Journal of Popular Culture*, the *Journal of Popular Film*, and elsewhere. He is working on a longer study of monster movies.

1. Curtis Harrington asserts that such movies are more popular in periods of depression and disorder. See "Ghoulies and Ghosties" in Roy Huss and T. J. Ross, eds., *Focus on the Horror Film* (Englewood Cliffs, New Jersey: Prentice Hall, 1972), 17–18.

2. Lawrence Alloway, "Monster Films," in *Focus on the Horror Film*, 123.

3. Frank McConnell, "Rough Beasts Slouching," in *Focus on the Horror Film*, 26.

4. R. H. W. Dillard, "Even a Man Who Is Pure at Heart: Poetry and Danger in the Horror Film," in W. R. Robinson, ed., *Man and the Movies* (Baton Rouge: L. S. U. Press, 1967), 65.

5. Lawrence Alloway, 124. He is speaking specifically of the effects of death and decay.

6. John Thomas, "Gobble, Gobble . . . One of Us!" in *Focus on the Horror Film*, 135.

7. John D. Donne, "Society and the Monster," in *Focus on the Horror Film*, 125.

8. Drake Douglas, *Horror!* Collier Books (New York City: Macmillan, 1966), 11.

9. The statement was made on "Frame of Reference," a discussion following the showing of *The Blue Angel* on the American public television program, *Film Odyssey*.

10. See Ernest Jones, "On the Nightmare of Bloodsucking," in *Focus on the Horror Film*, 59.

11. "The Child and the Book," in *Only Connect*, Sheila Egoff, G. T. Stubbs, and L. F. Ashley, eds. (New York City: Oxford University Press, 1969), 93–94.

8. The Boys on the Bandwagon: Homosexuality in the Movies

GENE D. PHILLIPS, S.J., teaches fiction and film at Loyola University of Chicago. A frequent contributor to U.S. and foreign film periodicals, he has been a juror or panelist at Cannes, Chicago, and Berlin film festivals. He is the author of *The Movie Makers: Artists in an Industry* and *Graham Greene: The Films of His Fiction*. He is currently working on studies of Stanley Kubrick and Alfred Hitchcock.

9. Sex in the Contemporary European Film

LESTER KEYSER, who teaches at Staten Island Community College of the City University of New York, is a contributing editor for the *National Catholic Film Newsletter*. His work has appeared in *Literature/Film Quarterly* and other periodicals, and he has contributed to the book *Ingmar Bergman: Essays in Criticism*.

1. Parker Tyler, *Classics of the Foreign Film* (New York: The Citadel Press, 1962), 79.

2. Andrew Sarris, *Interviews with Film Directors* (New York: Avon Books, 1967), 176.

3. Quoted in Ian Cameron and Robin Wood, *Antonioni* (New York: Praeger, 1968), 9.

4. Quoted in Sarris, 436.

5. Susan Sontag, *Styles of Radical Will* (New York: Farrar, Straus, and Giroux, 1966), 23.

6. Quoted in Joseph Gelmis, *The Film Director as Superstar* (New York: Double-day, 1970), 105.

7. Amos Vogel, *Film as a Subversive Art* (New York: Random House, 1974), 153.

8. Pauline Kael, *Deeper into Movies* (New York: Bantam Books, 1974), 475.

10. *I Am Curious—Yellow:* A Practical Education

DAVID S. LENFEST teaches satire and poetry at Loyola University of Chicago and is also a filmmaker. Radim Films distributes his *The Great Odor of Summer*, and he has recently finished another film called *George Washington Sleeps Here*.

1. Vilgöt Sjoman, *I Am Curious (Yellow)*, trans. by Martin Minow and Jenny Boh-man (New York: Grove Press, 1968). All quotations from the trial or the script are from this volume.

2. Bertolt Brecht, "From the *Mother Courage* Model," in *Brecht on Theater*, trans. by John Willett (New York: Hill and Wang, 1964), 215–20 quoted in Stanley A. Clayes, *Drama & Discussion* (New York: Appleton-Century-Crofts, 1967), 273.

3. Brecht, 272.

11. *Midnight Cowboy*

FOSTER HIRSCH teaches English at Brooklyn College, New York, and has written essays and reviews for the *Nation, Commonweal*, the *New York Times*, and many film periodicals.

12. *Carnal Knowledge*

RICHARD McGUINNESS is a film critic whose work has appeared in a wide variety of publications, including *Rolling Stone, Changes, Moviegoer*, and *Film Comment*. For two years he contributed weekly television commentary to the *Village Voice*.

13. *Deep Throat:* Hard to Swallow

ELLEN WILLIS contributes regularly to the *New Yorker*, the *New York Review of Books*, and other periodicals.

14. *Last Tango in Paris:* The Skull Beneath the Skin Flick

JACK FISHER, who teaches film and directs theater at Norfolk State College in Virginia, has written criticism for *The Film Journal, Contempora*, and other magazines.

15. Sexuality in Film: Reconsiderations after Seeing *Cries and Whispers*

DAVID R. SLAVITT, who was for seven years a film critic for *Newsweek,* has written several volumes of poetry and many novels, including *Rochelle, or Virtue Rewarded, Feel Free, Anagrams,* and *The Killing of the King.* As "Henry Sutton" he wrote the best-sellers *The Exhibitionist* and *The Voyeur.*